Understanding CPI(M)

Will the Indian Left Survive?

Understanding CPI(M)

Will the Indian Left Survive?

Diptendra Raychaudhuri

Vitasta

Vitasta Publishing Pvt. Ltd.
New Delhi

Published by
Sudesh K Verma for
Vitasta Publishing Pvt. Ltd.
2/15, Ansari Road, Daryaganj,
New Delhi - 110 002

ISBN 978-81-89766-59-7

Cover Design and Layout by Vitasta Publishing Pvt. Ltd.
Printed by Vits Press, New Delhi

Dedicated to

My father late Satyendranath Raychaudhuri and my father-in-law late Ajoy Sengupta, both of whom were associated with the Left movement in Bengal during its turbulent phase.

Contents

PART III

Present in Perspective of the Past

PART IV

Future: Dangers and Opportunities

Preface

As this book deals with the communists, I must confess one thing. I do not know, better to say I cannot understand who a communist is. Lenin was a communist and Boris Yeltsin too was a communist. Mao Ze Dong was a communist and Deng Xiao Ping too was a communist. Roza Luxemberg was a communist and Nicolae Ceausescu too was a communist. Che Guevara was a communist, Ganapathy (the general secretary of the Maoists) is a communist, Prachanda (the Nepalese PM) is a communist, and Buddhadeb Bhattacharya (the CM of West Bengal) too is a communist. These facts appear before me like a puzzle that has no solution, for each of them had or has different and contradictory positions.

And then there was Stalin, the great killer who succeeded to eliminate at least 3 million of his fellow countrymen. But we cannot disclaim Marx and his theoretical work for the demons his work produced in later ages. But, even when judged by his own work, Marx stands outdated as the society in a semi-advanced semi-primitive country like India has hundreds of classes. It leaves little scope of class struggle. However, surplus value is a simple concept that holds ground still today. Encouraged by this, some people argue that if one is a communist he should have faith in social ownership of the means of production. In other words, a communist should try to do away with the capitalist system. But all the communists in the world, except for some like those who are known as Maoists (or Naxalites) are just walking in the opposite direction. If it has to be admitted that they are communists, I must confess that they remind me of a childhood story of a doctor. The only thing the doctor could do was treating TB patients. So, he kept all the patients who came to him with some TB patients so they may acquire the disease. It was all done with the honest intention of curing them! Whenever I hear someone argue that he is now practising capitalism so that ultimately socialism can be achieved, I feel he is treating a society that has not been infected by TB and is trying to spread the virus like that honest doctor.

Forget that. Even this assumption that for the sake of equality and justice the means of productions should be owned by the society is fallacious. As in a liberal democracy the whole society cannot control the decision-making process, similarly in that utopian stage when the society will own the means of production, decision making will be in the hands of an oligarchy. That oligarchy will come from the party. So, instead of class division according to wealth, there would be a class division according to proximity to the party. Power will still be concentrated in the hands of a few, and the society will be worse off as people will not have the right to change the rulers. Very few people in India will voluntarily opt for such a system.

But, even in a free society this theory can bring in catastrophe. It can create an oligarchy of party bosses who control all mundane affairs like who will avail which government scheme, who will get employment in schools and government offices, or even who is at fault in case of a quarrel between two parties. The party bosses become all in one: the judiciary, the executive and even the legislature! People are subjugated to the laws these bosses create. And all this go on while individual ownership of means of production too flourishes. The government pick and choose a favoured one from a bunch of industries and give him all facilities.

Cannot believe this? Go and ask the people of Bengal.

But then, the Maoists say those who are governing Bengal for 32 years winning consecutive seven elections are pseudo-communists.

So I leave the impossible task of defining a communist to those who amuse us by claiming that Marxism is a science. I would like to use a simpler term: the Left. By 'Leftists' we understand a group of people who fight for the uplift of the poor. This term has nothing to do with communistic ideas like abolition of private property or social ownership of means of production and so on. It simply denotes a force willing to be with the poor and underprivileged, a force that fights for a continuous uplift of that section. We will examine in this book whether the Communist Party of India(Marxist) is still a Leftist party, and whether it will remain a Leftist party in the future. Here I must admit that I believe a true and strong Leftist party (or a bunch of parties) is vital for the survival of this country. Otherwise, the political opportunists or lackeys of crude capitalism will so dangerously widen the gap between the handful of rich and the overwhelming majority of the poor that the whole country would plunge into anarchy.

This book analyses the relevance (or irrelevance) of the CPI(M) and the Left in present day politics in India. It provides an interpretation of the recent past and the present of the CPI(M) and offers an analysis on their chance of survival in the future as a relevant political force.

When I talk about the relevance of the party, it has to be assumed that I believe the Left has a space and a role to play that is totally different from the others. However the world changes, new forces emerge, and the space or role also changes. From Keynesian theory to the New Deal to Reaganomics and then to the days of financial meltdown, the epicentre of world economic ripples have changed constantly. Thus the space the Left had or the role they were supposed to play half-a-century ago and the space they have now or the role they should play today cannot be the same. The CPI(M) and the Left too learned from their experience of running state governments. BT Randive, who was a revolutionary communist in his younger days, supported Jyoti Basu's line of 'mixed economy' and 'joint sector' for West Bengal in the mid-80s.

But, the contours of focus shifting cannot overrun the basic ideology (i.e., the very meaning of 'Leftism'). The Left stands for socialism. In other words, they stand for maximum state intervention to bring in maximum uplift of the unprivileged and underprivileged sections, who together are still two-thirds of the Indian population. Half-a-century ago, a communist could think about an armed revolution and a thorough change of the society and imposition of a state-controlled command economy. That economic structure had failed worldwide. Armed revolution everywhere brought in armed tyranny. Till now, there are organizations that believe in all these and have waged a war against the state from the jungles and remote areas of central-southern-eastern part of the country. This force, the Maoists, is essentially an anarchist force, but with a remarkable—if not huge—mass support. This support is the answer to the neglect of vast number of people still living in abject poverty, still failing to earn (or spend, all the same for them) 20 rupees a day per person. All the parties functioning in the system are answerable.

The relevance of the Left is to be seen in this perspective. They remain relevant if they stand against the onslaught of neoliberalism and try to exert themselves in favour of maximum state intervention; they remain relevant if they work for the bottom 50-60-70 per cent of the population, if they act as a buffer between the system and the Maoists. The first and foremost task of a Leftist is to ensure food, clothing, housing, education, medical facilities and a social security network for each and every individual. Otherwise, nobody will care whether any force using a signboard of a Communist party or anything else exists or not. There are so many parties that follow neoliberalism that nobody is interested to hear from a communist whether 'globalization is a must'. It only amuses the Rightists in the same way a trainer is amused when he sees his wildest horse tamed. Again, as the Maoists are out there, as it is evident that the traditional Left has become a part of the system, nobody is interested to hear something like 'CIA is out to tarnish our image'. What is needed from the Left is: (i) creation of an environment where industries and capital grow in a fair way without twisting the arms of the government or damaging the interests of either the workers or the common man, and (ii) ensuring that the revenue the government earns be dedicated to real uplift of the bottom.

I believe the relevance of Left politics lies in its pro-poor attitude and constant endeavour to intervene in the system in favour of the poor (which is impossible without continuous fight against corruption and communalism). This book is written from this broad angle. With the incredible record of opening fire on the poor rebellious peasants in Nandigram and, supporting neo-zamindary (SEZs) at the national level, and punishing one of the most honest chief minister of the country to please a dodgy state secretary in Kerala, it is highly doubtful whether the CPI(M) would be able to play such a role. Hence there is need to examine the cross currents in the Left camp and speculating on the future.

But the future or the recent past cannot be interpreted without referring to the past. So, at times the book deals with the past, but as briefly as possible. The aim is to provide a comprehensive understanding of the CPI(M) and the Left as a whole.

The book concentrates on the CPI(M) and does not go into the detail of other Left parties as those other parties do not have much independent existence. In the name of 'Left unity' they cling to the CPI(M). They have lost their ability to think about why the Left unity is needed: to kill poor farmers, to dish out huge benefits to industrial houses, to help the rich grow richer? These parties try to eat their cake and have it too. They take all the advantages of being with the CPI(M) and then criticize the CPI(M). They cannot live without the CPI(M). So, at the end of the day, they have no option but to follow their 'big brother'.

Terminology

Elite This term is used in a particular context. The elite refers to a particular segment of population (the rich and the upper middle class), who are totally cut off from the poor mass (two-thirds of the people) and live in a world where they themselves only matter. The Rightist elite (comprising of almost the entire elite segment) has no scruples and do not hesitate to push and pursue policies that harm the poor further. The Leftist elite (a miniscule section) is not indifferent about the poor, but generally knows very little about them.

Neoliberal A believer in an economic philosophy (neoliberalism) that argues in favour of achieving progress and even social justice by encouraging free-market mechanism and fewer restrictions on business operations or economic development. Thus it rejects government intervention in the economy to complement private initiative, and calls for promotion of globalization of the economy. It is a philosophy that has faith in a chain reaction: you implement business-friendly policies and the rest will follow automatically. Free run of business and capital will lead to growth of businesses; growth of business will lead to creation of jobs and other economic benefits which will lead to the welfare of the entire society. This is commonly referred to as 'trickle down economics' or 'Reaganomics'. Classical liberals like Adam Smith argued that in order to best serve human welfare, individuals should be left free to follow their own interests. So the logical corollary was a government that abstains from 'interference in free enterprise', and puts checks 'only on undue strife and competition'. This was the dominant economic thought in the West till the Great Depression and World War II. This was replaced by the New Deal and Social-Welfarism. Then from the 70s of the last century, and more vehemently from the 80s, Neoliberalism started dominating the thoughts and actions. There is a strong current of opposition to neoliberalism, particularly in developing and underdeveloped countries where often it brings in disaster by making the poor poorer. Detractors argue that government intervention is necessary to create an equitable society.

Rightist A strong believer in free economy and unlimited freedom of acquiring wealth (like freedom to hire and fire, pay minimum tax and to be involved in any sort of business activity, such as retail trade or creating situations in agriculture similar to that of indigo plantation). To most of these people, it does not matter whether the ruling party is communal or secular. What matters is their economic outlook. Some of them may have some commitment to social justice, but most of them lack it.

Leftist A believer in socio-economic equity and justice brought through maximum state intervention in economy and economic affairs. Generally, they vehemently oppose communal or any other divisive thoughts (except that based on real socio-economic situation).

Communist Theoretically, those who believe in social ownership of means of production are called 'communists'. They dream of a society where each individual will get according to his need and will give his best, and the state power will be in the hands of those representing the toiling class. In reality, all socialist countries run by Communist parties were and are autocratic and totalitarian. More confusing is the identity of a communist as different people doing diametrically opposites claim themselves to be communists.

Hardliner A communist who clings to the ideas of 60s and 70s and has faith in the concept of dictatorship of the proletariat. These people are generally Stalinists and see democracy as a tool to be used for reaching socialism. People have a penchant for dubbing a communist a hardliner if he carries anti-Congress attitude. But that is meaningless, as many neoliberal individuals and parties are also strongly against the Congress.

Radical The Leftists operating in democratic system but still opposing foreign investment, conditional international loans, or free run of private capital.

Moderate A person having faith in democratic set-up and also in as much compromise with the capitalist system as to allow a free run of the system but not at the cost of the poor. He may or may not focus on the uplift of the poor.

Revolutionary (Communist) Those who believe that a revolution, if it aims to bring in a new equitable social order, has to be a violent one. This term is applicable to the communists of older times and the Maoists of the present age.

Stalinist Those who believe in three principles: (i) If you are not with us, then you are our enemy; (ii) All opposition can be and should be silenced by using physical force, and (iii) The organizational interest is supreme.

PART I

A Prelude to a Bigger Tragedy: 2009

One

The Mortal Fear of Doom

IT WAS the darkest day for the bosses at AKG Bhawan, the headquarters of the second largest communist party of the world and the largest operating in a democratic country, i.e., the Communist Party of India (Marxist) or the CPI(M).

It was indeed ironical that the main office of the Bengal party that had reigned supreme over the eastern state for over three decades had now been put in the same spot as its national headquarters. Still, in Calcutta's Alimuddin Street state committee office it was business as usual, for it was still the headquarters of the ruling party of Bengal.

But the four-storey building by the side of a quite boulevard leading to the roundabout of New Delhi's Gole Market wore the look of a condemned house. Outside it was all bright: the afternoon sun was burning bright, a few children were playing merrily on the pavements, the traffic was light, and life was going on like every other day. Only inside the headquarters, it was dark as midnight.

It was 16 May 2009, and the results of the parliamentary elections were out. From 60 members in the 14th Lok Sabha, the Left Bloc led by the CPI(M) had been reduced to 24 in the 15th, making it almost irrelevant in Indian politics.

The CPI(M) itself had won 16 seats. The figure was three less than the number it got in 1967, in the first general election it faced after its birth in 1964. Ironically, this haunting figure of 16 came after its ever-best tally of 43 in the previous parliamentary election when the party performed excellently both in West Bengal and Kerala. Before that its best score was 37 in 1980, and it never went below 30 in the last two decades.

But, now it was all over. The CPI(M) was finally reduced to the level of the CPI, the smaller Left party that had had won around 10 seats on an average since 1977. The CPI was reduced to this sorry state since it supported a Congress government at the Centre in the 1970s. Interestingly, the CPI(M) too had faced its Waterloo after extending support to the Congress-led coalition for 50 months since 2004.

It looked like the party was going back to the womb after completing its life cycle of birth, growth and decay.

There was shock, either dismay or jubilance, in the political circles in Delhi at this ignominy of the Left. What most of the observers did not know was that even this electoral outcome was just the tip of the iceberg.

It was actually a legend coming to an end. A long story, a saga of defiance and sacrifice that started long years ago, and had lost its track in modern times, was finally coming to such an end that would ever remain unsung.

The movement from Telangana to Nandigram symbolizing the rise and fall of the Indian communists, however, would never be forgotten.

***

The electoral debacle of the CPI(M), and of the Left as a whole, came as a shock to the political leaders and observers alike. They forgot that it was bound to happen some day for the Left's importance in Delhi was disproportionate to its strength on the ground.

More significantly, it was bound to happen in 2009 itself as the ground for this debacle had been prepared by the Left in previous five years. The Left was not defeated by Mamata Banerjee's Trinamool

Congress in Bengal. The Left was not defeated by the Congress alone in Kerala. The present Left was defeated primarily by a spectre of the past also known as 'Left'.

For long years, the CPI(M) aspired to play a bigger role at the national level imagining themselves to be important players, even while their success was basically limited to one state that gave them their two-thirds strength in the Lok Sabha since 1977. That was West Bengal, a state in the eastern part of India with 42 parliamentary constituencies. It delivered the numbers till 2004 and kept afloat the party's simulated importance at the national level. The only other state that supported Bengal in this endeavour was Kerala which gave the party 15 (and the Left Bloc 19) of the state's 20 seats in 2004. It must be mentioned, for record's sake, they had a very solid base also in Tripura, a tiny north-eastern state, but it could add to the number only by 2, for the state had only that many constituencies.

Despite this tiny base, from where the party could expect to win a maximum of 10 per cent of the total seats (545) in the Lok Sabha, the Marxists aspired to intervene in the national scenario in a way that they deemed meaningful. The CPI(M) was, however, reluctant to share power at the central level, and limited itself to persuading the government, whenever possible, to follow certain policies of their liking. The number they brought together also allowed them to play an important role in the so-called 'secular' camp opposed to the BJP, the Hindu chauvinist party. This ultimately nudged them, in 2004, to side with and directly support a government led by the Congress, their one-time arch enemy. But, despite their pivotal role in the 'secular' camp, they did not try to corner much benefit from the government. Thus, they were respected for occupying a high moral ground: they were men (and a few women) with a difference, for they were not after power for power's sake, and would not join a government that would not follow the total bunch of their policies. This stand further legitimized their larger-than-number role in national politics.

Again, Indian political situation has always been presenting them a series of providential opportunities. Their small parliamentary strength in 1969 gave them their first big opportunity when Indira Gandhi, the then Prime Minister, found herself in a serious crisis with her path encumbered by the old and conservative guards of the Congress. After her sudden and dramatic decision to nationalize several banks to ensure a 'socialistic pattern of society', she got the much needed strength from the tacit support of both the communist parties. However, for the CPI(M) that period of proximity was short-lived.

The CPI(M) went whole hog against Indira Gandhi as soon as she emerged stronger after 1971 general election. They lost their ability to influence her from behind the scene like in the aftermath of bank nationalization, and so they decided to increase the distance. Again, the CPI(M) got a golden opportunity in 1977, when the first non-Congress government came to power in Delhi as a result of people's anger against the Emergency imposed by Indira Gandhi. The Marxists had significant influence on the Janata Party government as comrades-in-arms against the Congress. But, this influence was greatly reduced when Indira Gandhi returned to power in 1980, and then it was lost altogether when Rajiv Gandhi led the Congress to victory in 1984 by the highest margin ever. Fortune, however, continued to favour the Left as out of the blue emerged VP Singh, who showed exceptional courage by raising the banner of revolt against Rajiv Gandhi over the Bofors Howitzer gun deal. This gave an opportunity to the Left to again come to the forefront of Indian politics and play a role disproportionate to its strength. Naturally, they had considerable influence over the South Bloc during VP Singh's 11-month stint as Prime Minister. Again, the Left provided tacit support from the opposition benches to the Congress government of Narsimha Rao from June 1991 to June 1993. Thereafter, for the rest of Rao's regime, its importance was on the wane, although it was not over. It again went up when United Front (a conglomeration of smaller parties) government ruled the country for 23 months beginning June 1996. The CPI(M), however, lost all control over the Central Government when the BJP-led NDA came to power in 1998 and ruled till the first quarter of 2004. But during this time the CPI(M) had considerable influence over the whole of the opposition camp. It had a major role in bringing down the

13-month-old AB Vajpayee government in 1999, though that attempt did not bring any fruit as Vajpayee came back to power with more MPs in the ensuing general election.

Altogether, in the 45 years since 1964, the CPI(M) had major influence on the Central Government for 10 years and mild influence for another 15 years. One party from the Left camp (the CPI) strayed from the other comrades to support Indira Gandhi from 1970–77. If they are counted, another 7 years will be added to this period of influence of the Left. But the real glorious days of the Left commenced from 2004, when in the backdrop of a very long history of anti-Congressism, the CPI(M) decided to support a Congress government at the Centre, that too led by Dr Manmohan Singh, the architect of 'neoliberal reform' in India. The Left had their logic ready for this volta-face: they joined forces with the Congress and others to keep off the BJP, which it considered to be communal, from power. It was true that the Congress-led United Progressive Alliance (UPA) needed the number the Left provided. But what was interesting was the CPI(M)'s enthusiasm to extend direct support, ditching old partners like the Samajwadi Party of Mulayam Singh Yadav and, thereby, nixing the scope of consolidation of a third alternative.

Whatever, 2004–08 saw the zenith of the CPI(M)'s influence in Indian polity. But after 50 months of extending support to the Congress government, the Left withdrew its support. This did not come on any economic issue or an issue directly related to the common man. The withdrawal came on the Indo-US civil nuclear cooperation agreement. Known as the 'Nuclear Deal', this mandated India to accept certain conditions in lieu of resumption of supply of nuclear fuels (despite India's history of experimentation with nuclear bombs). The Left was opposed to the deal, and they believed they would be able to dislodge the government with the help of some other parties joining them.

They actually played a gamble to assert themselves. With their images taller than real in their minds, they believed the moment of their ultimate glory had come. Haunted by the spirit of 'lets make that happen', they went forward to bring a no-confidence motion to seal the government's fate. They forgot India is a nation of the corrupt. They forgot that politicians are just a commodity. They forgot how in July 1993 Narasimha Rao's minority government survived a similar motion of no-confidence. And history repeated itself. MPs started switching sides; MPs failed to be present in the House; MPs abstained. The Leftists were outmanoeuvred by the Congress party managers, and saw in dismay Mulayam Singh Yadav, their closest ally, paying them back in the same coin: 50 months back, they supported the Congress without caring for Yadav's Samajwadi Party. Fifty months later, the Samajwadi Party went away with the Congress to fill in the gap created by the Left's withdrawal.

With their pride hurt badly, the Left leaders acted with a vengeance and decided to form a Third Front to teach the Congress a lesson in the election to be held within a year. The Left still imagined itself as a major player, failing to understand that the Left's credibility as the fulcrum of the Third Front had melted away with its decision to directly support a Congress government at the Centre. Now, they were suspect in the eyes of the others. No one knew what deal they would make with whom and when. Probably, the Left leaders thought the others would accept them as superior beings and acknowledge whatever they said or did was always right. But this time, in 2009, no one embraced them except for those few who had no other option, like Deve Gowda and sons (Karnataka) and Chandrababu Naidu (of Andhra Pradesh). the Bahujan Samaj Party's Mayawati or the Biju Janata Dal's Navin Patnaik were in the neutral gear, but not keen to commit a long-term relation with the Left. With this Bloc, the Left hoped to cross hundred-mark and then play the role of a kingmaker. They did not have many leaders with them, but they were sure—even after the votes were polled—that people were still with them.

The day of counting however turned into the day of reckoning for them. The election results showed people, even the people of Bengal who were with them for 30 years, had all left them. The Congress increased its tally very significantly from 145 (2004) to 205 and the UPA led by it came close to the half-way mark. Immediately, there was a rush to extend support to it, and among those who rushed to do so were Mulayam Singh Yadav and Mayawati. The UPA formed the new government comfortably, and this time the second party in this government was the Trinamool Congress of Mamata Banerjee, the long-time archrival of the CPI(M) in West Bengal.

No one looked back at the CPI(M). A meeting of the Third Front scheduled at the party headquarters had to be called off. The plight of the Left was seen in the headlines that screamed its fate, justifiably, 'Left in the Lurch'.

The pundits of the media saw the obvious: the Left was punished by the people for withdrawing support from the government and trying to forge the impossible—a Third Front.

The obvious in this case was however an illusion. The Left could have done no better had it continued with the Congress even for the rest of their lives. Their nemesis was knocking at their doors, and that had very little to do with the Congress or the Third Front. We will soon come back to that, just after taking note of another point.

***

With the electoral debacle of the Left, a cycle that started decades ago appeared to have ended in 2009. It was a sudden end of glory.

This was waiting for them for a long time, for the importance they enjoyed was a simulated one: like fake currency notes it remained in circulation for decades without any intrinsic strength. It was illusory, for it did not stem from a wide mass base or an admirable capacity to launch a nationwide movement; it was a massive superstructure built in the air. The fellow-travellers did not respect them for their strength on the ground: they respected them for their dedication to the cause of the poor and the underprivileged, for their honest living and honesty of purpose, for their progressive attitude. Even after the ideology they believed in was defeated in countries after countries, no one pointed fingers at them; and they carried on advising different leaders, from VP Singh to Mulayam Singh or Laloo Prasad, no matter whether it was sought or not, whether it was abided by or not. Though the CPI(M) was anti-Congress for a long time, they always had a politburo member designated for liaising with the Congress: P Rammurthy in 60s and 70s, HS Surjeet in 80s and 90s, Sitaram Yechury in the present decade. Till 2004, no one slammed the door on the face of these leaders for it was known that they often extended their hand for the benefit of the country, and not for their personal aggrandizement. Their support to Indira Gandhi during the time of bank nationalization or Surjeet's effort to end Khalistan movement was examples of such acts.

The rise of Hindu chauvinist forces provided them with an excellent opportunity to add to their legitimacy and assume the role of a pivot in the 'secular' camp. But, somehow this also corroded their fame, their legitimacy. The fight against the growing forces of communalism, a large part of which was imaginary, blinded them. First they supported the Congress and lost their credibility among their old friends. Then they supported the Congress policies. Afterwards, they went further ahead on the Rightist track and lost their support base.

The bubble had burst in West Bengal. The Left had tested a defeat in the state at any level of election (be it Lok Sabha/state legislature/Panchayat) after 32 years. It had won only 15 out of 42 seats. Unfortunately for them, they failed to foresee the future or prepare themselves for the eventuality. They could not read the writing of the wall that was so evident even to some honest analysts who never before had inked such a gory picture for them[1]. If in Bengal they could still manage one-third of the seats, in Kerala it was meagre one-fifth (4 out of 20).

This was bound to create an atmosphere of gloom. 'What next' was the question. But it could not have been so dark if the disappointing calculations about the future were factored in by electoral outcomes only. After all, electoral reversals are like unavoidable pitfalls in a political party's road to power. And the CPI(M) was in parliamentary politics since its inception. The undivided party, which embraced electoral politics since 1952 (when the first general election took place in independent India), had seen even darker days before and just after Independence. It had seen the days of Emergency (1975–77) too. True, in those days, the cadre was charged with a dream of a revolution—bloody or peaceful—and parliamentary politics was not be-all and end-all in the lives of those thousands of communists. But now, in 2009, the party was entirely dependent on their success in parliamentary politics. However, that is true about all other political parties. And there are examples of how a party could reverse such electoral debacles by launching a movement, or simply by default. The 'Hindu' party BJP got only 2 seats in 1984, but jumped to 85 just five years later, and thereafter, within 12 years, was firmly entrenched in power in Delhi. They could create history by utilizing the vacuum in anti-Congress politics, and by unleashing a Hindu chauvinist movement in the name of Ram. So, why the CPI(M) and the Left were so down?

True, it was apparent from the results, almost a forgone conclusion, that they would lose both Bengal and Kerala in 2011 assembly elections. But a political party wants to fight back even when pushed to a corner. Why the CPI(M) should be an exception?

So, definitely, the darkness was not the consequence of the electoral debacle. It was surely indicative of some deeper crises in the party.

***

That brings us back to our earlier point: the Left could have done no better had they continued with the Congress even for the rest of their lives.

Let us see it from the affected parties' point. For them, the major question was whether a comeback was possible.

For staging a comeback, one needs to introspect, identify the reasons of failure, and take remedial steps as quick as possible. While the media pundits were speculating on the reasons of the debacle of the Left, party leaders knew it all. The CPI(M) had decided to withdraw support from the government about a year before they actually withdrew it. In the middle of August 2007, the Left would have withdrawn support, if the government had gone ahead with the Nuke Deal. The statement issued on behalf of the CPI(M) politburo on 18 August warned of 'serious consequences for the government and the country' if Manmohan Singh went ahead with the Nuke Deal. But they actually withdrew support on 9 July 2008. Why was this delay? For a single reason: the Bengal party needed time to prepare itself for facing the electorate. Why did they need time? Because mid-August 2007 was too close to 14 March 2007. What happened on that particular date? On that day, something happened in a place called Nandigram where villagers were resisting land acquisition plan of the state government. The chief minister had by then said that the government would not acquire land 'if the people do not want it'. People of Nandigram, and the whole of Bengal, knew why that phrase 'if the people do not want it' was always being added. They knew if the police, and under their protection the CPI(M) goons, could enter the area, no one would ever be able to say 'no' to the CM's industrialization plan. So, according to West Bengal DGP AB Vohra[2], on that particular day, 5,000 villagers resisted 3,000-strong police force from entering Nandigram. Just imagine, 5,000 unarmed (or armed with some *desi* weapons) people versus 3,000 armed police force! So, obviously a war was going on there. The locals were just fortunate that only 14 (official figure) died on that day. Many more were injured. The police and the CPI(M) people entered through some points and allegedly tortured and raped some women. Nothing serious! In every war, the victors do that with the vanquished.

The party leaders of all the Left partners in Bengal knew that Nandigram had gone into history. So they wanted to buy as much time as possible, hoping time would heal this wound.

That was why the Left could not withdraw the support in August 2007. Whatever, this shows that all the Left leaders knew the reasons of their debacle. And Nandigram was only one of the many. The reason taken together can be packaged as the Left's turning into a new 'Left', just like Labour's turning into the new Labour (in UK). The first question was, how to rectify the blunders. The question was whether the party (i.e., Prakash Karat, the general secretary) would be able to show the courage to take on those two mighty leaders—Buddhadeb Bhattacharya and Sitaram Yechury—who were the architects of the 'new Left' in India? But then, what about Karat's role? He posed himself as a hardliner, but had acquiesced with the track diversion that took place during his tenure as the general secretary of the party (He took over as general secretary in 2005).

But, those who could think and analyse, those inside the party or those sympathetic to the Left, knew it well that there could be no course-correction without getting at the root of the problem. The insiders were also suffering from what we may call 'limitations of perceptions'. Being involved with the process of the party's shift towards the Right, the whole of the scenario remained beyond their grasp: someone was seeing it from the Right, someone from the Left, and no one had an overview.

Now, let us move over the total scenario that brought them to their Waterloo. We must see it from the perspective of the people in general, and the supporters of the Left (including those who lived in its strongholds and had earlier voted for it, and also those who lived outside its influence zone) in particular. Seen from their perspective, it was clear that the reasons of the debacle in Bengal and Kerala were to some extent alike, and to some other extent different.

***

In Bengal, the reasons were strewn in the fields of the vast rural area, in the villages where the poor peasants lived, in the semi-urban areas where the poor were in majority, and in the pockets of Muslim settlements. Three factors were responsible for their turning away from the Left: i) the fear of forcible acquisition of agricultural land and use of brutal force to crush the protestors (by the police and the goons loyal to and part of the party organization), ii) the disillusionment of the people who expected, from those long 32 years of unbroken Left rule, real change in their lives (and not in the lives of a few others only), and iii) a callously partial administration (indifferent to the needs, sentiments and dignity of the Muslims, Dalits and *Adivasis*), both bureaucratic and political.

All these were sourced from a single criterion—the mindset and the changed outlook of the state leadership. The discordant voice of Rejjak Mollah (a minister in the state) on forcible acquisition of land was silenced, and since no one in the party dared to protest openly. Shedding their old identities, West Bengal CPI(M) went for a face-lift, and the look it assumed was that of a pro-industry, pro-development and modern entity. It planned forcible acquisition of tens of thousands of acres from the tillers, and doled out huge benefits to the favourite corporate barons (like Ratan Tata). Its top leader in the state, the chief minister, said openly that 'globalization is a must'.

People simply rejected this new Left after they saw its most barbarian face in Nandigram, where land acquisition was planned and denied, where the CPI(M) goons made endless attempts to 'recapture' the lost base from the rebels and allegedly raped the local women, where the police killed 14 poor men who along with other thousands of locals were resisting the entry of the joint force of police and the CPI(M) goons. People withdrew their support from the Left when they realized that the CM, in the garb of a democrat, is actually a Stalinist. Otherwise, when the goons finally reclaimed the area months after the police firing, the CM would not have rejoiced the victory with his notorious words that the rebels 'were paid back in the same coin' (13 November 2007)[3] . The CM, who was trying to build up a liberal image of his political self, failed to hide his Stalinist core in that moment of excitement. But people were not convinced that liberalism and Stalinism could go hand in hand. They opted for democracy.

The CPI(M) did all these in the name of the welfare of the people. But the people rejected the 'benevolent' slaughterers. They rejected the Left because its barbarism was unleashed against the backdrop of its failure in improving substantially the universal health or education system, its failure in following up the gains of remarkable growth in agriculture, or in providing an iota of justice to a Muslim boy who had to give his life for marrying a girl of a rich and influential Marwari family of Calcutta. The Left had failed even in staving off hunger of millions of people.

It is another matter that (on 16 November 2007) the High Court had termed the police firing wholly 'unconstitutional which could not be justified under any provision of law'. The CPI(M), a party that never cared for any democratic institution like the court, the governor, or even the Central Government, criticized this verdict. Binoy Konar, an important state-level leader who earlier threatened to exterminate the people of Nandigram by surrounding them from all sides, said the court verdict would encourage 'lawlessness'!

When all other efforts failed, the Left tried to stifle off the immense popularity of Opposition leaders Mamata Banerjee (who, otherwise, is not known for her statesman-like visions or political wisdom) by allowing Ratan Tata to withdraw his Nano project from Singur. Many believed the Left actually colluded with the Tata Motors to make this happen. We may discard that theory, but the fact remains that this trick too failed like anything. Along with the majority of the people of Bengal, even the residents of Singur assembly segment (and, of course, the Lok Sabha constituency) rejected the Left in 2009.

It was expected; it was inevitable, and it happened. But, it was not only Bengal that had rejected the Left. Kerala too did it. We should have a glimpse of the Kerala situation too.

The case of Kerala was different. Unlike West Bengal, the conflict between the neoliberals led by the dodgy state secretary Pinarayi Vijayan and the old traditional hardliners led by a-bit-too-radical Chief Minister VS Achuthanandan had not yet been resolved in Kerala at the popular level, the most important level in a democratic set-up. Vijayan controls the entire party machinery (i.e., the Stalinist 'organization' of the party), while octogenarian 'VS' is immensely popular among the supporters. They were locked in a fight to finish the other, and in the preceding years before the election it went to a bizarre level. VS called his rivals 'neoliberal' and 'corrupt to the core', while Vijayan and his men virtually called him 'senile' and a member of 'certain extremist groups'. This last epithet was used when the party rejected CM's plan to have a second land reform to destroy the land mafias. But as the fight has not ended, the Left, if not the CPI(M), still has a future in that state.

Again, unlike West Bengal, the rank and file of the CPI(M) in Kerala is not so corrupt, while a large section of the leadership has a very corrupt image of themselves in the minds of the people. About Bengal it must be mentioned that a large section of the top state leaders are not seen as corrupt: but it is just the opposite in Kerala. This contradiction between the base and the top may assume a significant role in shaping up the future of the Left in Kerala. Theoretically, the top cannot get rid of the base, it has to change the base through a long process, but the base can rid itself of the top in one felling swoop. At the practical level, it is difficult to predict what will happen actually. It all depends on how long VS will be able to carry on his fight against the neoliberal and perceived-to-be-corrupt leaders of the party.

Such grave contradictions were not present in Tripura, the third state ruled by the Congress. In that state there was no major shift from pre-2004 Leftism, no daring experiment with governance, nor any tinkering with normal functioning of Indian democracy and free economy. It was neither Rightist, nor excessively Leftist. This tiny state has two Lok Sabha seats, and both of them were won comfortably by the CPI(M) even in 2009.

Thus, at one level, the reasons of the debacle were clear and visible. But there were doubts whether these crucial errors would be acknowledged. Again, the question was whether those responsible should be punished. But, who would punish them? Even at the central level, the CPI(M) had betrayed the same neoliberal mindset by supporting the SEZs (Special Economic Zones, an euphemism for neo-zamindari of secondary and tertiary sector lords), by not resisting the entry of the big players in retail sector who are sure to damage the livelihood of millions of small retailers, by endorsing the patent regime, and by abandoning their comrades during the airport strike that ended (4 February 2006) in surrender after four days of crippling the airports. All these happened when Prakash Karat was at the helm. There were two reasons why Karat acquiesced. Whether under duress or on his own volition? We will discuss these later. But the very fact that all these had the nod of the party's top echelon left no one unscathed.

All together, what the party did in the states, particularly in Bengal, and the stands it took at the national level had stripped it from its old identities. It was true that at the national level it stalled some major disinvestment proposals and entry of FDI (foreign direct investment) in some crucial sectors including in bank and insurance. Thus, thanks to the Left, the effect of global recession was minimized in India. True that at the national level they fought pro-US avalanche and ultimately withdrew support from the Central Government. But that did not help them as they had by then turned into a faceless entity: sometimes-Left-sometimes-Right, a bundle of contradictions. Who is a Leftist and who is a Rightist is determined solely by its approach towards the economic issues, and definitely the CPI(M) had turned into a Rightist force.

So, the main battle within the party was to be fought on the question of its identity—whether it would remain on the Left, or would trudge a Rightist path. This was a dangerous battle for any communist party as it inevitably led to a split.

The gloom that descended on the party headquarters stemmed from this grave fear.

***

However, course correction would not have been difficult if the communists could only understand what the people expected from them. A section of the communists feigned to be old guards leading a proletarian party and comrades gathered around to cheer them with absurd slogans like 'down with capitalism'. Someone else fancied himself as Deng Xiao Ping's too-late Indian avatar and a large section of red guards drew them together about him. Both sections were on extremes, while many floated around in the interspersing space. No one realized that the need of the hour was simply a democratic socialist party. Someone, named Saifuddin Chowdhury, realized it long ago and left the party at the fag end of the last century to embrace political oblivion.

The CPI(M) or the Left is accepted by that section of the population which believes the Indian Leftists are actually democratic socialists. Nobody believes that someday they will abolish private property. Thirty years ago, when the habit of acquiring wealth had not made such deep inroads in the party, the myth that the communists were against the institution of private property, or against the industrial barons, did convince many people. But, not any more. How could Jyoti Basu do that when his son amassed so much wealth in last 30 years? How Prakash Karat can go for it when his close friends and relatives are so rich? Why Pinarayi Vijayan, accused of making unfair deals with a Canadian firm, should suddenly hit the interest of such firms? Why Buddhadeb Bhattacharya will work against the interest of Ratan Tata? People ask these simple questions and they know the answers as well.

Again, nobody believes that the CPI(M) is for overthrowing the system as most of its leaders and cadre are from the middle class who stand to lose from a revolutionary change.

In short, its support base does not expect anything radical from the traditional Left of India. Those who seek such changes have opted for the Maoists. Communists started losing the ground to them long ago. AB Bardhan (general secretary of the CPI) once told me how they lost Gadchiroli (in eastern Maharashtra). The official Left planned a movement for raising the wages of the *beedi*-leaf (*kendu patta*) collectors and *beedi*-makers; but as they delayed it for various reasons, the Naxalites raised the demand and started a movement that successfully carried away the whole area with them in the 70s. The communists also lost their hold over Telangana to the Maoists, and they lost out in all the regions where the Maoists are strong now. It was not that the communists were very strong in those areas of Bihar-Jharkhand-Orissa-Chhattisgarh. But it is an interesting that the Maoist organization was built up by those people who came out of the CPI(M) and then left Bengal and Andhra Pradesh to work in new regions. They tried, they made sacrifices, they got killed, but they tried on and on and won the hearts of those *Adivasis* and Dalits who were treated most insensitively by the whole nation. But, from the CPI(M) no one ever left Bengal or Kerala to live and work in adjacent states to build up the party there. So, the traditional communists could never penetrate the jungles or the remote areas of central India where the *Adivasis* or the Scheduled Caste people live. The traditional communists never stood by them when *Adivasis* or Scheduled Caste were evicted from their hearths and huts. The communists could never even identify themselves with those millions living the most wretched life in this country.

So, the traditional Left was freed from carrying the burden of serving the interest of these poorest of the poor population. After the split of 1964, they grew in areas where poverty was there of course—40 years ago the extent of poverty was much, much more even according to the sham poverty line used in our country—but the strongholds of poverty in Left areas were not so endlessly large like that in the central India. Bengal was the second most industrialized state with higher per capita income and higher state domestic product, and it provided a vast scope for emergence of a large middle class—upper, middle and lower. Kerala too was not so poor, and quick spread of education made it one of the most socially advanced states in India. In last 30 years, Kerala had been ruled by the Left and the Right by turn, and it has better records than West Bengal in social development.

Anyway, it was the poorer section of the population—the peasants, the mill-workers, the lower middle class—and a section of the middle class that came out to support the Left. However, the top leadership in Bengal came increasingly from the middle class only. Kerala party still can boast of having a CM (VS Achuthanandan) who came up from the lower rungs of the society. But, Bengal has no such leader in the uppermost layer. That was why Kerala party did not neglect the core ideological points like pursuing a pro-poor agenda, following anti-US anti-MNC line or fighting the Congress severely on the ground. Bengal lost sight of all these.

There were reasons for that. With growing affluence of a section of the support base in Bengal, the party started feeling contradictory pulls. There was demand of development from all segments of population and it further confused the leadership about the path of development. After Narasimha Rao started liberalizing the economy, the scope for any alternative line (like demanding more public sector units to be set up in the state) shrank. And when the push came to shove from the mid-90s, the leaders became desperate. In Bengal, over the years, different sections other than the poor or the lower segment of the middle class had come up to support the party. The reason for their siding with the communists was simple—to reap benefit of proximity to power that flowed from Writers Buildings of Calcutta to the Gram Panchayat offices at the village level. These upper middle class or rich and extremely rich people were left without any alternative as the CPI(M) was ruling the state continuously from 1977. Soon they had their presence felt in the corridor of power. It all started happening at the time of Jyoti Basu, but being an aristocrat Basu was not friend of anyone and no one could influence the policies at their will. As Basu retired, the upper middle class and the rich had their field day. The party that had once sworn to break the dark hands of Tatas and Birlas now became well-wisher of Ratan Tata. They started identifying them with the interest of Ratan Tata.

Matters have not gone to this length in Kerala because of VS and also because the Left had not ruled the state for long years together.

Leaving these richer sections and those who are with the party for vested interest (including a section of the cadre), the vast support base in Bengal and Kerala and Tripura had limited expectations from the Left. Even those, who would have voted for them if they were strong in some other areas, do not expect much radicalism from them. They expected them to practise a path of democratic socialism. A democratic socialist party in a country like India should strive, first of all, to ensure social security for all. It means everybody should have two square meals a day, enough clothes to protect oneself from diseases, proper home to live in a somewhat healthy way, proper treatment of all kinds of illness, and a guarantee of enjoying all these even if one cannot work due to illness or for any other reason. Democratic socialism also calls for stalling such developmental initiatives and policies that harms more than it benefits the poor, fighting for ensuring human rights, and taking initiatives for fair and eco-friendly development, the fruits of which will ensure socio-economic justice for all.

This public perception has, in fact, made the task of the Left easy. The CPI(M) knew this. Long ago they had prepared, and then updated, their concept of 'people's democracy'[4]. It reflects exactly what their supporters expect from them. But the Left failed to work for fulfilling these expectations. They failed not only their supporters, but also themselves.

***

That brings us to the real reasons of worry for the party that still calls itself a communist party.

Strangely, as days and weeks and then months passed after the election, it became quite clear that Bengal leadership was not ready to acknowledge the real reasons of the defeat. They forgot why they pleaded for time when the confrontation on the Nuke Deal was picking up. In a farcical manner they wanted to bring home the point that as the CPI(M) withdrew support from the Congress-led government, the party got doomed in Bengal. But when were the people of Bengal so devoted to the Congress? Last time they voted whole-heartedly for the Congress was in, well, many decades ago, in 1972. In the election after Indira Gandhi's assassination in 1984, when the Congress had its highest ever tally in the Lok Sabha, the national party could manage to get only 16 out of 42 seats of Bengal. That was the record tally for the opposition after 1977, to be broken only in 2009. This time the Left's vote went down by 7 per cent.

Actually, it was another calculation that they were doing—had the CPI(M) not withdrawn support from the Central Government, the Congress would not have allied with the Trinamool Congress in Bengal, and a divided Opposition could not get so many seats. What a pity! The successors of those mighty communists of the yore were trying to live a life at the mercy of the Congress party! And their argument had two major fallacies. The Congress would have allied with the Trinamool Congress anyway, as the leaders of the Congress were fade up with the 'Leftism' of the CPI(M) at the central level. They would have anyway betrayed the Left at the hustings. They did the same with Mulayam Singh Yadav of Uttar Pradesh who provided oxygen to the government after the Left's withdrawal, and also with Laloo Prasad of Bihar, who was a partner in the first UPA government. Again, even if the Congress and the Trinamool Congress did not forge a bond, it was the Trinamool Congress that might have swept southern Bengal and would have got almost all the seats except, at most, four. Out of 20 seats the Trinamool Congress or its small allies won, the gap with the Left candidates ranged from 60,000–200,000 in 15, and in none of these constituencies the Congress had polled even 50,000 votes in last few years. We can easily add at least one more to this list and that makes it 16. The Congress too would have bagged all the seats except one. In that case, the tally of the Opposition (including the BJP which won the Darjeeling seat) would have been 22 and the Left 20. It is still a defeat all the same.

But, why were the CPI(M) leaders of Bengal doing it? Probably, it was another example of their lie-campaign to confuse the people. They were spreading the canard everywhere in Bengal that had there been no adjustment between the two Congress parties, the Left would have retained its supremacy as before. Logically, next they will be at the feet of the Congress so that it does not go with the Trinamool Congress in 2011. If that materializes, then they will spread the canard that they are going to come back to power. This has worked for long years—out of fear that they would be back, many people did not come out to vote against them. But, there is negligible chance of this happening again in 2011.

However, all these efforts are indicative of the moral fall of the Bengali communists. The logical next question is, whether there is any chance of regaining their strength in near future. In the light of this, a detailed recount of what they have done in Bengal will make it easier to understand why they cannot expect to occupy the Leftist space again, at least in the short run. Bengal is an excellent case for judging the Left as it has provided opportunity to examine what a 33-year long (1977–2009) communist rule could achieve or failed to achieve.

But before that, let us take a look at what the party was in Bengal in earlier times. It will enable us to understand how they negated their past and gradually lost the credibility that the earlier generations of communists earned for the party. That will also help us understand why Nandigram was so significant.

This case of changing hues was full-blown in Bengal before the parliamentary election and showed the consequence it would have. This development is also likely to have a bearing on Kerala.

***

Now, let us examine briefly the contours of what we mean by negation of the past.

The communists in India, and particularly in those areas where they ever had any strong base, were known for (a) their struggles against the landlords and the capitalists, (b) solidarity with the mass and (c) their probity and their willingness to fight against corruption, black money and so on. Factors (a) and (b) earned them a very high degree of credibility among the population benefitted by these, like small peasants, the marginal farmers and share-croppers, the agricultural labour, the people working in informal sectors and in industries and in offices. Factor (c) popularized them among the middle class. These factors and the corresponding support base overlapped one another, and influenced a very large section of the students and intellectuals. This spilled over outside their bases to create a secondary base among the students and intellectuals in places where the mass was not with the party. Again those same factors strengthened their trade union bases scattered all over the country, though they failed to expand that base to cover sizable segment of the electorate. That happened mainly because of their failure to understand the reality and to use that. They failed to reach out to the unorganized sector (90 per cent of the total workforce) workers who live a wretched live, and thus failed to mobilize the real poor workers. Still, the trade union wings of the CPI and the CPI(M) have played a very crucial role in adding to the strength, recognition and respectability of their respective parties.

Whatever, after sustaining power for years in Bengal the communists of earlier generations started facing an acute problem. Compulsions of running government in the states compelled them to make compromises. Mostly, Jyoti Basu took lead in it and carried the day. People forgave such compromises as they had faith in the communists. It was a question of credibility. The credibility level was so high that nearly 50 per cent of people of Bengal believed that whatever they did was basically in the interest of the poor people.

And the leaders, despite their various shortcomings, were committed to the poor. Even Jyoti Basu, who was criticized inside the party for being soft towards the capitalists and the Congress, used to clarify almost in every meeting that they had to make compromises as they were working within a capitalist system. He used to articulate his awareness about the profit motive of the capitalists, and then explained why he still invited them to invest in Bengal. From a pragmatic viewpoint, one has to acknowledge that his approach was flawless, for he himself acknowledged that it was being done under duress. And all through his active career, he always had a heart for the poorer people—he was for their struggles and rights, he was for strengthening lower level democracy and consciousness of the people. Basu was for strengthening the mechanisms that would ensure some sort of safety network for the poor.

He was not a communist in traditional sense, but he was a Leftist.

And such Leftists were everywhere in the party. In the late 90s, when I told Madhu Bag, a district level leader in Bengal, that they had failed to do anything to uplift the condition of the Scheduled Caste and tribal population, he admitted it and confessed that those people were still with them only because they had earned social dignity due to the Left movement. He also conceded that they had failed to do something meaningful for their economic uplift only because they did not know how to do it. Of course he told me this on condition that I would not write it. Now, after a decade I mention this as an example of the efforts and consciousness of those leaders of the past.

People like Madhu Bag, and there were hundreds and thousands of them, earned the Left the credibility it had by not only through their deeds, but also by their style of living. In Bengal, that generation failed in various fields, failed to follow-up their initial success of agrarian labour reform, failed to boost the health facilities, failed to find out ways to move forward; but never failed to be with the weaker sections of the people.

It must be clarified that 'failed' here does not mean that everything remained standstill. Not at all. Things were improving, but that was quite natural with passage of time. It happened in every state of India and in the world. I use the word 'failed' with a different connotation. A Left government is supposed to focus primarily on livelihood issues, on health and on education. Had that been done, Bengal would have been far ahead in social indicators of development than any other state. Unfortunately, that did not happen.

And yet the people had great confidence in the comrades. They knew the communists were with them and for them. The communists stood by them in their fight for their rights on the land they tilled, for their rights in the factories, for their dignity in everyday life. Often the comrades were too militant, dangerously and irrationally militant, causing flight of capital from Bengal, but a great majority of them were honest. Such pre-77 trends continued for more than a decade, and then started rotting.

In the first 15 years of their rule in Bengal, the Left raised their credibility level to a new high. That was the time when land reforms took place, payment of minimum wages in the agricultural and industrial sector was ensured, Gram Panchayats took charge of local administration, and the dignity of poor people was certified. These were the steps that did the magic. These steps were the open secret of Left's incredible success in Bengal for long years.

In next 15 years, they continuously failed the rising aspiration of their support base, but did not lose much of their credibility among their supporters, neither among the poor, nor among the SCs, tribal population or the Muslims. Corruption started making inroads, but most of the middle level leaders were still clean. However, they were losing their popularity slowly, and their lustre quickly. As their support waned, they became more dependent on arm-twisting tactics consisting of creating fear in the minds of the people and favouring only those who were firmly with the party. The cracks in the castle were widening, but the castle was far from the stage of being condemned. In 2001 assembly elections, the Congress and the Trinamool Congress took them on jointly (like in 2009), and failed miserably. The reason was simple—the Left was still the Left.

But it took them less than three years to wash out what they earned and retained for roughly about 30 years. And ironically, Jyoti Basu played a role in it, albeit indirectly. In 1996, the CPI(M) rejected a proposal of some smaller parties that formed a United Front to have Jyoti Basu as the PM. The majority section of the party led by Karat rejected the proposal on the ground that the United Front government would not achieve anything significant as it would be dependent on the Congress. Later, Basu described it as a historic blunder. Probably, Basu broke party discipline to bring home the point that leading a government could give a great boost to the party. But, his statement opened up the Pandora's box. Comrades in Bengal thought the Congress was no more a rival. They started opposing everything that Karat stood for in those days. They started imitating Basu in breaking party discipline. However, Basu himself restrained this section from going too far. After Basu retired, it was the state party secretary Anil Biswas who, despite his vacillations, kept the party on track. After his untimely demise (26 March 2006) during the run-up to the assembly election that the Left swept, it was all open for the neoliberals of Bengal.

That was the beginning of losing credibility. That was the beginning of the end.

***

It all started from the second term of Bhattacharya, when he really unmasked himself. Deciding to sway the minds of the people by a slogan of 'development', Bhattacharya projected it just like the hardcore Rightists. What Basu projected as doings under duress, he presented as doing the right thing. Thus, compulsion gave way to conviction. Globalization changed from being perceived as 'inevitable' to a 'must'. While pushing the Tata Nano project, he harped only on the debatable employment side (though in all probability, much lesser number of people were to get employment than those evicted from their land and living), as though it was a philanthropy on the part of the Tatas. He and his team collaborated with the industrialists as friends and the elation in his face with every new big project signed said it all. This was accompanied by apathy, if not antipathy, to old industries and plantations that employed huge number of people. Jute industry became sunset industry. Tea gardens were left in the lurch. Plastic and petrochemical lobby had their field-day in Bengal. A certain foreign company and its Bengali representative became immensely popular among the journalists, media directors and some of the Left politicians.

From a moral standpoint, Bhattacharya's approach would have been welcomed only if he severed link with his party, denounced the ideology that he had used to rise up to his position, and sought mandate of the people for his new agenda. Years ago, Mamata Banerjee quarrelled with her party, left it to float her own party, and came out with flying colours. But, Bhattacharya decided to have the best of both worlds. He wanted to be regarded as a communist while making efforts to crush the rights of the toiling mass like right to strike, a right recognized in all capitalist countries and denied in communist countries like China. He imitated Chandrababu Naidu's, SM Krishna's and Narendra Modi's model of development while remaining in a party that continuously criticized those models.

And he was not alone. Biman Bose, Shyamal Chakrabarty, Nirupam Sen, Binoy Konar and a host of state's top leadership tagged along with him. Some of the central leaders clapped for him. Karat and others acquiesced.

No wonder that it led them to do certain things like firing upon the peasants that many neoliberal politicians will shudder to do.

Now let us examine what were the changes Bhattacharya brought, or tried to bring but failed due to the pressure from within the party or its affiliated units.

First, the economic policy. In last few years, the Bengal government proposed to do certain things. They proposed to open the doors for corporate farming that could have destroyed the land reforms they undertook three decades ago. They planned to transfer fertile agricultural land to industry at a concessional rate. They planned to give huge subsidy to a very few selected Indian and multinational industrial houses. They planned to invite all foreign investors (feigning that the party was following a different yardstick on this count than the Rightists) with the excuse that it would create employment. They contemplated having retail chains of big companies. They jumped up at the prospect of having new airports developed by private players. Those who resisted the party's policies, like MK Pandhe (president of party's trade union wing CITU) in Delhi or Rejjak Mollah (a minister in the state) in Bengal, were silenced. They wanted to get out of the state PSUs (Public Sector Undertakings) run by the West Bengal government and have a pension scheme for state government employees where the employee will not contribute. In some of these mentioned cases, the government yielded to the pressure from within and aborted its plans. But in most of the cases it went ahead. Nandigram (where police firing killed farmers) and Singur (where land of many farmers was taken away forcefully), were just two most infamous cases of Bengal government's brutality that attracted the national media's attention.

The labour policy of the government was the same story of negation of the past. First, Bhattacharya clamoured for banning strike in the IT sector. Then he opposed *bandhs* (general strikes) by the unions. Such strikes were always called by the trade union wing of his party and other Leftist and Centrist trade unions. On 26 August 2008 he declared: *"I am against bandhs. Unfortunately, I belong to a political party, which calls bandhs. I have kept quiet. But, from now on, I'll not keep quiet."* His attempt to smother the democratic rights of the working class was confronted by the central leadership, who issued an open statement that censured him by saying that the party's opinion differed from the CM's. There is little doubt that Bhattacharya treated the statement as a wastepaper. Ironically, the CM's statement neither evoked any respect for him in Bengal where people were otherwise fed up with the overuse of general strikes and non-functioning of various government organs. People took the statement just as a gimmick as they had seen that this man had never even cared to go by his constitutional responsibility of making efforts to give protection to those who wanted to work on the days the Left unions called *bandh*.

In fact, the issue was simple: a trade union may exercise its right to call a general strike, but a government has to fulfil its constitutional obligation of taking all measures to keep normal life going. Had that been done, there would have been no issues at all. But, Bhattacharya was always confused. That was probably normal for any man who stayed, for reasons unknown, in an organization that carried on doing things he considered 'unfortunate'. Otherwise, he would have understood that people could see through his designs. He did not fulfil his constitutional obligations. He did not try to make the police administration (a department he was in charge of for many years) impartial so that it did its duty properly instead of carrying out diktats of the local party bosses everywhere. Had that been done, a *bandh* call by the Left that people disliked would have never succeeded (as those willing to join work would have got police protection, and life would have been normal in the state even on a day of *bandh*). Then, the Left would have stopped calling general strikes. But, following this course was an arduous task. Giving a statement against *bandh* is a cheap way out. Industrial barons clapped for the CM, media barons found in him a reincarnation of Deng; but, people could easily realize that the CM was going for gimmicks only.

Again, the CM also lost the sense of priorities. What is more important: clamouring for keeping open the call centres to ask someone whether he wants a banking facility, or making arrangements for banks to be open? Who decided that IT is more important than all other sectors including banking and commerce or factories? What about making arrangements for daily wage earners to earn their *roti-chaal* (chapatti-rice) on the day of general strikes? What about stopping forcible downing of the shutters of any establishment? What about stopping the *dadagiri* (use of force to intimidate people) of Bengal party and Bengal CITU? Do not expect any answer from the Bengali communists. They are confused about everything—about democracy, about citizen's rights, about the distinction between the government and the party, and about reforms and the means of reforms.

Let us move over to another point. The CM's efforts to wind up as many state PSUs possible also clarified things further before the labourers. When in 2007 the jute strike reached a critical stage and Union Labour Minister Oscar Fernandez took initiative to settle the matter, state government remained indifferent because, reportedly, the CM believed jute was sunset industry! For the sake of record, more than 400,000 people are directly or indirectly dependent on the jute industry, which has a tremendous potential market throughout the world with growing consciousness about environment.[5] I do not know whether the Bengal government had the same attitude about the tea gardens. But the CM and his government remained cynically indifferent about the plight and reported starvation of the tea garden workers for a very long time. Finally, Governor Gopal Gandhi went there (1 March 2007) and attracted media's attention by touring the gardens and commenting that it was shocking 'to find people dying of starvation in a progressive country like India'. Thereafter, the state government took some steps.

Next, the policies about the minorities. The CM once commented (in the aftermath of attack on American Centre in Calcutta on 22 January 2002) that the madrassas of Bengal were breeding ground of terrorism. Following his words, a drive against the Muslims began in Bengal. Jamat-e-Islami Hind dashed a protest letter to the then party general secretary HS Surjeet. Finally, the then Bengal party secretary Anil Biswas countered the CM and clarified that no such sweeping statement was justified as only one or two of the madrassas could be involved in nasty things. In those days, the corridors of power in New Delhi were abuzz with stories of Bhattacharya's proximity to and his 'breakfast' with the then Home Minister of India LK Advani, the mastermind behind Ram Mandir movement that demolished Babri mosque. Thus, from the very beginning of his innings as CM (since 6 November 2000), Bhattacharya became a suspect in the eyes of the Muslims, a large section of whom had voted for the Left for decades. The Sachhar report on conditions of

Muslims in the country laid bare the neglect of the community in the state by the great secularists of Bengal. But, the way the government dealt with Rizwanur Rahman death case disillusioned a very large chunk of the Muslim population. The police commissioner of Calcutta remained in office for weeks even after strongly defending the role the police played in separating Rizwanur from his wife who belonged to an extremely affluent Marwari family. The whole state was shocked. The reason for keeping that man in the office? He was close to the CM. The whole thing had two connotations—one was the anti-Muslim mentality and the other was the pro-rich attitude of the police administration headed by the CM himself. Thus, it also had its effect on the Hindu middle class and poorer sections. Calcutta saw a novel scene when hundreds and thousands came out and silently marched on with candles in their hands to protest. Caste, class and religious division became non-existent for a while, and this new movement was, alas, against the Left who had convinced the whole country that they were champions of castleless, classless and secular society! Then to appease the Muslims the government did exactly what the pseudo-seculars should do. It denied a home to anti-fundamentalist Bangladeshi writer Taslima Nasrin and opposed her entry in Bengal. This decision further alienated the progressive Muslims of Bengal. Here it must be mentioned that in Bengal one out of every four persons is a Muslim.

There is no point in digging out many such other skeletons. The inefficiency of the government was staring at its face in the abysmal failure in implementation of hundred days work scheme.[6] Curiously, that happened when the party leaders were out with their trumpets in the rest of the country to convince people that this scheme had become a law only because of them. It is another matter that people rejected their claim. On the front of public distribution system, which the party regularly took up in Delhi, people's revolt in 2007 against the malpractices in different districts said it all. According to reports the chain of localized revolts started on 16 September 2007 at Radhamohanpur village in Bankura district. On that day, a few CPI(M) leaders were trying to educate the villagers on the dangers of the Indo-US nuclear agreement. A group of people were not interested and asked them to provide food grains for them. Reportedly, the CPI(M) cadre tried to chase them away, but the villagers beat the CPI(M) leaders and burnt their flags. As usual police came to rescue the CPI(M) people and opened fire to quell the mob. But the news spread like wildfire and in four districts, all of which were the CPM bastions, unorganized crowd assembled spontaneously. They attacked ration dealers and the abettors in their crime, the local party leaders. Hundreds of such incidents were reported and police opened fire at various places. Three people died in the firing. This story of food riot in Bengal was not reported widely in our national Press and thus people were caught unaware and surprised at the Maoist take-over of Lalgarh. Joint forces of the state and central paramilitary are guarding Lalgarh for months now, but have achieved little. As in Jharkhand hundreds and thousands come out to support the Maoists in their operations. Why has this very poor region of Bengal revolted against the CPI(M) establishment? It is their answer to tall words and little work, to deprivation, to partisan attitude of the communists. Significantly, these people, the traditional base of the Left, have not tilted towards Mamata Banerjee's party, but selected an alternative to the traditional Left. It is another matter that the Maoists will, in the long run, fail them. This alternative CPI(M), i.e., Communist Party of India (Maoist), is caught in a time warp and does not understand the strength of the democratic process.

Enlisting more such facts here will run the risk of becoming boring. But I cannot desist from stating about another revolutionary act of the mythical Left of Bengal. A girl protesting against the government for months in Singur (against the Nano factory) was raped and murdered. There were several allegations of such rapes in Nandigram too. But as in Nandigram the culprits absconded and the delay in testing the women destroyed the cases, in Singur too the charred body could not bear testimony to rape. However, the killing could not be denied, and for that the lower court convicted the zonal committee secretary of the party (quite a high level leader in a district) and another comrade. The CPI(M) went about with a campaign that the party leader Suhrid Dutta was falsely implicated by the CBI and made that very man (freed on bail) their campaign manager in that constituency for the parliamentary election in 2009. And then, during the campaign, a so-called intellectual came out with a CD (produced by CITU, the trade union wing of the party) that revealed a new truth about the incident—the girl was not raped and murdered by the CPI(M) people, but by her father! Bhattacharya, the CM, reportedly supported making of such a CD in a television interview. I think I need not tell you they lost the constituency (Hoogly) that was regarded as their citadel.

Now, it maybe clear to the reader that this party and this government was destined to be doomed in Bengal. And remember, it all came in the backdrop of huge corruption at the lower level of the party and totalitarian control over life and living of the people. Thus, it was destined to pay the price of planning development of the state at gunpoint. It was destined to pay the price of robbing the people of their dignity that they had earned under the guidance of the older generation of the communists three decades ago. It was destined to lose in Bengal because the captain of the communist party there followed, in his gestures, thoughts and acts, the captain of one media house.

And, the party in Bengal continued with the propaganda that West Bengal was a heaven in India. Everything deteriorated in Bengal. While the central CPI(M) was furnishing its image by shouting for social security measures, in Bengal industrial sickness was going up, PF dues was rising, ESI scheme was falling through.[7]

The CPI(M) believed all such facts would ever be under carpet and their campaign that the people of Bengal are overwhelmingly with them will succeed forever. They thought their lie-campaign on Nandigram, Singur and every other happening in Bengal will win.

But, the skeletons have all tumbled out of the cupboards. There are so many of them that no place is enough to bury them.

***

It was farcical that after the election results were out in 2009, Bengal CPI(M) tried to project that there was nothing wrong in Bengal and everything happened due to the failure of the central leadership.

Here we should take note of another interesting fact that proves Bengal Left's logic was not only confounded, its claims smacked of political dishonesty. Extending its own logic to the defeat it suffered in the by-election of 10 assembly constituencies (the counting took place on 10 November 2009), one has to assume that the people were punishing them even in the by-elections of the state assembly for withdrawal of support from the Congress-led government at the Centre and trying to forge a Third Front. The CPI(M) lost all the five constituencies (including those three it earlier held) it contested and the Trinamool Congress won all the seven it contested. Surely, if we go by the argument of the state CPI(M), people should have voted whole-heartedly for the Congress. The reality, however, was just the opposite. As an ally of the Trinamool Congress, the national party contested three and won only in one. The Congress conceded its sitting seat Goalpokhor to Forward Bloc (the only party of the Left Front that managed a seat). In Kalchini, it came fourth while an Independent backed by the Gorkha Janamukti Morcha won the seat and the Adivasi Bikash Parishad came second. The CPI(M) would do well to prepare a document explaining this rejection of the Congress. People of Bengal of course knew the reason. Only a few weeks before the by-elections, the Congress took support from the CPI(M) in forming the board of Siliguri corporation leaving out the Trinamool Congress, with which it allied to fight the election. People punished the Congress for plying this fraud with them.

So, there is no love lost between the Congress and the vast majority of voters in Bengal except in three districts (Maldah, Murshidabad and Dakkhin Dinajpur). People were voting against the Left, plain and simple.

One can easily guess the degree of political fraud the state leaders of the CPI(M) too were indulging into, only to throw dust at the eyes of the central leadership, the cadre, and the support base. The reality, however, was simple—the new Left was losing its ground to the Trinamool Congress, a party that was now following a Leftist agenda like opposing forcible land acquisition, tyrannical rule, disinvestment of PSUs and so on. True, Mamata Banerjee was dithering from the beginning (and the

Central Government of Manmohan Singh had decided to go for another round of disinvestment just days before the polls), but the people of Bengal had overlooked it.

Whatever, as things showed up through passage of time, it was clear that apart from West Bengal, Andhra Pradesh and Tamil Nadu units too were unhappy with the withdrawal of support and the breakdown of relation with the Congress. In these two states, the CPI(M) earlier (2004 Lok Sabha election) aligned with the UPA and got one MP from Andhra Pradesh and two from Tamil Nadu. They failed in 2009 going against the Congress.

So it was not surprising that a sizable section of the party tried to find fault with the national leadership, namely Prakash Karat. Obviously, Karat's tenure had seen remarkable self-contradiction and had suffered from utter directionless political posturing. At times it supported utter Rightist legislations, at times it blocked softer Rightist proposals. It lodged a mild protest when the Indo-US defence deal was done; but it withdrew support from the Congress-led government on the Nuke Deal. For a hardcore Leftist, the first is naturally much more objectionable than the latter. However, those who criticized national leadership had only one point: Why they withdrew support from the Congress-led government? And why they wanted to forge a Third Front? Though these people failed to articulate things properly, it was clear that they wanted the party to be a subsidiary ally of the Congress like the Rashtriya Janata Dal of Laloo Prasad Yadav.

The CPI(M) was in real crisis. A party, particularly a Left party that is afraid of facing the reality, or truth, and wants to impose its lies on the people runs the risk of annihilation. That is what history tells us with examples abound.

This was the true nature of crisis in the CPI(M). And it was not only Bengal. The Kerala state secretariat, that earlier had sought the CM's resignation as he did not support the party's effort to suppress a corruption case (SNC Lavalin deal) against the party state secretary Pinarayi Vijayan, found fault with the CM for the rout. They initially defended their opportunistic alliance with the PDP led by Madhani (who had been cleared of charges of terrorism, but had the image of a fundamentalist) and blamed the CM for his utterances against it. True, the CM breached party discipline by expressing reservation about the party decision: but there was nothing called discipline in the party during Karat's regime of last four years. And there could not be anything called discipline when a party's top man in the state was accused of corruption and the party sought to throttle a proper investigation. Curiously, but expectedly, the state secretariat did not enlist how many times it itself had overruled and heckled the CM—starting from rejecting CM's call for second land reforms to compelling him to not to proceed with Lavalin case—and what message it had sent to the people. Instead, the state secretariat (where like in the larger body called state committee Vijayan group had huge majority) members started writing articles in the party mouthpiece *Deshabhimani* explaining why Vijayan should not be blamed for the rout. Later they had to concede some of their faults, but their attitude did not change. Thus, Kerala too, organization-wise, was a lost case.

I have not dealt with the details of Kerala only because such a defeat in Kerala was normal and the prospect of purification still exists there as the supporters and organizers of the puritan line are still agile under the leadership of VS Achuthanandan, the CM. We will examine the Kerala case in detail in later chapters.

However, the chances of rectifying the Bengal party appear to be nil. But, it was also true that a large section of the national party was pushing for return to the Leftist path. And that gave birth to acute suppressed confrontation inside the party. The risk of split was there and is still there, but it may not materialize as the whole party is getting an emaciated look day by day. So, the confrontation too is getting milder.

The characters and patterns of groups and subgroups within the party are complex and overlap one another. We will examine that later. More important is the acute confrontation between two of these groups, a neoliberal pro-Congress group led by Bhattacharya and Yechury, and a somewhat-hardliner anti-Congress group led by Prakash Karat. All other factions are aligning with these two groups according to their preferences or political positions.

The neoliberals of Bengal were trying to storm the party headquarters and oust Karat. They were peeved with Karat because he had spoiled their four-year long party with the Congress and had pushed them into hardship. They were peeved with Karat because he was trying to point out the real reasons of the debacle. He had warned them earlier, he stopped them from going ahead with their inhuman industrialization plan after Nandigram, and he tried to change some of the candidates the Bengal party nominated. But it was a coterie that was ruling Bengal and only those who were favoured were given tickets. They saw in Karat's attempts a threat to their peaceful coexistence and decided to fight him jointly. It is the common trend of all the coteries: all the members of a coterie know each other's weakness and that keeps them together. They protect each other's interest and retain their control over the organization. Thus Biman Bose, earlier perceived to be a communist who had excellent grass-root contact, Bhattacharya, a liberal who loved both intellectual exercises and the police, and Binoy Konar, a rustic hardliner who believed in the principle of might is right; all came together.

And in Yechury they found an able leader. Yechury himself was too sad at the loss of his clout after his party's withdrawal of support from the Congress. He was eager to get it back. The only way to regain his lost glory was to oust Karat and making an arrangement with the Congress to share power at the Centre as a junior partner, just like Laloo Prasad's party, or the DMK. As soon as the results were out, Yechury started contacting possible partners of his 'oust Karat' campaign. His point was simple: the responsibility of the defeat should be laid at Karat's door, so that he could be forced to resign. Everyone of the Bengal coterie agreed, except Nirupam Sen, who had fallen out with the chief minister and had turned close to Karat. Tamil Nadu and Andhra Pradesh also ratified the plan. This made the group sizable, but still in minority. But the onslaught started.

Naturally Karat had to defend himself. As his main rival was the Bengal party, he sided with Vijayan to get support of the entire Kerala unit. For that he was ready to oust VS, the hardliner and the most popular leader among the supporters, from the chair of chief minister. This attempt was resisted by Yechury and some others. So VS was ousted from the politburo of the party, but not from the post of the head of the state government. Personal rivalry between Karat and Yechury came handy for VS, and the chair of a rabid hardliner was saved by a neoliberal!

This is the best example of how compromises are being charted out inside the party. The confrontation in the party is now more personal than ideological. The two main players are Karat and Yechury. Both of them are trying to undermine the position of the other and wean away sections of the supporters from the other camp. Karat is, without doubt, miles ahead of Yechury, but to ensure his lead he has made compromises (like siding with Vijayan) and will have to make more comprises.

***

At the conclusion of this chapter, five points should be noted.

First, the CPI(M) lost the election because it itself had prepared the ground for it. Its sudden shift towards crudest capitalist policies was bound to be rejected by the people of Bengal. Again, the way the party cornered VS in Kerala, the level of infighting that strained credulity to accept both VS and Vijayan as comrades-in-arms, and the allegations of corruption against Vijayan and company had spelled doom for the party in the southern state.

Second, to save himself from the charges of destroying the party, Karat had pointed out 'the local factors' which were the real factors for the debacle of the party.

Third, Karat cannot be too aggressive against his main rivals for a few reasons. He too had acquiesced with the neoliberal pro-Congress group for last few years and cannot absolve himself from his responsibility. Again, for his survival, he has to win over a section of Bengal party (like a group led by Nirupam Sen, another hardcore neoliberal but personally close to Karat) and the largest section of the Kerala party. So, he cannot take on the neoliberals of Kerala led by Vijayan.

Fourth, this makes Karat's attempt to purify the party at the best half-hearted. He may steer the party towards a clear anti-Congress line, but the influence of the neoliberals will not diminish significantly.

Lastly, it will not help the party to regain its credibility in the near future. It is also doubtful whether it will ever become a Leftist party again. In that case its survival will depend on the failures of its opponents in its strongholds. People will not vote for the Left because of their positive agenda anymore.

So, it was not for nothing that the gloom that descended on the party headquarters in Delhi after the parliamentary election was so thick, so heavy. It was a Catch-22 situation for the party. Going deep into the reasons of the great defeat was pregnant with the possibility of a split. That would bring in organizational disaster. Ignoring the real reasons would doom the party in the long run. The party will be over ideologically.

Apparently, as things stand now in November of 2009, the party is confused, and is slowly drifting towards management of contradictions through compromises.

Probably, the party has no other option. The contradictions have become unmanageable. The contradictions are not only ideological, those are also philosophical. For long years, they have created (and probably they themselves also have believed in) different myths—the myth of invincibility of Marxism, the myth of ultimate victory of communism worldwide, the myth of monopoly of truth. When all those myths that many followers out in the fields too believed in turned into lies, they started building new myths. They did not realize that these myths had bled them severely each time they exploded, making way for the truth to emerge. These myths are at the root of their confusion and are eating away their sustainability. These myths had waylaid them.

And yet, they created and nurtured a new myth in last 15 years. That was the myth of 'secularism' or 'secular unity'.

The biggest myth of the recent years was that the Left supported a Congress-led government for the sake of secular unity, or, in other words, to keep the communal forces out. All of them had endorsed this myth. All of them, with a few exceptions like, maybe, the octogenarian MK Pandhe. All others started believing in it. This time the myth was more successful as a large section of common people in general started believing in it.

In the next chapter we will see why this was a myth and not a reality.

References

1. Interested readers may see my article in '*newsinsight.net*', dated 3 April 2009, in which I predicted: "...*the TMC-Congress pickings commence at eighteen Lok Sabha seats and could top twenty-four.*"
2. As quoted in the *Indian Express*, 15th March, Delhi edition.
3. "*They have been paid back in the same coin. Our supporters, after remaining away from their homes for 11 months, were desperate to return. They risked their lives and returned home.*"
4. This document is available in the CPI(M)'s official site: '*cpim.org*'.
5. Another 4 million people, the jute cultivators, are also partially dependent on it.
6. The average days of employment under NREGA in Bengal was 14 in 2006–07, 25 in 2007–08 and 26 in 2008–09. (*Source:* CP Joshi in Lok Sabha on 17 July 2009.)
7. A detailed report by Nagarik Mancha on factory closures and plight of workers published in 2006 is available on *net:www.sarai.net.*

Two

Myth of Fighting Hindu Chauvinism

CERTAIN THINGS, when repeated day in and day out, become axioms. Then no one challenges it. One such thing was the Left's proposition that they were supporting a Congress government to fight communalism.

A close look at things will prove there was never much of truth in it. In fact, there was never a secular camp in this country. The parties that came together against the BJP were never bothered about the secular camp or secular politics. It was only a politics of convenience. But that was wrapped with a colourful paper on which the word 'secularism' sparkled bright. It was a trap for the Muslims, all other minorities, and a section of well-meaning Hindus.

It was just a word, hollow but magical. It was to be uttered loudly, day in and day out, and its magic would charm everyone. If you want to share power in a coalition, you just utter the magic word. You are not ready to give up your post, just repeat it. You want your government to stay in power by dividing the opposition, just mutter it. It was like a mantra that washed away all sins. You do not have to act, all you are required to do is deliver a long speech, or write a long essay. Even a long letter will do. You may stop at this point, or may go further to get kudos from the Rightist media who makes little distinction between the others and the BJP. You give arguments in support of your act. Say that you cannot vote along with the BJP. Forget how many times you have done it earlier. Just put forward your argument strongly. Just leak your letter in the Rightist media. Forget that Narendra Modi is one of the heroes of the Rightist media.

Suppose your country is under attack and the BJP brings a motion that says we should have to fight the enemy. If you are secular, you must reject it. You cannot vote along with a communal force. You cannot dare to be a patriot, if the BJP men are also patriots. Never.

Thus goes the logic of 'secularism' in this country.

A leader called LK Advani brought back Hindu chauvinism at the core of the BJP. This man started a *rath yatra* in September of 1989 to mop up votes by rousing bigotry and intolerance. His *rath* entered a state called West Bengal where a force called the Left was in power. It allowed the *rath* to roll on.

That is secular act in this country.

A fool called Laloo Prasad arrested Advani when the *rath* was passing through his state (Samastipur, 23 October 1990). He did it to stop Advani from reaching Ayodhya which was in another state, Uttar Pradesh. But Laloo Prasad decided not to pass on the buck. He was eager to become a 'secular hero'. Whatever, two years later, Advani's men razed the Babri mosque. The Left shouted the most. The Left became champion of secularism and overshadowed Laloo Prasad. Seventeen years later, in 2009, the 'secular camp' about which the Left talked of so often rules the country. Laloo Prasad did not find a place in it. Of late, Laloo Prasad has realized that bigger parties are trying to gobble down the smaller parties (he has still not understood that upper caste elite does not want to see people like Laloo Prasad by their side). He still weeps copiously, telling everybody about that he is for 'secular unity'. But, he himself tried to finish off the Congress in his state.

That is secular politics in this country.

In 1984, about 3,000 Sikhs were massacred in Delhi. For four days (31 October–3 November, 1984), the administration abdicated its duty.

It was reported in the media that the then Prime Minister Rajiv Gandhi said[1]: *"Some riots took place in the country following the murder of Indiraji. We know the people were very angry and for a few days it seemed that India had been shaken. But, when a mighty tree falls, it is only natural that the earth around it does shake a little."* The mighty tree was Indira Gandhi, who was assassinated by her Sikh bodyguards (31 October 1984) to avenge for 'Operation Blue Star' in the Golden Temple. No one was punished for the pogrom. Cases were not recorded even when people came to the police station. All fingers, all needles of suspicion were at some influential Congress leaders. Later they became more important men. They became ministers in the Congress governments.

That does not make the Congress communal. True, the Congress leaders instigated the mob to butcher thousands of Sikhs. So what? The BJP's pogrom in Gujarat was pre-planned. Accept it. Never talk of Godhra. The BJP is communal and the Congress is secular.

The Congress was secular even when it nullified Shah Bano verdict and passed Muslim Women (Protection of Rights on Divorce) Act, 1986, to deny alimony to Shah Bano, the hapless Muslim divorced women. The Congress was secular, so it must be the Supreme Court (that invoked Section 125 of Code of Criminal Procedure, which applies to everyone regardless of caste, creed or religion) that was communal.

In a magical way, the Congress remains secular even if its Prime Minister starts an election campaign from the vicinity of Ayodhya, as it happened in 1989. It remains secular even if its Prime Minister goes into slumber while a mosque is razed, as it happened in 1992.

This is the core of 'secularism' in this country.

And about communalism, that is like a robe. If you are in the BJP, you are communal. If you are in the Shiv Sena, you are communal. You leave your party and come to the Congress or any of its friendly parties, and you become secular. Like Chhagan Bhujbal or Babulal Marandi. You leave the Congress and join the BJP, you become communal. Parties like the Telugu Desam Party, the Biju Janata Dal or the Trinamool Congress can travel down to the BJP camp and then can breeze up to the secular camp. No problem.

We can add on to this list. But, the point has already been made. Our point is not that the BJP is not communal. It is. It has a Hindu core. It is the political wing of the Hindu chauvinist social organization, the Rashtriya Swayamsewak Sangh (RSS). But, many of its 'communal' ideas are shared by many non-communal people. No one can deny that a uniform civil code is an ideal thing. Many Muslim countries do not allow its citizens to marry more than once. Most of the Muslim countries do not allow 'triple *talaq*'. And then, civil code is not only about marriage. It is also about inheritance, it is about a lot of other things. If a religion sanctions inequality in the mundane life, whichever religion it may be, that part of it should be changed through new laws. Then no communal party will be able to point finger at any community. It is the behaviour of the political leadership of all other parties, it is the Shah Bano case and its aftermath, it is the appeasement of a handful Muslims by the 'secular' governments that swelled up the support for the BJP in the second half of the 1980s.

Again, there are people inside the BJP who are not communal. When Atal Behari Vajpayee was its president in the first half of the 1980s, the party was gradually shedding its communal character. Advani and his disciple Narendra Modi gave it back its ugly face. Yet, till Vajpayee was the Prime Minister, the communalists could be put in check as far as governance at the central level was concerned. And it is true that its communal agenda is obsolete in modern India. That was why Advani was so desperately trying to cover his face with a cheap secular mask in the post-Vajpayee era. His attempt failed. It showed time had changed. It showed that rousing bigotry was no more a political alternative. It was not an alternative even in 1999, or in 2004. Then the alternative was a man called AB Vajpayee. With his virtual retirement from politics, the alternative became non-existent.

The people of this country have no reason to vote for a communal party even in the future. There is communal hatred, better to say antagonism, in the minds of a large section of the people. But that is at social level and no political party fights it at that level. It will not come up at the political level if the politicians do not go to the Imams to extract a fatwa for the Muslims to vote for a certain party (which the Imams are actually not entitled to issue), if the leaders of the Muslim community unequivocally condemn terrorism (as they are doing now), or if during a match between India and Pakistan no Muslim locality raises the flag of Pakistan (which is a rare sighting nowadays).

It was many such acts—condoned and even encouraged, if not being involved in, by the secular parties—that reacted in the minds of the people. This pushed many people to look at the BJP as a saviour. If this history is not repeated (and probably no one would dare again to reject another Shah Bano verdict through enactment of another law), then communal politics would always be rejected by the overwhelming majority of the Hindus.

The BJP in power at the Centre was an ominous sign when seen against the Ram Mandir movement of Advani. But with AB Vajpayee at the helm it was not as dangerous as the Left tried to show it.

About Gujarat genocide, Narendra Modis can do it anytime anywhere, and it matters little who is in power at Centre. Of course a real secular government will be a constraint for such people. But where do we find a real secular government? Two years after the genocide, a so-called secular government supported by all secular parties from inside and outside was firmly in saddle. For that government, it was business as usual with the Gujarat Chief Minister. True, by then Modi had won another assembly election. But extraordinary wrongs call for extraordinary actions. The US denied him visa. But the secular front denied him nothing.

So, it is obvious that 'secularism' or 'fighting Hindu chauvinism' or 'keeping the communal forces out' are all mere ploys to enhance one's strength and status, an excuse for a share in power. Laloo Prasad used it to have a place in the Central Government that he could not get otherwise. Mulayam Singh used it to get Muslim votes. And the Left? Let us examine their extension of support to the Congress-led government through the same prism.

***

What prompted the Left to directly support the Congress in 2004? Was it a spirit of fighting communalism or a fallacious strategy of gaining importance?

The suspicion stems from the fact that the Left forgot to exert pressure to compel the Central Government to take a very important step as far as the stability of the 'secular polity' was concerned. It forgot to push the government to take extraordinary measures to punish the real culprits of Gujarat genocide. Those men, believed to be the masterminds of the killing of Muslims were sitting pretty in high offices in Ahmedabad. The Left decided not to disturb them.

This single instance raises serious questions about the real intention of the Left in 2004. It was not that extraordinary steps on Gujarat pogrom were not possible. Like in so many cases, here again finally the Supreme Court asserted itself and ordered enquiry into the role of the people in high offices (27 April 2009). The court had to come forward as the political class abdicated its responsibility of doing justice to the mothers of those who were killed. The secular parties and their government forgot to take initiatives to come before the Supreme Court with new ideas. The cue was, however, there. The Apex Court had earlier moved the riot-related cases out of Gujarat. Thus the ground was ready.

It is understandable that the Congress did nothing out of fear that Gujarati Hindus would go against them if the party went overboard. The Congress believes in please-all politics and it will continue with it till the people reject it vehemently. But what about the Left? Why they did not put effective pressure on the government? Why they did not threaten to pull out if the government failed to take positive actions? Had they done that, it could have been assumed that 'secularism' was a real concern for them.

The communists were happy that the discourse of politics had changed after the installation of the UPA government. That was what Sitaram Yechury used to boast about. But what did the party actually mean by it? Did they mean that number of stories appearing in the media on Ram Janmabhoomi or such trivia had decreased? Well, the communal discourse did not occupy much space during the Vajpayee regime either. Stories appeared in the Press on Vajpayee versus the Sangh or Vajpayee versus Advani and so on because it was a favourite topic of the media. Those stories went out of circulation after the BJP lost power for a simple reason: readers are more interested about feuds in the ruling party and not in the opposition camp. And about genocide in Narendra Modi's Gujarat, well, it could have taken place under the UPA regime also. Thus, the change in discourse did not mean much.

If the CPI(M) bosses in Delhi had alluded to the absence of Ram-type issues in election, well, they had no role in that. It was decided by the common men, the vast majority of the voters, and a large chunk of them did not even know about the CPI(M). The communists never fought the BJP on the ground, except for in a small part of Kerala. They uttered tall words about secularism in the rallies where no one listened to them. They penned even stronger words in party papers and magazines which no one read. They scored points in the elite circle that has little impact on the lives of a billion plus people. It was the common man who looked up at the BJP expecting some relief from their miseries and rejected it when the 'party with a difference' failed to deliver on that count. In either case, they had no option—they had to vote either for the BJP or its allies, or for the Congress and its allies. They may again vote for the BJP someday, if the Congress ditches them and go too far with its neoliberal plans.

So, the CPI(M) was just creating an illusion of fighting the menace of communalism. Actually, communalism had nothing to do with their mundane political games. They had earlier joined hands with anybody and everybody to oust the BJP from power. People rejected such backroom plotters in 1999. But the communists learnt nothing. They rather created a phantom of 'communalism' to go closer to the Congress. A weak Congress suited them best. It provided them an opportunity to busk in the reflected glory of power. It allowed their leaders to appear on the TV screen every now and then. It provided safety to the government of Bengal that was the source of their importance and other facilities.

***

Now, look at the central point of the fallacy of 'secular unity' logic.

According to this logic, all the anti-BJP parties should unite under a common umbrella to defeat the BJP. Then such parties will come together to prevent the BJP from coming to power. That really diminishes the BJP to an opposition force with little chance of coming back to power.

But, does it damage the Hindu party, or actually help it?

First, look at the political scenario at the party-level. This two-front system will add to the BJP's claim and credibility to be the central and rallying point of anti-Congressism. If a political party feels that the Congress party or the Congress-led government is not allowing it enough space, it will look up to the BJP. Whenever the BJP or its allies will be able to create a situation in which the national opposition's chance to wrest power in the country or in a state will brighten, many others will join them. Again, there are certain regional parties whose main rival in the state is the Congress. These parties will inevitably be pushed to the BJP camp if the polity is divided in two camps. The Telugu Desam (Andhra Pradesh), the Akali Dal (Punjab) and the Asom Gana Parishad (Assam) are examples of such parties. So, in the long run a bipolar polity helps the BJP more than it damages it.

Now, look at it from the viewpoint of the politicians. Many people in politics have very high ambition. They hope that someday they will become the Prime Minister, the Deputy Prime Minister or the President of the country. If these posts remain beyond their reach, they will vie for any of the four most important ministries in the Central Government—home, finance, defence and foreign. A bipolar polity will compel these people to join either of the two giants, the Congress or the BJP. The days of Morarji Desai, Charan Singh, VP Singh, Chandra Sekhar, HD Deve Gowda and IK Gujral will be over. It will benefit the BJP most, for it is a family leadership in the Congress. The Congress is a close shop. But the doors in the BJP are open. Ambitious, intelligent and bright people, who may enter politics later, will prefer the BJP.

Now, come to the popular level. People will vote for the BJP in many states like Rajasthan, Madhya Pradesh, Gujarat, Maharashtra and so on whenever they will be peeved with the Congress. In the same way, when peeved with the BJP they will vote for the Congress. That is the scenario in more than 200 seats now. The Congress high command will not allow any other party to enter into its regions where these 200-plus seats fall. Ditto with the BJP. Being big brothers of their respective fronts they have the power to punish and crush the smaller partners. Having learnt the art of coalition from a leader like AB Vajpayee, the BJP has not practised this tactics yet. But the Congress has done this to its partners and wannabe partners.

Thus, a detailed analysis shows that by joining hands with the Congress the smaller parties damage themselves and help the BJP to grow as a potential alternative. If the Left had not extended direct support to the Congress in 2004, if it had formed a third alternative with Mulayam Singh (which could have been joined by Chandrababu Naidu, Deve Gowda and a few others later) to extend issue-based support, the third alternative would have grown in importance, strength and stature. The advantage of this was that the Third Bloc would have been a permanent entity. If none else was around, at least the Left would have been always there. Such defiance and determination helps a political party or a group of parties the most. This was how the communists gained the respectability decades ago.

One more point. When the Jan Sangh, the BJP's previous avatar was trying to make a dent with its slogan of 'Hindu, Hindi, Hindutva', the communists joined hands with it in 1967. Many coalition governments were formed in different states, and in states like Bihar the communists associated themselves directly or indirectly with it and other retrograde forces. The objective was to corner the Congress. In 1977, the Janata Party was formed after a merger of several parties, like the forces now denounced by the Left like the Jan Sangh, the 'reactionaries within the Congress' who after the split in the party was known as Congress (O), Socialists and rebel Congress forces. The Left was friendly to this party and went for seat-adjustment with it. It was from the womb of the Janata Party that the BJP was born. Only the name changed under the insistence of

AB Vajpayee, who was eager to free it from the hardcore Hindutva forces. The Left had made indirect adjustment in 1989 even with the BJP by keeping VP Singh in the middle. All these were done for weakening and defeating the Congress.

***

So, the question of 'secularism' was never uppermost in the minds of the communists. Always, it was the scope of intervention in the political arena that was the driving force. Whenever the Congress had turned weak, they had supported it. When the Congress grew strong, they moved over to the opposition camp where the Hinduites were present. True, since the razing of Babri mosque the communists had not made adjustments with the Hinduites. But then it was not possible also. The Hindu chauvinist force had acquired enough mass to be at the Centre of an opposition camp. Thereafter, the BJP decided to set aside its core agenda (like making India a Hindu state with a uniform civil code, finishing off the remnants of special power to Kashmir, and building a Ram Temple at the site of the Babri mosque) to draw other smaller parties to its orbit, and successfully implemented the plan. It gave up its burden of communal ideology to a great extent. The Advani-era ended, and Vajpayee-era came back once more. Advani was not acceptable to many other parties, but Vajpayee was.

As a consequence, the polity changed qualitatively: in place of a simple division between the Congress and its rivals (amongst whom centripetal and centrifugal forces worked by turn), a complex scenario emerged. The Congress and the BJP emerged as the two big parties and covered about three-fifth of the political space, while the rest two-fifth was with regional or semi-national [like the CPI(M) itself] parties. Depending on who is better posed, either the Congress or the BJP could drag smaller parties to cross the magic figure and form the government at the Centre. This process has started from 1998.

So, the phantom of communalism was never really as big as the Left tried to project. It was not the Hinduite BJP that came to power. The

Hindu chauvinists had already defanged themselves, and thus attracted 'secular' parties like the Telugu Desam Party or the Trinamool Congress. It was a coalition that came to power. The BJP could have been isolated by preventing many of the regional parties like the Telugu Desam Party or the Asom Gana Parishad or even the Shiromani Akali Dal from supporting it. The Left could have played a role in it if it stood firmly by Third Front politics. It could have done so if it had resisted the Congress' attempt to change the United Front Prime Minister in 1997. The Left could have played a role if it had remained at the core of anti-BJP anti-Congress third force. But Jyoti Basu and HS Surjeet loved the Congress. The duo brought the party to the door of the Congress when their contemporaries who could resist it were all dead. The ploy was 'secularism'. For that everything else could be sacrificed.

A petty political motive was camouflaged as an ideological package, and we all started believing in it. It gave the Left further legitimacy to follow the line.

So the Left sabotaged the third platform by supporting the Congress in 2004, leaving forces like the Samajwadi Party (Mulayam Singh Yadav's party) in the lurch. Mulayam Singh retaliated in the same way in 2008 by supporting the Congress when the Left withdrew support.

There is no denying the fact that support to the Congress government opened a new horizon before the Left. They got recognition, and their veto power attracted who's who of India towards them. Had they not extended such support, would Mukesh Ambani, the richest man of India, have cared to visit their headquarters more than once? For record's sake, it must be mentioned that what transpired between Ambani and the top-most leaders of the party was kept a guarded secret. Again, for record's sake, the CPI(M) did not oppose entry of Indian giants in retail trade. They only prepared documents containing many pages, but that was only to gift it to the government. That benefitted Ambani.

The CPI(M) sabotaged the third alternative to busk in the glory of power and authority even without joining the government. But they did not realize that the Congress is like a wild elephant that likes subordination, not challenges. Even if the Left became a subordinate ally like Laloo Prasad, it was doubtful whether the new leader Rahul Gandhi would have spared them. The second junior-most Gandhi in politics wants to rejuvenate his party one by one in all the states, and definitely in West Bengal and Kerala. He had proved it in Uttar Pradesh by dumping Mulayam Singh and in Bihar by dumping Laloo Prasad. Even after that, both had announced support for the government but had not been invited to join the government! In all likelihood, the CPI(M) could have faced a similar fate in a similar situation even it became a subordinate ally of the Congress as proposed by Basu–Surjeet and their followers like Yechury–Bhattacharya.

Altogether, the myth of building a secular polity is now over. The Congress has not cared for other secular parties. Thus 'secularism' was only a ploy of the smaller and weaker parties to go close to the Congress. That was the case with Laloo Prasad, with the Left, with Mulayam Singh, the Congress knew it well. It took help from them and then dumped them. That is politics. Only the strong can play this game. The weak, the subordinate allies, cannot survive long.

Now, after examining the myth of 'secularism', we must probe why the CPI(M) built this up, who exploited it, and how it damaged the party.

References

1. Addressing a rally at the Boat Club, quoted in *The Tribune.*

Three

Influence of Media and Glamour

IT WAS strange that the erstwhile hardliner Prakash Karat, the man who refused to let Jyoti Basu head a government dependent on support of the Congress in 1996, lost track of his politics in the new millennium. Or maybe, he was forced to make compromise with the followers of Basu–Surjeet duo. His position in the party was compromised by Basu himself with his public uttering that the decision of the party was a 'historic blunder'. This statement engendered sentiment in the Bengal party against the 'diktats of the people in Delhi who have no base'. This was basically against Prakash Karat and Sitaram Yechury. Karat fought it with grace while Yechury joined hands with the Bengal CPI(M). Yechury became a darling and later managed to get a Rajya Sabha seat from Bengal. Karat too did not or could not resist the attempt by Basu–Surjeet to drag the party closer and closer to the Congress.

Karat and Yechury rose like meteors in the CPI(M). For some years, they were together. But after 1996, the year of committing 'historic blunder', Yechury gradually drifted towards the liberal camp headed by Surjeet and Basu. Karat remained firm on his line—he was a hardliner—and fought the stalwarts alone.

However, the Bengal party is not against Yechury anymore. Why? One explanation can be that now he toes the 'Bengal line' and so he is no more an enemy. But, there is another explanation also. Bengal party, in last 10 years, is increasingly being run on the diktats of the media, and particularly the biggest media house of Calcutta. Yechury is a darling of the media.

We have noted that the politics of secularism was, in fact, a clear ploy to drag the CPI(M) closer to the Congress. But, encumbered by their ideological moorings, the communist cannot speak the truth straight and simple. So, they had to have an ideological package inside which the truth should be laid hidden. This package was 'secularism'. The then general secretary of the party, Surjeet tried to sell this package from the early 1990s. Yechury was still with Karat, planning assertion of the younger generation in the party. At that time Saifuddin Chowdhury advocated a pro-Congress line rather openly. That gave Yechury an opportunity to throw Saifuddin, another leader of the same generation, out of the central committee. It cleared, for Yechury, the path of hogging the entire limelight. Surjeet's proposition was rejected by the party in Chandigarh Party congress (1995). But, Surjeet did not give up. Finally, it was endorsed in 1998. It was a line of 'secularism' that the party congress endorsed, but not collaboration with the Congress. Let us see what Surjeet said about it:

> "The basic document to guide the working of the Party remains the Party programme. The strategic objective outlined in the Programme remains valid for this stage of the revolution. However, the realization of this ultimate goal is connected with other tactics, depending on the situation. The tactical approach that the CPI(M) has adopted since its formation in 1964 is directed towards the achievement of this long-term goal. It has changed from time to time depending on the concrete situation existing at a particular point of time. In 1969, during the Presidential elections, when there were two contenders from the Congress party itself, we lent our support to VV Giri. We wanted to ensure the defeat of the other candidate who at that particular moment represented forces that were more pro-imperialist. Later on, in the 1977 elections, we supported the Janata Party (the Jan

Sangh the predecessor of the present BJP was part of it), because at that particular point of time, the dismantling of the Emergency framework and restoration of democracy was the prime concern. When the issue of dual membership of both the RSS and the Janata Party came up and the erstwhile members of the Jan Sangh were unwilling to give up their membership of the RSS, we withdrew support. In 1989 at the 13th Congress we called for the defeat of the Congress party, while simultaneously, we called for the isolation of the BJP. The situation had changed radically by the time we went to the 14th Congress. The Congress taking note of the growth of the BJP gave a call for the defeat of both the Congress and the BJP. This slogan was reiterated in the 15th Congress. The 16th Congress Political Resolution noted that 'in the present situation, the struggle against the BJP-RSS combine and the communal forces assumes utmost importance. There must be a proper appreciation of the danger posed by a communal party holding the reins of State power. The Party will have to make the fight against these forces its central task in the coming days.'"

Further, it stated:

> "Struggle against the communal forces, their designs to disrupt national unity and the democratic movement assume importance. This can be done only on the basis of a broad-based mobilization. The efforts to forge and strengthen the third alternative, in electoral terms, will have to be renewed. While there is no question of an alliance, or, united front with Congress with its present policies, efforts must be made to reach out to its mass following which has a sizeable section of people adhering to secularism."[1]

This was Surjeet's own explanation of things. He wrote this in 2002, whereas the 16th party congress was held in Calcutta in October 1998. The communists can interpret things in different ways unimaginable and incomprehensible for us. But look at what Surjeet wrote. He is categorical that in 1998 the CPI(M) decided two things—first, that the main task of the party was to defeat the communal forces, and second, to accomplish it they would have to forge and strengthen the third alternative.

But strange things had started happening during 1998 Party congress. Without caring for what they had written in the party document, Surjeet declared before the Press that the third alternative had lost credibility. Yechury declared that if the government fell, the Left would support the Congress to form an alternative government. All the papers reported these things.[2]

Seven months later, when AB Vajpayee's government facing a no-confidence motion lost by one vote in April 1999, the CPI(M) really announced its support for Sonia Gandhi, who was eager to form an alternative government. But she could not do so as the Samajwadi Party led by Mulayam Singh and two small Left parties (the Forward Bloc and the RSP) declined to offer support. They alternatively proposed that Jyoti Basu should form the government and the Congress should support it. The CPI(M) politburo members discussed it unofficially and took an informal decision that if Sonia Gandhi proposed so, the party would form the government. It is believed that the then President KR Narayanan also requested Soniaji to consider this as Basu was in a position to form a stable government, but she did not agree to make 'a communist' like Jyotibabu the PM of the country. There was total stalemate. No alternative government could be formed. Sonia Gandhi made it clear that she was not bothered about secular unity, she was eager to see a resurgence of her party. The CPI(M) was snubbed by the Congress, and that made the attitude of the bigger party clear. Sonia preferred election. In the election, however, Vajpayee came back to power bagging a greater mandate for the NDA.

Still, the CPI(M) did not give up its appease-Congress attitude despite what the 17th Party congress said in 2002. HS Surjeet wrote about it:

> "The understanding of the 16th congress was that to be able to advance the struggle to isolate the communal forces and to resist the attacks on the livelihood of the people, it is necessary to project a third alternative. We have been pursuing our efforts to reforge the third alternative. This, as the 17th congress resolution notes, 'is necessary to meet the current situation wherein both the BJP and the Congress are gathering parties around them and trying to see that two combinations emerge.... A step towards this was the formation

> of the People's Front, which comprises the Left parties and some of the secular opposition parties like the Samajwadi Party and Janata Dal(S). This combination is a partial expression of the immediate need for a third force. Some of the secular bourgeois parties will come and go out of this formation, but its existence will help meet the needs of the current situation.'
>
> At the same time the Party congress emphasised that the real alternative is the Left and democratic front. This, however, should not be confused with the People's Democratic stage. Until we reach the People's Democratic stage where the working class will have leadership over the other allied classes, the Left and democratic front is a slogan for the interim period till we reach the goal of People's Democracy. The Left and democratic programme spelt out in the congress resolution should form the basis for developing, organizing and expanding the Party's multifaceted activities enabling it to rally all other Left and democratic forces and the mass of the working people who constitute the base of the Left and democratic front.
>
> The correlation of class forces in the world has changed radically after the disintegration of the Soviet Union and restoration of capitalism in the countries of Eastern Europe. It has made our task much more difficult. We have to take these factors into consideration while working out our tactical line. A communist party has to integrate national developments with the international situation as both cast an influence over the other."[3]

So they knew everything. Insiders said at that time that all those sentences on Third Front were incorporated in the party document as Karat insisted on them. Surjeet reiterated those and even explained them in context in his afore mentioned article. But in reality Surjeet and Basu, and Yechury and Bhattacharya had planned out the future course.

Probably, no other party in India had suffered from such contradiction between two sections of its leadership, or between what it put in black and white and what it did.

***

Whatever, Karat finally decided to retaliate against the pro-Congress communists in 2007. He started preparing the ground for withdrawal of support. By doing this, he antagonized the Rightists to the extreme. His anti-America stance infuriated the elite for whom the US was like a heaven. Karat's earlier acts like stalling the disinvestment process were still pardonable, but this was unforgivable. When it seemed that the government would fall if it went ahead to sign the Nuke Deal, the media swung into action. The spokespersons of the Rightists, who praised Narendra Modi so many times, unabashedly brought up the issue of 'secularism'. How could the CPI(M) break the unity of the secular front, they asked.

Soon, the question was echoed by some of the communists. Someone echoed it to retain his post, someone else echoed it to protect the Left in Bengal. But finally Karat came to his own self after many years. He did not budge. And then, in the next parliamentary election, the CPI(M) was routed.

But the pro-Congress section of the party had gone so close to the Rightists during 2004–08, was now so obsessed with the rightness of the Rightist path, was under so much influence of the Rightist media, that they refused to acknowledge the real reasons of the great defeat. After the election, this section created an example of a new low for the communists by aligning with the Rightist media and by playing at the hands of the Rightist elite.

Very interestingly, after the inevitable happened in Bengal and Kerala, the big media houses clamoured for the blood of the party general secretary Prakash Karat for this debacle. Not directly, but in almost all their stories had the same slant.

I wonder, if in future the Congress faces a debacle whether the media will have the guts or willingness to raise a demand of Sonia Gandhi's resignation. Or that of Manmohan Singh. Or that of Rahul Gandhi. I do not remember any one of them carrying a single copy in their papers containing the same message after Rajiv Gandhi brought down the Congress from 404 in 1984 to 197 in 1989. No such concerted effort was seen after Sonia Gandhi failed in 1998 and in 1999. And here I must mention that five years ago, this same Karat, acting as a *de facto* general secretary, led the party to attain its highest tally ever. Harkishen Singh Surjeet was the *de jure* general secretary, but constrained by his ailment he gave up the charge of the organization years ago. Surjeet's activities in those days were mainly limited to behind the door confabulations for making a 'secular' government.

It is media's old strategy to raise a point that they want to raise by quoting those who are ready to spell it out. Accordingly, the first opportunity to the Rightists was provided by an expelled member of the party. He, Somnath Chatterjee, was in the Parliament only because his party nominated him as a candidate and got him elected. Then he became the Speaker of the Lok Sabha because his party nominated him to that post. But when the party withdrew support from the Congress-led government in 2008 and asked him to resign, he decided to ignore the party's wishes and remained in the Chair for the rest of the tenure. For this, he was lauded as a hero by the Rightists and was expelled from the party. Here, it must be mentioned that the Speaker's post in our country is not a non-political position. A Speaker faces the next election after his term as a candidate of his party. Whatever, when the results were out, he brought to the fore the question of 'conscience' and floated the suggestion of Karat's resignation. It was immediately picked up by the Rightist media.

Now, there were many in Bengal, from a state secretariat member of the party to a band of intellectuals, who were only eager to echo what the most powerful Rightist media house of the state thought and wanted to project. Probably, Bengal CPI(M) was the most glaring example since 2006 of a political party dancing to the tune of a Rightist media house. The party under Buddhadeb Bhattacharya was implementing the agenda of the Rightists and, in return, getting full support and protection of that Rightist media baron. This made Bhattacharya so jubilant that he started dictating that house what should be written and how any story damaging for him that somehow appeared in that paper should be countered. For professional reasons, I will not elaborate this point further, but I have enough material to prove it.

After the defeat, and even for months and years preceding it, that very-influential media house in Bengal was trying to split the party and free a large chunk of the party from the clutches of its perceived-to-be hardliner general secretary Prakash Karat. For the media, both regional and national, Karat was enemy number one for his socialistic thoughts and for his anti-Americanism, while Buddhadeb Bhattacharya and Sitaram Yechury were their blue-eyed boys. Bhattacharya, the CM of Bengal, and Yechury, the second most influential politburo member, were loved by the Rightists for their readiness to follow and implement all sorts of neoliberal policies, and also for their habit of sharing details of the party matters with them. Yechury was cleverer, for in his articles and opinion-pieces he often opposed neoliberalism, while inside the party he was trying to drive the party continuously towards a definite Rightist path. Bhattacharya was less tactful and had stated without ambiguity that 'globalization is a must'. He was actively supported by the largest media house of Bengal in his endeavour to break open all Leftist prejudices against the role of capital or the capitalists.

I must take a pause to explain certain things as I have mentioned about the role of the media, a subject generally left untouched. Firstly, when I mention the media as 'Rightist', I do not hold it against them. Ideologically, Right and Left are two paths to prosperity and better life for all. The Rightists believe in inequality according to ability and in free initiative, while the Leftists believe in equality and state intervention. One may support or oppose either of it. Secondly, I must mention that the largest media house in Bengal was much more open than many others in the country. Its chief editor had openly stated that he wanted the political parties to follow (in his words, to be satellites of) his ideology, and he proudly announced that he was a Rightist. There was no ambiguity. He stated this clearly at a function on the occasion of 75 years of the *Anandabazar Patrika*, and added that he would support only those parties who would toe his line. He wanted to see a hardcore

Rightist regime in Bengal, and when he felt that Bhattacharya as a CM was prepared to serve his purpose, he supported him to the hilt. So, on the part of *Anandabazar Patrika*, the effort undertaken was primarily from the ideological commitment to free market economy. And there was nothing secret about it. The openness of *Anandabazar Patrika* group in charting out its goal is laudable, for some other houses in the country try to camouflage their real intentions. I know it better, for I was associated with that house for long years.

We must keep it in mind that despite of the prevalent puritan ideas that people of this country still cherish about a newspaper or a TV channel (that it should be neutral and only defend the rights of the people), the big media houses have their own ideology and moorings and they try to mould their readers or viewers in that shape. This is true about all the media, be Rightist or Leftist, all over the world.

What was shocking was that a section of a party that called itself communist decided to follow the Rightist media. What was shocking was that they were jubilant when the biggest media house of Bengal started supporting the Bhattacharya government. As a total ideologically bankrupt force, they felt that *Anandabazar* supporting them meant *Anandabazar* was being converted. Poor fellows! This ignorance took them to the bloody fields of Nandigram, where they fired upon and killed 14 peasants. Sadly for them, *Anandabazar* did not support them on this—rather it tried to expose some of the culprits.

Another Rightist paper the *Indian Express* hailed the election mandate in its headlines made with a very big 'YES' and then following it up like this: *'That's the national mandate for the 15th Lok Sabha giving the Congress most seats since 1991 and the UPA a stunning entry into its second term—liberated from the Left'.* It did not try to camouflage its jubilance. Its chief editor wrote a well-argued piece in the front page where he welcomed the verdict as one in which 'politics of aspiration has won over the politics of grievance'. He argued that the voters were unforgiving with those who were victims of hubris, and he mentioned three categories whom the people had rejected—those who announced themselves as next PM without being even sure of 40 seats (must be people like Sharad Pawar), those who built their statues (Mayawati he was talking of), and *'those with a fraction of seats in the Parliament aspire to control the nation's foreign and economic policies without, of course, being accountable for anything'* (directed against the Left).

From a Rightist viewpoint, he argued his position very well. But a philosophical question remains unanswered. Even if only one person thinks that some prevalent faith (whether that be 'Nuke Deal is good for the country' or 'the sun revolves around the earth') is wrong, should he not fight the prevalent faith till the last with all his might, even if there are millions or billions of people against him? The question is not whether that single individual is right or wrong in his perception. The question is whether one should or should not stand up and fight for one's conviction.

Next the *Hindustan Times*. They had a copy on Karat with a headline 'How Karat nuked his party'. And they enlisted three reasons for this debacle—withdrawal of support on Nuke Deal, forging new alliances and dumping the old, and cobbling up a non-existent Third Front. It was typical Rightist analysis aimed at punishing the bad boy.

Well, without adding more newspapers, we can say every Rightist newspaper had a common trend, to lay blames on Karat's door. Though the papers argued their cases well, they all decided to overlook the real factors that brought in the disaster for the Left in Bengal and in Kerala. But, definitely the media knew the real reasons. It was not only the local media of Bengal and Kerala that had written about the factors that resulted in the ultimate fall of the Left. The Rightist newspapers of Delhi too had, very successfully and very rightly, brought out the reality of Bengal and Kerala consistently for months and years preceding the election. The *Indian Express* did it tirelessly. But after the election results were out, all those papers forgot that a careful reader could relate the reasons of the defeat with what he had read in these very papers earlier.

When the newspapers targeted Karat, they were actually reflecting the mind of the Rightist elite as a whole. The Rightists had obsession with core issues like forging close relation with the US. This was for them the road to faster growth and conquering new heights. That was true about the Rightist elite as a whole. They expected that the Nuke Deal, if implemented properly, would not only benefit many big US or other Western companies, but would also bring luck to many Indian partners. So, they saw in Karat a threat to their prospects. So they tried to turn the table against Karat and lift their poster-boys Yechury and Bhattacharya to a position of more power. Pinarayi Vijayan, the neoliberal secretary of Kerala state committee, was not a poster boy because he was not 'pally' with the Press and had old-time arrogance.

In this game, many people came together, like a section of the Congress party, business magnets and industrial lords, high government officials, and the media barons [reportedly, the US ambassador to India also had a role in it, but it is not certain whether his alleged role was against Karat or against the CPI(M) as a whole]. They had one-point agenda—to finish off Karat. They played their games all through the first term of the UPA regime. Their activity peaked when Karat decided to withdraw support from the government, but they failed to contain him.

While the Rightist political and business classes limited themselves to enjoying the riddance of the CPI(M) after the election, the cudgels were now taken up by the Rightist media to continue with its old agenda of finishing off Karat. They knew Karat was the last man in Indian political circle to raise voice against the US, and if he was around he might block the road to building an America-dependent India once again.

Of course, the Rightists had more reasons to do that. The Rightists try to eliminate the Left from the political process so that the road to their prosperity is cleared of all obstacles. The Leftists also try the same, often more crudely, in the political societies they dominate. As Mamata Banerjee now follows a somewhat 'Leftist' path, she too has become a target of some of the Rightists. They will break Banerjee sooner or later; but they failed to break Karat.

It is not so that the Rightist elite in general are still as indifferent about people's poverty and deprivation as they were even a decade ago. If you remember Manmohan Singh in his first years in politics as the Finance Minister, you may also recollect his jihad against subsidy, particularly those targeted to the wretched (maybe those earning up to 25 rupees per day per head) or the poor (earning up to 50 rupees per day per head) and the low middle class (earning up to 100 rupees per day per head). He was not willing to spend money for PDS (public distribution system through which cheap and bad quality food grains and some other essential commodities reach the poor). But during the last two years of his tenure he started changing. This trend continued and widened during his premiership. We all know he is not a politician and works mainly as a chief executive officer of the government, while the political decisions were earlier being taken by Narasimha Rao and now being taken by the Gandhi family. But even if we assume that he acted on these matters as instructions came to him, it is noteworthy that the elite and particularly the political elite were catering to the needs of the poor. The hundred days work guarantee scheme was an excellent example of it. Whatever, our point is that while the Rightist elite have turned more sympathetic to the poor, they still try to streamline the system so that no Leftist voice exists. The reason is simple. A Leftist always demands more intervention by the state, for which more money is needed and that can only come from more taxation and stringent implementation of laws aimed at stopping leakage. That is what the majority of the Rightists, in general, loathe.

The media in India is controlled by the Rightist elites and it is quite natural that they will make continuous endeavours to defeat and defang the Leftist elite and waylay the Leftist mass. We have discussed what the intention of the Rightists was, and the ideological reason behind that. Now let us see how this voice was echoed by the party leaders.

***

Many from the party, particularly the expelled comrades and defeated candidates, came forward to lend the Rightist media more credibility.

The first reaction from the West Bengal state party secretary Biman Bose (the man who could come to the post only because his junior comrade and the much-more-efficient party secretary Anil Biswas died suddenly in March 2006 at the age of 62) was no less amusing. After a meeting of the state secretariat, he attributed the defeat to the surge of support for the Congress and the failure of convincing the people about the concept of a Third Front (that Karat proposed and tried to implement). We have seen earlier that this showed his ignorance. His statement showed his ignorance on two counts. First, he did not know that the percentage of vote the Congress got in 1999 (114 seats) and in 2009 (204 seats) was not much different, only about 2 per cent more. So, theoretically, either it was actually an indication of the Congress vote-base shrinking geographically while becoming more concentrated in its strongholds, or else, opposition parties got more fragmented while retaining their individual vote-shares. One can win more seats even after getting less votes if the number of its opponents increase and the opposition vote gets divided. The rise in the number of seats the Congress got was actually a mixture of both. This electoral arithmetic eluded the perception of the state leaders. They did not know that half of the people (who had cast their votes) of India had voted for parties other than the Congress or the BJP. It did not matter whether those parties were aligned to any of the two big parties or not. The votes they got were their votes. Otherwise the BJP or the Congress would have jettisoned them and fought those seats on their own.

More amusingly, the state secretary could even see a 'Congress wave'[4]. He negated the argument that the defeat had anything to do with local factors. In his defence he had fantastic points—he asked why the same pattern was observed 'everywhere'. It was not clear whether he imagined that the Congress had won in all the states or he believed that his party had fared equally badly everywhere.

Neither was true. The Congress fared badly in many states like Bihar, Jharkhand, Orissa, Karnataka, and did not do well in some other states. The CPI(M) did very well, rather superbly, in the tiny state of Tripura, where it won both the constituencies the state had.

It was clear that Bose was trying to shift the focus to Delhi by fabricating stories of a Congress wave and thereby underlining the fact that the responsibility was with the central leadership, namely of Karat.

Now, we know successful politicians are neither fools, nor totally ignorant people. So, we assume, the same is true about Biman Bose. So why did he speak like that? The only plausible reason is that he was not speaking his mind. He was following a line that was decided by someone else. The made-easy interpretation that he presented bore the imprint of the media persons. Those in media go for quick interpretation and miss the finer prints as they fight against the time. But generally they rectify the mistakes later on as more facts come. But Bose was trapped. He had said what he was fed.

Otherwise also Bose had to find some way to wriggle out of his responsibility of the debacle. After all, his report to the central party stated that the total number of losing seats and seats where they had a 50–50 per cent chance of winning taken together was 22. But, they had lost 27. He stood exposed in the eyes of his own cadre and the leaders of all others states of his party. So to wriggle out of the situation he raised his finger towards Karat.

It was politics of convenience. Here Bose's line and the Rightists' line merged. Both found in Karat a common enemy, a man who was not ready to accept the argument that neoliberal policy had nothing to do with this electoral debacle. The easiest way, therefore, was to, weaken and if possible remove the man.

Another pundit and member of the state secretariat of the party, Subhash Chakrabarty, was quoted in the *Indian Express* as saying, "*The collapse of the party began to accelerate after it withdrew support to the UPA government at the Centre.*" And many of the defeated MPs attributed it to an imaginary Congress wave and party's failure to lend credibility to the slogan of a Third Front. At least five of them, including veterans like Tarit Topdar and Rupchand Pal, were quoted by the Delhi papers.

By their uttering, these leaders betrayed either their puzzled mind after the defeat, or else their mediocre political understanding and detachment from the mass. Not surprising. Many of them were known as having won election with bike-riding cadres (in many places of Bengal people shuddered at the sight of those bike-processions), loyal police force (red guards of the government) and pliable administration. The two hotbeds of the new industrialization plan of the Left were Nandigram and Singur. Left parties continuously carried on their lie-campaign that the people of these two regions were with them. But the reality was altogether different. Rupchand Pal, the five-time MP of Hooghly and the most vocal proponent of local people's great excited support to the Nano project, lost the election. We may hope someday he will explain why those great supporters with whom he used to take out historic processions left him for Mamata Banerjee. He lost by more than 60,000 votes from the same constituency that five years ago he had won by a margin of more than 166,000 votes. That time, he got 96,000 more than the combined vote of the divided opposition, i.e., the Trinamool Congress (his main opponent) and the Congress. In 2009, even in Singur assembly segment, the ground zero of abandoned Nano project, he trailed by more than 6,000 votes than the margin by which his party had lost the assembly seat in 2006. Again for the record, after losing Nandigram assembly in a by-election a few months ago, the CPI(M) finally lost the parliamentary constituency by about 160,000 votes. Five years ago the same Lakshman Seth got 23,000 votes more than what the Trinamool Congress and the Congress (then fighting separately) got.

What is clearly discernible to a sane intelligent mind, was not understood by some: forget about the rest of the Bengal, even the people of Nandigram and Singur (the supposed centres of prosperity) had not endorsed the industrialization plank of the state government. So, somewhere something went wrong seriously. People everywhere are for development, for balanced and eco-friendly industrialization, for prosperity. If they rejected certain things, there must be some reason. The reason could not be Prakash Karat's effort to forge a Third Front. It just cannot be so. The Rightist media ignored it for philosophical reasons. But most of them too stopped doing it when the Left lost one after another local elections after the parliamentary poll. Only a few journalists continued with it as they were paid to do so. But what about the Bengal party leaders?

The question is, are we supposed to believe that Bengal leaders of the CPI(M) were so naïve that they could not understand why they lost. All factors, however, indicate that it was it not naivety, but calculated efforts to achieve a target.

The orchestra of the Rightist media and Bengal leaders were amusing for us, the common men or observers. But, it was a tragedy for the party that for many decades fought against similar designs of these very Rightist media. For long years, in every public meeting, Jyoti Basu used to say that five big media houses were against him on policy grounds. It convinced his listeners about the propriety and the rightness of what the communists were doing. After all, the Rightist media takes up cudgels for Rightist ideology and policies and in the process throw up Rightist icons—so the Leftist leaders will have to counter it continuously to convey their messages to the masses. The tradition was alive till Jyoti Basu's days in Bengal and is still alive in Kerala (and the state committee there did not blame the central leadership for the debacle). But Bengal communists created a new milestone in their ideological history by collaborating with the Rightist media barons backed by Rightist elites.

Nothing surprising. We know, from our experiences all over the world, that communists are capable of doing everything, every single thing imaginable, by the name of their ideology. That is why they have become almost a near-extinct species surviving mainly within the iron curtains of a barbaric regime in China.

***

Clearly, it was the beacon of the glory associated with the Centre of power called Delhi, and all other comforts associated with it that goaded the CPI(M) to directly support the Congress in 2004. The myth of 'secularism' was put forward to misguide the common man. And then, once they were in—more powerful than the king—they got stuck. Yechury and Bhattacharya were in the thick of the actions, true partners of the Central Government. They basked in the reflected glory of the Congress.

And the unwilling man Karat too got his share. It was not only the Prime Minister Manmohan Singh who was to call the shots, he could not do so without Prakash Karat's nod. Karat gradually started enjoying this position. Still, he tried to throw spanners when things went too far. His obsession was with the PSUs, and for them he fought. However, his strong anti-Americanism brought him back to the track. But it was too late; by then, he had conceded too much. His party had lost its identity. It had become a Rightist party. And then he tried to impose on it his version of Leftism. Naturally, there was confrontation of a very high intensity that threatened the existence of the party.

So, at the core of the spasm the party is reeling under at the moment is one worrying factor—a section of the party loves the Congress (and the glory, power, facilities and opportunities associated with it), the other section hates the Congress party and wants to be at the Centre of an alternative to the Congress. This dispute is threatening the unity of the party.

That it was simple love for the Congress that propelled Yechury and Bhattacharya and the Bengal party will be clear if we study the days of confrontation between the Left and the government on the Nuke Deal. We will do so in the Part II of the book. We will also see how the same debate—relationship of the communists with the Congress—remains unresolved for almost a century.

But before winding up this part, we must go through an interesting fact. It will show that the party was fully aware about the fallout of tailing a big party. The party was fully aware of it from its own experiences in different states. They even decided, in 2002, on the course that the party should stay. It is amazing that within two years they forgot it, and invited their doom.

Now, have a glimpse of the Andhra Pradesh party's report placed in the state conference in 2001. This report was about the experience of alliance politics of the state CPI(M):

> "The long association with the TDP resulted in wrong approaches and trends of the bourgeois parties having an influence on our following. All this contributed to weakening of our popular base. There were some lapses in maintaining our Party's independence while dealing with TDP. Due to the lapses in drawing very clear demarcation line between us and TDP, the harmful impact of TDP was felt on people and our followers in some areas. Some activists in some districts due to alien class influences and illusions left our Party. An ex-MLA and two district committee members and over 15 sarpanches left our Party after elections in Khammam district. Similar such instances were also seen in some other districts. Drawing proper lessons from these experiences we should very carefully protect our independence while dealing with bourgeois landlord parties in future."

This discussion was necessary in the state conference as the party's vote percentage had gone down after its supporting the Telugu Desam Party in the state from 1994–1998. Forget that in 1967 Andhra Pradesh assembly election the CPI(M) fought alone and got 6.7 per cent votes. Even after the Naxalites broke away from them, they got 5 per cent votes in 1972. But in 1999, they could secure only 1.7 per cent.

If you have found in it any parallel with the national situation in which the CPI(M) discovered itself in 2009, then there are more amazing information for you. This Andhra report was discussed and incorporated in the political-organizational report of the party congress. It was not only the Andhra experience that was deliberated upon—they studied the experience of all other states like Tamil Nadu or Bihar or Uttar Pradesh where the CPI(M) was aligning with bigger state parties for years. Everywhere the experience was the same. The party was losing its ground. In the light of these facts, the political-organizational report made this observation:

> "In many cases, the electoral understanding does not remain limited to the elections. After the elections, our relations continue either as a 'supporting party' or through 'informal' or 'formal' coordination. This has been the situation in states like Bihar, Assam, Andhra

> Pradesh and recently in Maharashtra where we were in a co-ordination committee which supported the Congress–NCP ministry. Such an approach has prevented our demarcation from the ruling party and its bourgeois landlord policies. It has not been conducive to fostering our independent role and activities which is the basis for strengthening our Party. When our electoral allies win the elections and form the government, the tendency has been to treat them as allies throughout their tenure in office. Such state governments, often headed by regional parties, adopt the same economic policies of liberalization and generally pursue bourgeois-landlord policies and it is inevitable that we come in conflict with them. Opposition to these policies, demarcation from their political-ideological positions are absolutely necessary. If these are muted, it harms the Party's image and affects its mass base.
>
> From the PB and CC, we have failed to stress this important point and intervene to provide a correct orientation, as our preoccupation has also been with rallying and maintaining good relations with these parties.
>
> Our alliances with all India bourgeois-landlord parties have also been developed at the national level since the 10th Congress. One of the results has been that in certain states we have been continuing with our relations with the concerned state units of the bourgeois parties as allies, because of the national level combination. When state governments are run by these parties, we have adopted an approach of a friendly or constructive opposition which does not pay priority to developing the struggles against the bourgeois landlord policies of that government or strengthening the independent activities of the Party, which means also politically and ideologically demarcating from these parties."

At the end of the same report, the party stated certain things clearly:

> "In the present situation when the BJP–RSS combine is running the Central Government it becomes all the more important to rally more allies to isolate the BJP and defeat it. The self-critical lessons that we have drawn about our experience with bourgeois parties and

> the emphasis we should give to develop the independent activities of the Party and projecting and building the Left and democratic front must be integrated into our united front tactics."

Two years later, the party joined hands with the Congress, violated the directions of the party congress and forgot the experiences of Andhra Pradesh and other units. It did not only damage them in West Bengal and Kerala, it damaged the image of their trade union wing (CITU) and that has made the comeback all the more difficult. Electorally, they may stage a comeback after a few years. Both Kerala and Bengal have bipolar polity. People were fed up with the CPI(M) and they decided to vote for the Congress. And what is the point of voting for a party which will ultimately support its rival? The CPI(M) thought its mass base was its slave, and they went ahead for dangerous experiments. Whatever, in Bengal also people may vote for the Left again in the future if they feel disillusioned with the Congress–Trinamool Congress alliance. It may happen anytime after 2011. But electoral comeback is not so important for the Leftists. They have to be different. They have different dreams, different commitments and different dedication. Whether the CPI(M) and the Indian Left will be able to become Leftist again is not known.

Equally difficult will be charting an independent path. Trying this path is boring, tiring, not fit for the persons who believe in flamboyance or who seek shortcuts. That was why the CPI(M) raised the bogey of 'secularism' and went for comfort and power. But Karat threw stones at this glass house and broke it. Out in the cold, they found the people who were with them had left them long ago. They could not see them going as from the glass house the outside could not be seen. The glasses were tinted.

And now both the groups inside the party are attacking each other, bleeding each other, and then making compromises.

So, they failed to point out the real reasons. They had their compulsions too. They had to hide the fact that Bengal comrades were disappointed with Karat because withdrawal of support from the Congress-led government had resulted in an understanding between the national party (that became a junior partner) and Mamata Banerjee's party, thereby taking away more seats from the Left. They had to hide that for the Bengal party ideology and commitment to the people, particularly poorer people, were all things of the past—what mattered was power. The US imperialism was no threat to them. They loved the Congress and its policies. They could not concede it because it was a pity for the Left—those who once contested on the strength of huge popular support—to depend on division of opposition votes to survive. According to insiders, the CPI general secretary AB Bardhan took up this issue with Karat and advised him not to surrender before such nasty designs.

The most difficult question is, however, a different one. Will those leaders of Bengal, Kerala and Delhi who had tasted media glare be able to live a life outside the orbit of limelight? Only those who have tasted it know how difficult it is to live without it. PC Joshi, BT Randive, Jyoti Basu or HS Surjeet lived most part of their lives without it. They rather deliberately avoided it. The media is Rightist, and it carries with it all the vices of the Rightists. It compels one to dance to its tune. For the Leftists, it is like an insidious malignant cell that grows within, and then leads to death if not countered at the proper moment with proper medicine.

The helplessness of the party was clear when they used 90-plus Jyoti Basu to make a statement (1 November 2009) before the November round of by-elections in the state. The statement said: *"We gave unconditional support to Congress to counter communalism and save the country. Now, when the state is facing a severe crisis, I would ask Congress supporters to back Left Front candidates for peace, order and development."*

The statement was not an appeal to the Congress leaders as made out by the media. It was an appeal to the mass base of the Congress. But the Bengal leaders failed to understand that such an appeal has no value, no meaning, no significance at all. The state is not in crisis, it is the party that is in crisis, that too because of its own doings.

The crisis is only deepening. A section of the party will like to forge an alliance with the Congress in future. They will try to join a Central Government led by the Congress. The other section will oppose it tooth and nail.

The malignant cell in the CPI(M) is easily detectable now. It is up to the party to decide how they will counter it.

References

1. 'Significance of the 17th Party Congress of the CPI(M)' by HS Surjeet, *The Marxist*, Vol. 18, No. 1, January–March, 2002.
2. One such writing available on the Internet is in the *Outlook* October 19 issue.
3. 'Significance of the 17th Party Congress of the CPI(M)' by HS Surjeet, *The Marxist*, Vol. 18, No. 1, January–March, 2002.
4. The *Indian Express*, Delhi edition, 17 May 2009.

PART II

Prakash Karat and the Nuke Deal

Four

Autumn of the Left

LET US wind back the time to 2008.

It was autumn, but there was merriment in the air. Three months ago, the Left had withdrawn support from the government. But the government had survived.

The market was buoyant, the establishment happy and the investors were free to look forward for a kill. With the prop in the form of the Left thrown away, the Union Government opened up the corpulent Provident Fund (25 trillion rupees) for management by the private sector players like the ICICI, the HSBC and the Reliance Capital. Anil Ambani, the owner of Reliance Capital, had this prize catch soon after his friend Amar Singh's Samajwadi Party bailed out the government of Manmohan Singh. Others were preparing for some other grab somewhere else, and the growing economy was shining bright. India was on the threshold of being unleashed, we were told. What was implicit in it was that the elite India was on the threshold of being unleashed after the signing of the Nuke Deal.

Nobody had the answers of how and why, but the media pundits elevated the campaign launched by a section of the Congress party to an unprecedented high. They wrote in their columns full of slant comments against those opposed to the Deal that India would just become a world power after inking the Deal. The golden future they portrayed left the common man wondering why such a grand step had not been taken so long.

It was almost party time for the elites of India. The government was rid of the entity called the Left, and the neoliberal policies of the government could now run amuck. So, there was merriment in the air, and it mattered little if Kashmir was lost for yet another time due to the Amarnath crisis, or if the vast majority was constricted by bear-hug of price rise, or if three-fourth of the population could not earn even 50 rupees (then equivalent to 1.25 US dollar) per head per day. Nothing else mattered, for India had clinched the Deal and was on the threshold of a golden age. It was not surprising given the fact that a certain rule of the game had emerged in India—a government must work for the elite India while promising tall things for the vast majority. Manmohan Singh had opened the exchequer for the elite of the elites, and had promised new deals to rural India. At the end of the day the poor got only a truncated guarantee for 100 days work, and the private players had it all.

Rid of the Lefties, the elite of India could really rejoice then, for the great juggernaut of growth and development was moving. Question like 'for whom' was irrelevant.

But the crisp autumn failed to do away with a nip in the air. After all, autumn is autumn.

This autumn came a couple of months after the Left's withdrawal of support on 9 July 2008. The withdrawal by the Left and consequent filling up of the vacuum by the Samajwadi Party immediately resulted in India going to International Atomic Energy Agency (IAEA) for stipulating India-specific safeguards. By August, IAEA Board of Governors endorsed the conditions of the Deal, and the Nuclear Suppliers Group (NSG) gave their nod in early September. The rest was just procedural follow-up. Now, the Deal done, the polity was gearing up for the election that was six more months away. Thus, it was autumn for the 14th Lok Sabha too, and the leaders of different parties showed signs of slight disquiet. It was now time for a curtain over a historic five-year term of a Congress-led government that had the exclusive identity of being supported by the Left for first 50 months. Some leaders were worried about the Left's withdrawal of support, and were wondering what next.

However, the top leadership of the Congress party was not that worried. They had started receiving encouraging signals from the CPI(M). These signals were not coming from the national headquarters of the Marxists—they were coming from the distant East. They were harbingers of a rapprochement: if a similar situation like 2004 arises again after the polls, the Left will, once again, extend support.

***

The recent political history took certain new turns by certain decisions of the Left. They first decided to support the government and then started working on snatching away parties from the BJP camp. Those 50 months showed that the broad camp against the Hindu chauvinists was capable of keeping the BJP out of power for long, long time. But after the completion of the fourth year of this new unity, everything changed with the Prime Minister's 'do or die' attitude.

The battle had started from the middle of August 2007. First, the Left threatened to withdraw support. Then the government pulled the brakes. The ruling UPA and the Left began a discussion on the merit and propriety of the Nuke Deal. Pranab Mukherjee, the second man of the government tirelessly worked on brokering peace between the warring camps of Manmohan Singh and Prakash Karat, and he was being ably assisted by Sitaram Yechury. The discussion dragged on, meaninglessly, for six months. Then managers of Manmohan Singh started their preparations for taking the final call. And soon the government started insisting on allowing them to approach the IAEA for a discussion. The Left protested firmly. A few days later, suddenly they backtracked and allowed the government to go ahead.

It was known in those days that the Left had allowed the government to go to the IAEA for a discussion after getting a firm commitment from

Sonia Gandhi. The commitment was that the government would not proceed further without the nod of the Left after coming back from the IAEA. It was not known (because it is a matter of interpretation) what actually transpired in that particular meeting attended by Sonia Gandhi and her closest aides, and the two topmost leaders of the two communist parties, Prakash Karat and AB Bardhan. That was why it was difficult to judge whether Sonia Gandhi played an active role in trapping the Left, or she really assured the Left and later could not stand firm in the face of Manmohan Singh's threat of resignation. But at least one leader from the Left opposed the proposal of allowing the government to go to the IAEA—Debabrata Biswas, the general secretary of the Forward Bloc. After coming out from the UPA–Left formal meeting that saw the Left backtracking, he told a few reporters that the Deal was now destined to be through.

What Biswas could see, Karat failed to imagine. Even when the government was closing the Deal secretly, Karat told reporters, off the record, that the Deal was dead. By then, he too had become close to the Congress, had developed personal equation of trust with some of its leaders, particularly Sonia Gandhi, and had fallen victim to such practices that he at one point of time was vehemently opposed to. But that was only natural. Power corrupts—not always in materialistic way, but more often mentally.

So, Karat felt betrayed, and cheated, when finally Manmohan Singh pulled off the biggest coup of his life.

Naturally, the end was bitter, so bitter that the PM openly said that the Left (without whom he could not become the PM or remain PM for four years) tried to make him behave like a bonded slave. One wondered why. Lal Krishna Advani agreed to keep aside all contentious issues he had cherished all through his life for the sake of a coalition government. Then why Manmohan Singh felt that abiding by coalition *dharma* (i.e., avoiding issues that may break the unity) was tantamount to behaving like a slave. The question was not raised by the elite media, and thus it never became a moot point in a public debate.

Miffed with the PM for his constant tirades against them, the Left too retaliated very bitterly. The CPI(M) leaders said the PM had finally found his master (the US). Those who claimed themselves to be communists in India had always used such language (a well-known example was their description of Subhash Chandra Bose as 'Tojo's dog'). But what was surprising was that these two parties were living together for four years like close friends.

It was also true that the Left could not point out much objectionable things in the Deal that called for such bitterness. After all, if the controversial Hyde Act had empowered the US government to terminate the Deal in case India had not followed them, India too was in no way bound to accept the US diktat or return the facilities. If such a situation arises in the future, it all will depend on the future government's sense of dignity or eagerness to defend the country's sovereignty.

Thus it all seemed that so much fire and hate were instigated by exterior factors. Non-pundits could not understand what was so great in the Deal or how it would brighten the future of India so much that anything could be put on stake: non-pundits also failed to understand what could be so bad in it that it should tantamount to eclipse of India's sovereignty. Again, it was fine that there was difference of perception on the Deal. As it proved to be irreconcilable, the Congress and the Left parted ways. There is no solution of an ideological debate, we all know. But the bitter end gave birth to certain question—What was the reason behind such irate uttering by both sides? Who provoked them? And the most important one, who benefitted from it?

It all boiled down to a simple formulation. Definitely, a section in the Congress was peeved with the Left for their last remnants of Leftism that they imposed on the Central Government. We know this fraction of the government consisted of the hardcore neoliberals like Manmohan Singh, P Chidambaram, Kamal Nath, Kapil Sibal, and Deputy Chairman of the Planning Commission, Montek Singh Ahluwalia. We also know the man who was blocking the path of disinvestment and such other measures was Prakash Karat. So, initially the Prime Minister and his men took a different course. For clearing the path for new pension fund, or labour reforms, or for introducing hire and fire policy, Mammohan Singh depended on Buddhadeb Bhattacharya. The trick he used was praising Bhattacharya at regular intervals. Obviously, it was a shrewd political tactic to divide the communists. Singh and his team understood that a section of the communists were no more in a position to realize that praises from the architect of neoliberalism in India is no certificate for a Leftist. Along with Bhattacharya, there emerged Yechury who was too willing to make a deal with the government on every matter. Manmohan and company decided to extract support from the Left on every disputed issue through this channel.

Soon, things became obvious to Karat and company. They realized that these two politburo members were actually working as spokespersons of the Central Government. Karat realized that Manmohan Singh and other ministers were trying to cut into his authority inside the party. So he became a bitter critic of the PM. As such he personally suspected Singh to be a man whose loyalty was to the US. Singh on his part believed Karat's loyalty was to China. Singh's perception got strengthened as Karat and AB Bardhan insisted, debunking the security concerns, to allow China to invest more in the country. Karat's perception about Singh too got strengthened when he sent Pranab Mukherjee to sign an Indo–US Defence Agreement. Thus the two, Karat and Singh, were bitter about each other much before the Indo–US Nuke Deal assumed the shape of a crisis. Thus, the rift was accompanied by an unprecedented shrill.

Consequentially, what generally was referred to as 'secular polity' was fractured. The media, an overwhelming chunk of which is controlled by the elite, had never pointed out that Manmohan Singh had put an end to the unification process of the 'secular forces' for the sake of a deal with the US.

The whole episode proved that this battle was between the hardcore Rightists and the hardcore Leftists. It proved that secular unity was less important for all the players. It exposed each and every player of the secular camp. Thus the autumn of 2008 turned ominous for the so-called secularists. It brought in a prospect of long and bitter winter, if not the end, for them.

***

In the autumn of 2008, the prospect of a long winter also loomed large over the leading Leftist party, the CPI(M). That was because the image of the party had taken a severe beating after Nandigram incident, and because of cracks and fissures appearing in their house that had the potential of bringing down the structure itself.

In this chapter, we will see the nature and extent of these divisions in the party. And throughout this Part II of the book we will try to ascertain why Prakash Karat, considered as a hardliner, failed miserably to stop the party from wearing the face of the Rightists. That is important for our study, as this vertical rift denied them the opportunity of reaping any harvest out of their last Leftist act, as a consequence of which the path ahead is tapering.

Apparently, this division in the party was an offshoot of support to a Congress government. Curiously, the 50 months of support had endowed Bengal government with much benefit, while the other government led by the party, Kerala, got much less. The great geographical divide in the party was staring at the face of the leaders who decided to ignore the ramifications of one incident: after the Railway Budget of 2008 was presented in the Lok Sabha, the CPI(M) MPs from Kerala walked out of the House, while those from Bengal sat tight. That single incident proved that the comrades of Bengal had no feeling of camaraderie for the comrades of Kerala. It was height of provincialism. It was provincial chauvinism.

It was unthinkable even a decade ago that MPs from Bengal would not share the voice against deprivation raised by the MPs of Kerala, even after being requested to do so. It was a sure sign of a rift in the party that was too deep to have a cure.

The Bengal MPs did not walk out because (a) they were happy with what the rail budget provided for Bengal and (b) they did not want to embarrass the government. Everybody knew that the parliamentary party leadership consisting of people like Basudeb Acharia or Rupchand Pal or Niliotpal Basu[1] or Mohammad Salim and others were all from Bengal, and did neither know nor bothered to know about Kerala. The situation was the same for more than a decade. The regular parliamentary party briefing during the session was thus reduced to briefing by parliamentary party of Bengal. Even earlier leaders like Somnath Chatterjee or Saifuddin Chaudhury too were from Bengal. Curiously, no other national party, not even the CPI, was in such a pathetic situation. Things changed only when Sitaram Yechury became parliamentary party leader. But then he too started behaving like a Bengali comrade. What else could he do when he too was elected to Rajya Sabha from Bengal? Thus for a reaction on matters like budget, rail budget or any other pan-India matter, the Kerala journalists had to look for reactions from the central party office, as parliamentary party always failed them.

Again, in matters related to governance and legislation, Bengal's point was heard and taken into account by the Central Government, but Kerala was never consulted. This did not change a bit even after Yechury came to the Parliament. On every debatable issue, Pranab Mukherjee used to call up Bhattacharya. VS was an unknown name.

But the geographical rift that was manifested in the Parliament was just a tip of the iceberg. In reality, the other type of rift was much more severe than that. What happened inside the party during the 50 months of support followed by its withdrawal actually was itself an indicator of a long-term rift.

***

Let us now examine the exterior and the interior of the rift and how the CPI(M) behaved in those 50 months.

We must remember that the decision to support the Congress directly was almost unanimous as far as the leadership of the party was concerned. Only a handful like the party's till-then-strong trade union wing CITU's leader MK Pandhe resented it. We must keep it in mind that the CPI(M) was the only party in this country that was electorally not in contest with the BJP (in its core area hardly there was any presence of the BJP), and yet identified the BJP as its main enemy on 'ideological' grounds. Thus it had proved itself to be the most principled party in the eyes of the people.

But, the CPI(M) was also known as a principled party because of its pro-poor attitude, thoughts and ideology. Traditionally the communists were known as hardliners, having faith in maximum state intervention to ensure maximum social justice and uplift of the poor. Over time the connotation of 'maximum intervention' has changed, and those who disliked private investors had to settle with the fact that private investors will be there. But the 50 months of its support to the Congress-led Union Government showed it was ready to sacrifice this valued principle to uphold the premise of 'compulsion of governance', a theory the Congress bosses constantly hammered at their ears. The Left was not in the government. They were 'outside supporters'. But they were told that the supporters would have to understand the compulsions of the government (for example, ratifying some legislation related to patent regime), and they should support every legislation the government brought. Though it was not morally obligatory for a party or combination of parties (the Left consisted of the CPI(M) and another smaller communist party called the CPI, and two smaller parties, the RSP and the Forward Bloc) who were not part of the cabinet, the Left bought this argument. Probably, they thought they would be able to block some regressive legislation planned by the government using this principle of governance. At the end of the day, it was clear that they had paid much more than they had earned.

What they did was a case of surrender before the Rightist ideology on the excuse of fighting communalism. Otherwise, they could have provided issue-based support that would have no compulsion, but would allow much more space to exert their wishes.

The Leftists, who for years fought the patent regime and the very existence of what they felt 'discriminatory' trade agreements through GATT and WTO, approved the Patent Bill. The elites were cruel enough to overlook that the sanctimonious communists, who pledged their existence to fight the 'bourgeoisie-landlord' ruling class, and particularly landlordism, raised their hands to support the new SEZ scheme, which was a euphemism for industrial fiefdom. The elites were not satisfied with this great sacrifice by present day 'communists' who once used to sacrifice their lives fighting a battle for poor tillers' right to land. The Leftists then concentrated on the probable foreign investors to stop them from entering retail trade in India that was being carried by millions of low-earning people. But, it must be kept in mind, that at the same time they allowed Indian giants to enter this sector. They sacrificed all logic in favour of the poor and the unprivileged only to please Manmohan Singh, the PM. Was it so that if a poor man lost his livelihood because of Reliance it would hurt him less than if he was thrown out because of Walmart or any other foreign company. Everybody knew it was not so. So it could not be that the Left leaders did not know that. They knew, and yet they sacrificed their love for the poor for the sake of a government. It even surprised Mukesh Ambani, the top businessman of the country, who said that he apprehended much more resistance to his (Reliance) company's plan for entering into retail trade.[2] No, his apprehension was ill-founded. He did not know what great sacrifice the Leftists could make. Earlier they sacrificed their lives, now they were sacrificing their principles.

Thus, the Leftists did their best to be treated as a 'good boy', but the elite wanted much more from them. New entrants need to be ragged, so that they become perfect part of the system. The elites failed to understand what a terrible wrench it was for someone to leave its old world all on a sudden, to deny one's past so brazenly, or to capitulate before its once-upon-a-time enemies in such a humiliating way.

But it was not so that all those decisions—which were rare examples of communists supporting neoliberal and ultra-neoliberal policies—were endorsed without fierce debate inside the party. On all these counts, there were debates in the politburo, central committee and even in the state committees. But finally the opposition had to bow out. I remember one of the staunchest fighters against this new outlook, MK Pandhe, often used to tell me that the party would some day understand that there was no difference in the outlook of the UPA and the previous NDA as far the economic agenda was concerned. But, the majority faction was not convinced.

Even after doing so much, the majority faction failed to satisfy Manmohan Singh and his team, and their supporters, the elites. In fact, the elites were peeved with the fact that Prakash Karat was still acting as a last line of defence of the Left. He had conceded many points, but on three counts he did not yield ground. One, he was dead against weakening the public sector and was vehemently opposing disinvestment to swell the exchequer. Two, he was not allowing foreign investment in certain crucial or sensitive sectors. Three, on foreign policy matters, he was steadfast in his opposition to forging proximity to the US. Though he was not very comfortable within the party on these three fundamental points, he somehow managed to carry the party with active help from people like Pandhe or VS.

I know I am making things complicated. First I said the majority faction, which included Karat, ignored the perceptions of Pandhe. Again I said Karat held ground on certain issues with the help of Pandhe and the party decided to oppose the government on those points. Then, how many groups were there?

Broadly, three at the politburo level. One was of the neoliberals led by Bhattacharya–Yechury duo. Vijayan too sided with them on pure economic isues. On the opposite extreme, there were hardliners like Pandhe, late Chittabrata Majumdar and VS Achuthanandan. This group was against supporting any neoliberal idea. Finally, there was another group consisting of Karat, SR Pillai, Manik Sarkar and Brinda Karat. This group, given a free run, would have acted like hardliners. But crushed between the two extremes they were constantly siding with the stronger group on a certain issue. This group was vacillating from one extreme to the other and was acting as a balancing factor. So we can call this group a 'moderate' group. At times, the neoliberal camp took recourse to 'compulsion of governance' theory and convinced the moderates of the need of supporting the legislations of the government that was dependent on them. The deal was that the government would not press for any legislation that the Left was opposed to. At other times, the neoliberals argued that there was no point in blindly opposing all neoliberal ideas. Rather, it would be better to press for amendments to smoothen the rough edges of the policies. The moderates agreed.

However, this classification was effective for the period of supporting the government and was applicable only on economic matters.

In other matters and in other contexts, this division in the party took different shapes. We will come to that a while later.

***

In an overall scenario, the CPI(M) stopped the government from doing certain things, but the government extracted much more concessions. The government stopped it from following its ideological core.

At times, the Left leaders went directly to Sonia Gandhi to seek her help and succeeded in melting the hardened attitude of the government. Two such issues on which help came from Gandhi were PSU disinvestment and pricing of petro-products. This irritated the PM's camp and it decided to play the same trick on the CPI(M) to get things done. PM's camp started appeasing and using Bhattacharya and Yechury. This trick worked. The signals that went from this influential group of the party, basically Yechury–Bhattacharya faction, were quite contrary to what Karat was saying publicly. This emboldened the government to ignore Karat's line. The common perception in the government was that ultimately what the Bengal unit would say would be carried out. That was also the impression of all those connected to the corridor of power, including most of the journalists.

Bhattacharya and the neoliberal group proved their ability by helping the government to avert the crisis on Indo–US defence relation. Karat was furious when the government quietly signed it, and he planned to withdraw support. It was discussed in the politburo. But with

Bhattacharya's help Yechury mediated with the government and brought a compromise formula. It was decided that it would not be any exclusive agreement with the US and similar 'agreements' would be signed with other countries including China. Thus the government went ahead to do what it wanted, while providing an escape route for the Left. The agreement with the US was carried on further and further, while the agreements with the other countries remained on paper. This crisis, thus averted, was never reported in the media.

Whatever, the consequences of the Indo–US Defence Agreement emboldened the government and it decided to go forward with its own agenda. So, one day the 'communists' woke up to a scenario that they interpreted as one where India was on its way to be a junior partner of a world vision prepared by the US to serve its interest. That world vision of the US under George Bush was aimed at containing Russia and China, and finishing off Iraq and then Iran. So the hardliners and the moderates of the CPI(M) together decided to stop the finalization of the Nuke Deal.

Again, the elites succeeded to win over the neoliberal section of the CPI(M). This section now demanded that the government should not be overthrown. Thus a clash started within the party between two groups—one group was just like the neoliberal elite and had little difference with the leaders of any other party, the other group was a motley combination of various shades of opinion united on the point of anti-Americanism. In reality, one group was trying to cling on with the Congress, while the other was preoccupied with theoretical obsession on an elitist point.

History has thus witnessed a bizarre clash within a communist party of a Third World poor country on issues not directly related to the people's life. It bore testimony to the fact that the whole approach of the party towards the Congress-led government was convoluted. Under Karat, they wanted to assert themselves. But, their assertion lacked direction. If their past was any indication, they were to oppose both SEZ and Nuke Deal, and the resistance should have been more vehement against the SEZ policy.

But the policies of the new Left could not be measured with any yardstick. They welcomed and implemented SEZs in Bengal, but not in Kerala.

***

Now, let us take a pause. We need to analyse why the CPI(M) sacrificed its pro-poor ideology. Why they, or let us say Karat, did not fight on SEZ and surrendered before the extreme right designs, and then suddenly decided to put stiff resistance to the Nuke Deal? We will discuss it in the next few subsections. First, let us start with the incidence of total break with the past as evident in case of SEZ.

Earlier, we took note of the 'compulsion of governance' theory, but it does not come up with real explanation as far as the Left is concerned. The Left were known for their frayed tempers (hundreds of examples can be cited to show they never cared for judiciary or any other institution in Bengal and Kerala), known for scanty regard for this 'bourgeois democracy' (four decades ago, when they were in a government in West Bengal in which communist leader Jyoti Basu was the deputy CM, the CPI(M) state secretary Pramode Dasgupta suggested that Union Home Minister should be arrested as and when he would come to Bengal), and they were never conformist. It was rather surprising how they became conformists like the other, in their own terminology, 'bourgeois' parties.

The truth was, the party (or a large section of the party) started remoulding itself as a social democratic party without denouncing, like the Social Democrats, the basic tenets of Marxism. This remoulding had started long ago and the process was on for decades, but it got a very major boost during 2004–08. We may say, they went further, as evident from their stand on SEZ, and started supporting extreme neoliberal policies. This support to SEZ was a very major break—we may say a critical break—with the past so far as the Left was concerned. Let us see how and why this concept of SEZ was being opposed even by the neoliberal economists. Here, it may suffice to say that SEZ is just the opposite of state intervention: it is giving away fiefdoms to industrial lords on a platter with not only tax concessions and subsidy, but also with near-absolute rights.

SEZs, as contemplated, were to be a conglomeration of a lot of things—real estate, tax haven, lax laws, much lesser governmental monitoring, and a new heaven for shifting industries from the mainland.

That was SEZ as contemplated in 2005 when the Bill was passed in the Parliament with Left support[3]. The amazing rush that followed showed how great the benefit was for the industrialists or service sector barons. Advantage number one, only 35 per cent of the land was to be used for production unit. The rest was for infrastructure including thriving real estate business. Advantage number two, there were huge tax concessions. Advantage number three, relaxed labour and other laws. Those were enclaves under industrial barons permitted to start neo-zamindari in free India with the active support of the Left.

Strangely, even after supporting the SEZ policy, quite brazenly the Left every year gave memoranda to the finance minister asking for cut in tax concessions and levying more taxes on the rich! Recourse to such double standard further exposed the party. Under duress, they started suggesting some changes in the SEZ Act. It was again another attempt of hoodwinking the supporters, as by then almost all the SEZs that exist today took their sanctions from the government and started building upon their new estates. MK Pandhe and Chittabrata Majumdar of the CPI(M) and Gurudas Dasgupta of the CPI later fought against the concessions to be given in labour laws and could restore a significant part of it. But, that was victory on paper only, as in these fiefdoms, where contractors were to thrive, nobody was supposed to care for what was written in the statute book.

Now just see how some of the Rightists viewed the SEZ policy.

The Reserve Bank of India (RBI) had stated that SEZs must be treated as commercial real estate rather than a priority sector proposition for bank lending.[4] The Finance Ministry was worried about the estimated revenue loss of a whopping Rs 175,487 crore in taxes between 2005 and 2010 because of SEZs and feared that it could lead to large-scale dislocation of industries from domestic tariff areas. The then Finance Minister P Chidambaram said, *"The SEZ Act allows for too generous tax concessions."*[5]

Dr Jagdish Bhagwati of Columbia University, an ardent advocate of globalization, felt that India did not need SEZ for the simple reason that it had passed the phase when such instruments were required. After denouncing its need theoretically, he advocated additional reforms for reducing trade barriers. In September 2006, Raghuram Rajan, the then IMF Research Director, described India's SEZ policy as a tax give-away that was likely to shift Indian production to SEZs rather than create new economic activities. He too felt that the subsidies, guarantees and tax sops on offer were misdirected. Rahul Bajaj said SEZs are land scam. (*Business Outlook,* 5 October 2006).

But the Leftists of India of modern times found the idea fascinating. While the Left supported it and West Bengal government applied for many SEZs as though it was the latest toy available in the market and must be grabbed, the Finance Minister of Maharashtra (a 'bourgeois' politician called Jayant Patil) came out against his own government's policy on the issue. After raising his voice against farmlands to be acquired for setting up SEZs, he questioned the sagacity of doling out sops to those zones when no consideration was being shown to the country's 150 backward districts.

It all became terribly confusing. Who was a Rightist and who was a Leftist could not be identified anymore. This single decision of the Left deprived them of their legitimacy—whatever they did or will do to show their Leftism, whatever claim they would make to show their concern for the poor, whatever they would write in their magazines in favour of state intervention would be just mocking them till they declare that supporting the SEZ policy was an unforgivable blunder on their part.

Contrast this position with what the Left stood for throughout its history. Even when they started traversing on the path of social democracy, they did not sever their link with three segments of population. First, following the legacy of Tebhaga–Telangana, they stood by the tiller for his right to till the land and get appropriate share of the yield. Second, they stood with the labour for their rights. Third, they opposed land grabbing, tax concession and such other benefits to the industrialists. But, they lost themselves in 2006.

It was basically a reflection of the mindset of the new Left. It was the mindset of a group of people who had sunk totally in what they called 'bourgeois vices', without acknowledging the fact that the 'vices' were now 'virtues' in their eyes. So, the other part of this mindset was to hide facts and behave in a way as though nothing had happened. Like true social democrats, they tried to reform the SEZs with imaginary suggestions like allotting more area for manufacturing purposes and other insignificant details. Of course all these came as an afterthought, knowing fully well that even before considering all those there would be hundreds of SEZs.

And I reiterate, all these were done deliberately. There were objections from within the party. There were detailed deliberations on this at the politburo level, where Achuthanandan and Pandhe and Chittabrata Majumdar tried to raise the alarm, but failed. Theirs were the last faint echoes of the values and principles of what people knew decades ago as the voice of the communists, the voice that could be trusted. They fought, but lost. Still, at least, they fought.

The neoliberal CPI(M)'s experiment with SEZ landed them in Nandigram. It is only irony of history that in recent years wherever people have started movement against efforts of forcible eviction, be that in Rajasthan, Maharashtra, Uttar Pradesh or Haryana, they had sworn by the people of Nandigram and their heroic struggle. Nandigram became a symbol of people's resistance. It became the Telangana of modern India.

Whatever, Indian Left's support and implementation of SEZ thus became a historic event in the world communist movement. It was another matter that the financial meltdown ultimately killed the enthusiasm for SEZs as the export market shrank. That had nothing to do with the Left's sin.

***

Now, this could not happen unless a neoliberal section had come up in the party and was strong enough either to take-over, or to threaten to take-over, the party. This has happened many times in the past all over the world, and it was true (and still is true) about the CPI(M). Whether such developments should be hailed or condemned depends on one's mindset. If a communist party renounces its faith in seizure of power by use of guns and accepts democratic competition, it grows above the main drawback of its demoniacal existence in many other countries, and thereby becomes a democratic force. But if in its attempt to adopt the system it adopts neoliberal mindset, then it loses its bona fide reason to exist and becomes irrelevant. This was the case with the CPI(M) in the autumn of 2008. And it deprived them of their *locus standi*.

Consider this. While the Left restored to firing and kicking people in Nandigram, the government of Maharashtra restored to referendum to decide whether the Reliance SEZ should come up in Raigad (September 2008) district. The SEZ was cancelled after the locals said 'NO'.

***

Essentially, all these are questions of mindset. The mindset was vividly reflected in their attitude towards compensation given to the people of Singur. Their attitude was like they had given best compensation (for land, and not for loss of livelihood!) and people should be indebted to them. But what was the reality?

They ousted many thousands of poor peasants and poorer labourers from Singur without giving them a small share of the prosperity their land would bring for the others who owned land in the adjacent areas. Surprisingly, the Tatas bought land in suburbs of Chandigarh for a project for Rs 2.5 crore per acre in 2008.[6] It is to be noted that Chandigarh administration offered only Rs 14 lakh per acre for third phase of Rajiv Gandhi Chandigarh Technology Park at Manimajra. But even that was more than the highest Rs 12 lakh paid in Singur. At Dankuni, which is 25 km from Calcutta, a private company proposed to buy land for more than Rs 50 lakh per acre. At that rate, Singur land, 40 km from Calcutta, should have been priced at Rs 30 lakh per acre), while the unfortunate peasants of Singur got maximum of Rs 12 lakh per acre.

There was nothing wrong in this attitude if only one accepted capitalism as the last truth and renounced one's faith in Marxism, which had anyhow failed all over the world. There was nothing wrong in this attitude if only one announced one's conversion to neoliberal camp. Otherwise it was doublespeak, manifestation of sheer opportunism, a fraud on the people.

But, apparently the mindset had not engulfed the whole party. The party was divided. There were people at all levels who opposed this mindset. I have said that at the politburo level there were, in those days, people like Achuthanandan, MK Pandhe and Chittabrata Majumdar, who were opposed to supporting or implementing the concept of SEZ. They were real hardliners, and compared to them Karat often looked a moderate. Though in Bengal, the traditional hardliners were badly cornered, Kerala proved to be a different story. When, after the 2006 election, the neoliberal party secretary Pinarayi Vijayan (who had absolute control over the party organization) made efforts to stop Achuthanandan from becoming the CM, the ground level supporters of the party almost revolted. It pushed back Vijayan and his nominee, and put Achuthanandan, the hardliner, on the CM's chair. This was a major development that should be taken note of, for it showed that unlike in Bengal, in Kerala the party's lower level had not turned Rightist. And as the Congress is the symbol of neoliberalism, the cadre-base there remained anti-Congress and anti-America. Vijayan and his men were neoliberals, but they too were against the Congress and the US. But that was not the case with Bengal. When protests against Coke–Pepsi was planned and launched in Kerala by the party—first during the US invasion of Iraq and then on the basis of an allegation of misuse of water resources and pesticides found in it—West Bengal party undertook nothing of the sort. They were not against multinationals anymore.

***

This brings us to an interesting aspect. Whatever we have observed till now shows that there were three sections in the party. At the highest level of leadership the hardliners were represented in those days by VS Achuthanandan, MK Pandhe and late Chittabrata Majumdar. Then there was a moderate section like Prakash Karat, Brinda Karat and

S Ramachandran Pillai. However now we will not count the moderates as a separate group, for they either sided with the hardliners or else with the neoliberals. And yes, there were the neoliberals, who had become majority in the middle and lower level of the party. This was proved in 2005 Party congress where a party document defining the new approach to counter the economic reality was prepared. But the neoliberals in the party were not united on political question.

We have seen that a section of the party had started supporting the neoliberal measures of the Union Government out of their faith in it, and this section consisted of an overwhelming majority of the Bengal party and a large section of the Kerala party. They were not ready to admit the fact that they were following the age-old capitalist path. However, these neoliberals themselves were divided in two camps. The Bengal neoliberals were pro-Congress, and the rest of the neoliberals including those from Kerala were anti-Congress. This was basically out of obligation.

The Bengal comrades believed that if the party sided with the Congress at the Centre, it would be able to divide the opposition in the state in two camps. In the state the Left would not ally with the Congress, and the Congress would fight elections against it. However, because of the understanding at the Centre, the main opposition of Bengal, the Trinamool Congress (a breakaway group of the Congress) would not join hands with the Congress in the state. Thus the opposition, which had the support of half the voters of Bengal, will remain divided, thereby losing the assembly elections for many more years to come.

But in rest of India, particularly in Kerala, the party was engaged in a direct fight with the Congress. So, proximity to the Congress was risky. It could benefit the Congress, or even create a vacuum in the state as people might start believing in the RSS campaign that both the parties were on the same side of the fence and the electoral fight was a mock one. So, despite the fact that Vijayan was a neoliberal, he was also anti-Congress. The other group, the hardliner group led by the Chief Minister VS Achuthanandan was against the Congress for ideological reasons. Thus the whole party in Kerala was against the Congress.

So, on this line, the rift was a complicated one. In a sense, it was a peculiar situation. The neoliberals outside Bengal were still squeamish about unmasking them, nervous about risking a sudden total break with the past. They continued with old habits of opposing the multinationals, opposing America, while actually they loved to be close to the *crorepatis*. But their continuation with the old line actually kept the hardliners of the party more relevant than them. It also strengthened the overall anti-Congress attitude of the party.

This probably explains why Karat, earlier known as the hardliner, failed to stop the Yechury–Bhattacharya as far as economic questions were concerned and succeeded in overrunning them while political questions like withdrawal of support were concerned. There were three distinct segments in the party—a hardliner segment (Pandhe, VS and others), a pro-Congress neoliberal segment (Bhattacharya, Yechury and others), and an anti-Congress neoliberal section (led by Vilayan). Whenever any of the segments came together, they carried the majority with them. Karat as general secretary sided with the majority group, for he had no option. On economic questions, both neoliberal segments came together. And on political questions, the hardliners and the anti-Congress neoliberals joined hands.

Thus, when the question of withdrawal of support came, only the pro-Congress neoliberal group was out in the market to stall it. However, the neoliberal effort to transform the party to be at peace with the possibility of India becoming a junior partner in the US alliance was too much for two other sections (the hardliners and the anti-Congress neoliberal). They were afraid that if they went on supporting the government despite the Deal, the party would lose its popular base in Kerala and the secondary base it had among the students, intellectuals and other segments of population. This secondary base had little electoral value, but it gave the hardliners their courage of conviction. We will explain that later.

Here, our point is how the party was placed in the autumn of 2008. To understand that we must study minutely what the different factions of the party (whom we have divided in three: the hardliners and the two sections of neoliberals) did before and after the final call of withdrawal of support.

***

On the question of anti-Congressism and anti-Americanism, the hardliners and the anti-Congress neoliberals were together, and on the basis of this solid majority they took a decision in the central committee meeting in September 2007 to withdraw support from the government if it went ahead with the Nuke Deal. The pro-Congress neoliberal group then took recourse to the theory that Left's withdrawal of support would strengthen the 'communal forces'. The other side was not ready to buy this argument. They felt it was an attempt to make the party a permanent junior partner of the Congress. If the BJP was to be fought, they pointed out, it was the Congress who should shoulder the maximum responsibility. They argued that the threat of communal forces was not a licence to the Congress to do whatever they wished to do.

Thus, for the first time, the myth of secularism was exploding.

But, Buddhadeb Bhattacharya and Sitaram Yechury carried on their manoeuvres even after a decision was reached. They started negotiations with the government, came out with different proposals (like having a legislation in India to counter the effects of the US Hyde Act) that the majority group led by Karat rejected, and forced the party to spend many months in dilly-dallying. By giving an impression that the hard decision taken by the party under pressure from the hardliner general secretary Prakash Karat could be annulled, they fooled the gullible reporters and editors, and tried to fool senior leaders of the government. They also got a promise from Laloo Prasad that he would not allow the government to go ahead with the Deal by sacrificing the government itself.

Yechury and Bhattacharya (brought in use by 90-plus Jyoti Basu to pressurize Karat) created sufficient confusion in the minds of the people. Basu had proposed a fantastic line that could be dubbed a line of permanent settlement: *'Negotiate, but do not disturb the government, and oppose those policies and decisions not of our liking outside the Parliament.'*

Never blame his age, Basu had always been soft on the Congress. Bhattacharya went a step ahead. At the height of Nuke Deal dispute, he openly spoke of the necessity of nuclear power for West Bengal's development.[7] Then Basu supported him. It seemed that the principle of discipline of the communists that was invoked so many times to silence all dissents by lesser comrades was given a quiet burial. The Stalinist structure crumbled at the top. It became free for all. In Kerala two groups (led by Vijayan and Achuthanandan respectively) were already fighting bitterly, and now it became Bengal versus the party centre.

By indulging in a futile exercise of having a series of meetings which carried on for months, the divided house of the CPI(M) allowed the government time to make all the preparations for the Deal and for life without the Left. Karat had said much earlier that no one would be able to convince him that the Deal was not against the interest of India, but he too participated in the proceedings of a UPA–Left committee to discuss the pros and cons of the Deal, and allowed the government to go to the IAEA for an informal negotiation. According to insiders, Karat himself attended the meetings for he and his team was apprehensive of compromises that Yechury could make in the committee in his absence. But, at the end of the day, Karat stood fooled by the cunning political moves of Manmohan Singh and his team.

It was true that the majority section of the party stood firm on their decision. However all of them avoided stating the simple position that the people at large could understand, that they would withdraw support if the government went ahead. As it was shrouded in mystery with contradictory signals from two quarters of the party, their final call seemed an abrupt one, incongruent with their earlier decision of allowing the government to go to the IAEA.

We must have in mind in this context that a decision which in the eyes of the people seems sudden or impulsive cannot ensure any political gain.

So the autumn did not bode well for the Left. The party had supported the Congress for a historic 50 months, and then made futile attempts to bring it down, but neither of the acts had any lasting impression on the common man. It was not clear what they either achieved by supporting the government or by withdrawing it. True, like Chandrababu Naidu extracting concessions from Vajpayee, Buddhadeb Bhattacharya got many projects from the government. But, according to knowledgeable bureaucrats of Bengal, the degree and extent of this favour was not significantly higher than what Andhra Pradesh got from Vajpayee. Thus at the end of the day, what mattered to the leaders of the Left was their basking in the reflected glory of the power of the Congress, and their influence on top level bureaucrats and politicians.

We all know power corrupts. The CPI(M) proved, using someone else's power corrupts more. At the end, they belonged to nowhere. The Rightists and their followers never accepted them really. The Leftist mass too turned away from them.

***

This open division in the Left that had continued for months together harmed them in ways more than one.

We have seen the dilemma and divisions among the Left from the organizational angle. Now, let us move over to real politik to find out the real undisclosed reason for their dilemma and its fallout.

***

Ironically, the Left could not snatch the initiative because they had skeletons in their cupboard. As a consequence of their West Bengal unit following neoliberal policies, Nandigram had become a symbol of common man's resistance. The party was scared that if election took place within one year of police firing and killing of farmers in March 2007, they would lose many seats in Bengal. This was a major reason for the West Bengal unit to oppose the decision of withdrawal, and as they explained it to the national party, other leaders had to be considerate. Ultimately, the party failed on many counts.

First, it failed to dislodge the government. It was a political failure as it was the Left who gave time to the Congress and other parties in the government to redo their arithmetic of majority in the Lower House and snatched away the initiative from the Left.

Second, it failed to stall the Deal. Thus the Left would be seen in the future as a force that cleared the path of signing the Deal by tagging on with the government till it was too late to stop it. However, I am not sure whether it would really count in the future, for I believe the Deal was neither demoniacal as the Left portrayed, nor angelic as the Congress and the elite tried to demonstrate.

Third, they failed to show their influence over other regional parties, despite the fact that they were instrumental in cobbling up a Third Front only a decade ago.

Fourth, they failed to show up as a cohesive and disciplined party.

All this happened because they had no firm public position. For many months, Karat appeared to be weak and Yechury carried the day. The ordinary middle class was confused. The silent majority was not concerned.

It had put a question mark on their capacity of manoeuvrability in the future.

More importantly, it had put a question mark on the Left's ability to reinvent them and their ideological position in a space where they would have to fight both the BJP and the Congress, the two pillars of Indian elites.

The most hurting fallout for them was that they failed to prepare the people for it. Their decision was not preceded by proper political campaign. They never came out with an unambiguous 'threat of withdrawal' that the people would have understood clearly. It seemed that they left hurriedly the negotiation table and ran to the President to give the withdrawal letter. The common man did never understand what they negotiated, why they allowed the government to go to the IAEA and why they took the final call one fine morning. And they never understood how this was related to their lives.

So the Left did not get any benefit of it in the election. It proved secret deals and clandestine understandings do not help in popular politics.

And for records sake, the West Bengal unit of the CPI(M) decided not to raise this issue of the Nuke Deal in the hustings.

All this happened to the Left because of two factors.

First, they were a house divided on the question of withdrawal of support, and were caught on the wrong foot. They were neither straight nor bold. They were not communicating to the people. They were making tawdry compromises to keep the government alive for few more months. Thus the man on the street was confused. The often-heard question in those days was why the Left was still supplying oxygen to the government if they felt the Deal was so bad. Their posturing, timing and shrewd calculations, all aimed at managing differences between the two groups within the party, did not cut any ice with the people in general. By dawdling for months, they failed to project what they wanted to project, that the Deal was against national interest. If one believed something was going to happen that was against the interest of the nation, someone was to act urgently. Pathetically, there was no urgency in their actions. And the government utilized this time for making all preparations. It must also be mentioned that the top managers of the CPI(M) were under the impression that Sonia Gandhi would not allow Manmohan Singh government to proceed with the Deal. Again, Karat took it for granted that Mulayam Singh Yadav was with him, when in reality Yadav sealed the deal with the Congress to support them after Left's withdrawal. Yechury boasted that Laloo Prasad would stop the Congress from going ahead, while Laloo was indifferent to the issue and limited himself to pressurize the Congress to go ahead in a way so that the government would survive. Thus, the end came like a bolt from the blue to the leadership itself.

Secondly, and this one is a derivation of the earlier point, they forgot to link it with the people's lives. In the run-up to this decision, AB Bardhan, the general secretary of the Communist Party of India (CPI, the original party, and now a smaller communist party) linked the nuclear issue with other policies of the government, like the price rise, farmer's plight, lack of social security of the majority of people and so on. He raised all these points in an impromptu Press conference after a party meeting. But the CPI(M) discarded it. They felt that if it was done then it would look like that the Left had decided to withdraw support and was just making a ploy. It was strange, may we call it bizarre, that Karat and company—who had inherited the tradition of Left movement in India that for long years stood for protection of the poor and weaker sections—failed to realize that their withdrawal of support had to be linked to the interest of those sections.

Might be, they no longer believed that they were to stand for those sections. Might be, but it was strange that they forgot even for their political survival, for their future, they had to do it. Even the Congress or the BJP—the parties of the elites, for the elites and by the elites—try to do that.

It was really odd that the Leftists failed to realize it! Simple political sense demanded that they would have either followed Jyoti Basu's prescription (oppose the government outside the Parliament and go to the people, but do not topple it), or should have gone whole hog against the government policies. These two paths went completely in different directions. Basu's path would finish off the communist movement and Leftism in India, and the other path would once again mark the CPI(M) as a militant party. But Prakash Karat and his core team's obsession with the single issue of Nuke Deal showed that they too were too much elitist in their approach. They thought in terms of the elite. Thus, there was a huge disconnect with them and the poor of the country. This was sure to tell upon them in the future.

Forget about the people at large. They lost moral right to forge a 'Third Front based on alternative policies'. Politically, of course, they can do anything, for nothing can stop any party from functioning in its own way in a democracy.

***

We have reached to a very important point of our discussion. We know Karat ultimately compelled the whole party to toe his line on withdrawal of support. But, what was the secret of his power? How he could overrule Bengal unit? We have observed that the CPI(M) got divided in three factions. Let us examine them further.

One faction, led by Prakash Karat since the mid-90s, was socialistic in its outward expression. To go by their economic view, we find they were in favour of maximum state intervention to ameliorate the condition of the poor, and in political field it was essentially anti-Congress.

We may say that this faction was the continuation of the old mindset of the Indian communists, sans the concept of a revolutionary change. However, we must note here that the undivided CPI accepted peaceful means of transition (that is through the democratic process of participating in election) to power way back in 1950s. We may like to ignore their own assessment of it as a tactical line (a line taken for a short span of time to reach a goal). We know after participating in elections one seldom goes back to the jungles to fight guerrilla warfare. Thus, after the split (in 1964), the CPI(M) too traversed the same path. That was why the Naxalites left the CPI(M) and went to the jungles. So, the mainstream communists had abandoned the concept of revolution decades ago. But an urge for sweeping changes in favour of the poor stayed on in the minds of the old leaders. Karat is an inheritor of this trend, though he acquiesced with the neoliberals on many occasions during 2004–08, to save his chair to fight it out another day.

The second faction was led by Pinarayi Vijayan. This faction was neoliberal in its outlook, but retained the old anti-Congress mentality. The overwhelming majority of the leaders of Kerala had rallied around him by the initial years of this century. This group may have in some way drawn on the legacy of the group led by late EK Nayanar, a man from a rich family with legendary background of fighting the British and feudal powers. It may be said that Nayanar, like Jyoti Basu, planted the seeds of liberalism in the party. Strangely, Vijayan was once known as VS Achuthanandan's man, but then he started consolidating the neoliberal section. And naturally, VS clashed with him and tried to oust him. On his part, Vijayan retaliated vehemently. The situation deteriorated day by day and got a boost when VS became the chief minister. The feud between the two groups made the CPI(M) a butt of ridicule in Kerala. Vijayan has won the day inside the party, but is still in a cleft stick as an accused in a graft case. Here, he has a major difference with Bhattacharya against whom no charge of corruption surfaced ever.

The third faction, led by Yechury–Bhattacharya, was both neoliberal and pro-Congress.

However, the relevant questions that should be asked about Karat include why he could not resist the onslaught of neoliberal thinking in the party? Why he had to make so many compromises with Yechury–Bhattacharya group after becoming party secretary while he was an adamant fighter earlier? On political front, he had realized earlier that heading a government could not be so bad an idea as he thought in 1996. That was why in 1999 he was prepared to let Basu occupy the Prime Minister's chair if only Sonia Gandhi agreed. But on economic front his ideas had not undergone radical changes. Otherwise he should not have withdrawn the Left from the UPA–Left Coordination Committee on disinvestment issue. So, why he made so many compromises? Why he failed to resist the pressure of the neoliberals?

***

But generally, people ask the opposite question: why Bengal party, which was the most important branch of the party, more important than the rest of the party in electoral terms, could not force Karat to toe its line? This is a natural question, given the fact that in any other party it would have been the Bengal party that would have dictated terms.

Maybe, an exception could be the BJP. Suppose, what would have happened if, 10 years ago, the BJP could get 50 seats from Uttar Pradesh and less than that number from the rest of the country. Could it be so that the Uttar Pradesh CM, suppose Kalyan Singh or Rajnath Singh, would have dominated over LK Advani or AB Vajpayee, or say, the RSS? No. But if in place of Vajpayee–Advani, the national leaders were Arun Jaitley and Sushma Swaraj? Probably, yes. But, what about the domination of the RSS?

This dilemma comes in case of all regimented parties. The whole framework of the CPI(M) explains why Bengal could never dominate over the national party. When the question of withdrawal of support from Morarji Desai government came in 1979, Bengal party was opposed to it. But they failed. The same was repeated in 2008. It is not as simple as Bengal line versus Kerala line. It is a more complicated one. It is a legacy of the past that the CPI(M) organization carries till today. Success is not measured in electoral terms: it is measured in terms of ideology. So along with the state units, mass fronts like CITU or Kisan Sabha and so on are given due importance in the party organization.

In the CPI(M), no leader can rule the roost unless he has the support of the majority of the politburo and central committee members. Contrary to the common belief, the CPI(M) is apparently a very democratic party. Every three years, they hold a congress where party delegates come up from the lowest level through elections. A draft goes down to the lowest level and opinion starts building up from that level. Groupism plays a great role in it, and though it blurs to an extent the outcome of the ideological discussion, we have to admit that it is part of a democratic process. Finally, the delegates are elected from all state units and all frontal organizations like CITU and Kisan Sabha and so on. These delegates elect the central committee in the Party congress, which is a convention attended by all elected delegates. True, a panel is generally selected through discussions among the top leaders. But anyone is free to challenge it. If people do not challenge it, that is because they do not want to put their career at stake. But, supposing the present rift in the CPI(M) remains and widens, it may be so that in next Party congress Yechury will propose a different panel, if he has the guts to do that. Of course there is risk in it: if his panel gets defeated he may not find a place in the next politburo or even in the central committee. To avoid this risk, the leaders make compromise formula and the panel goes unchallenged. Unless there is a great rift, this process of inclusion carries forward a communist party. It ensures that those who have some support base in the party will not become victim of politics of exclusion.

In this organizational structure, Bengal party cannot dictate terms. In case they have lost faith in Leftism, they have two options before them—either to take-over the party by converting the majority of the party to their faith, or else to split the party.

Now, similarly, after taking over of the party as its general secretary, if Karat tried to upturn the ideas of the neoliberals, he would have become a minority in the party. He became general secretary of the party because the majority of the delegates wanted him to be. And, majority of the delegates in 2005 when Karat became general secretary were either neoliberals, or were leaning towards neoliberal ideas. That destroyed the old Karat, and compelled him to wear the face of a moderate.

Here, it should be mentioned that at times a man who had lost majority support of the politburo or the central committee, and was also in minority among the Party congress delegates, had worked as the general secretary. HS Surjeet functioned like this from 1996–2004. But that could happen only because Karat, the leader of the majority faction, wanted him to continue as the chief of the party. Surjeet was the last veteran around, and the leaders of the majority section did not want to see him go. Karat himself was in minority when he proposed to withdraw support on the Defence Deal. But, he was never in a position when he could be overthrown, only because he made quick compromises with the majority section. This happened particularly on economic questions: Karat tried to resist the onslaught to some extent, and then came up with a compromise formula which actually resulted in say 75 per cent victory of the neoliberal group. This discredited Karat in the eyes of the Leftist mass, but kept his position inside the party secure.

Probably, 2005 was a bad time for Karat to assume the post of general secretary. Theoretically, he should have declined it and offered it to Yechury. After the debacle of the neoliberals, he could have claimed and gained the leadership. In that way, he could have ever retained the image of a hardliner. But, in practical politics, no one can see through time, and no one lets a chance go. So, Karat went for it in 2005. As a consequence, he now stands in the midway, neither here nor there.

Whatever, we have noted that the organizational structure is such that Bengal, or Kerala, cannot decide party line alone. Maximum number of delegates from a single unit come from the Kerala party, as it has the largest number of party members. Even then, Bengal and Kerala delegates together are less than half the number of delegates of the Party congress. For the party organization, the frontal organizations are also very important. Mostly these frontal organizations are dominated by the hardliners. And there is no flaw in this organizational structure. What the CPI(M) is today is the result of the work of Centre of Indian Trade Unions (CITU) and the peasant front. The Rightists had insisted that the party organization should be dominated by the parliamentary wing. But for a Left party, mass organizations should have equal importance. Mass organizations are important for launching agitations against various types of repressions against the people (by the state or by the society) and without such agitation a Left party ceases to exist as a Leftist entity. The parliamentary party can be of sole importance to those parties who do not depend on mass movement.

***

So the secret of Karat's power lies in his ability to carry the majority with him. At times, he too gets carried by the majority. It has happened on economic questions. And that made Yechury the second most important player in the party. But, how the shift suddenly started from 2005? The answer may be found in a document the party adopted in the same year. Sitaram Yechury and Buddhadeb Bhattacharya were the two main proponents of this document. It was discussed in the Party congress (where Karat was elected general secretary) and due to differences was referred to the next central committee that adopted it. Karat-loyalists and the radical section of the party fought parts of it tooth and nail, but failed to change its spirit. It defined a new approach of the party. It said they would have to engage themselves with reality rather than opposing things blindly. It said: (i) Neoliberal trends had brought to the fore difference between finance capital and industrial capital: while industrial capital was welcome as it created real opportunities for employment and upgrade of technology, finance capital was not as it took the speculative routes.

(ii) The communists should not oppose everything blindly as they had done so far: they should get associated with the process and try to change the policies keeping in mind their ultimate goal, i.e., socialism.

That was what they called their new pragmatism. Have a look at what they said in their own language:

> "The struggle for an alternative socialist order has to be based on the revolutionary transformation of the existing order. This, in turn, needs an engagement (i.e., joining issues) of the revolutionary forces with the existing world realities with the sole objective of changing the correlation of forces in favour of socialism. This process of revolutionary transformation has to be based on such an engagement and not on the wishful thinking of escaping from the existing realities. The entire history of the revolutionary movement led by the working class is the history of such an engagement with the existing realities in order to shape the material force required to establish the alternative in socialism."[8]

Even before this document was placed or passed, the party had started engaging with the reality under the leadership of Sitaram Yechury. The first occasion was a Bill on the patent regime and they accepted what the Government of India proposed with minor corrections. They negotiated for a few amendments and then voted for it believing that those amendments had ensured a change in correlation of forces in favour of socialism.

Meanwhile let us see what they said about investment. This is important as the passing of this document enthused Bhattacharya to don the robe of a reformist and start a jihad for industrialization:

> "...the CPI(M) Programme notes that following the completion of the democratic stage of the revolution, the People's Democratic State will:
>
> 'Allow foreign direct investment in selected sectors for acquiring advanced technology and upgrading productive capacities. Regulate finance capital flows in the interests of the overall economy.' Till this stage is achieved many interim

> slogans and approaches will have to be worked out. Under such circumstances, the flow of foreign capital into our country, in the present conditions, must be regulated by stipulating the following conditions:
> a) Such capital should augment the existing productive capacities in our economy,
>
> b) Such foreign capital must upgrade the Indian economy technologically, and
>
> c) Such capital must lead to employment generation."[9]

Again, keeping certain questions that arose in Kerala, the party gave certain dictates to the state governments on various subjects. One of those was its line on foreign loan:

> "These governments, therefore, may accept aid for developmental projects but the important criteria that needs to be adhered is that there should be no conditionalities which are against our basic interests and policies. In no case should we go in for loans which involve structural adjustment programmes. Such programmes entail conditionalities like privatization of certain sectors, downsizing staff, cutting subsidies and fiscal conditionalities."[10]

See the contradiction—in case of foreign loan, they stuck to their old policy, while in case of investment, they had drafted their decision in such a way that makes way for everything. Can you think of any modern industry, that too such one that is so big and so ambitious as to invest in a foreign country, which will not augment production capacity (then what will it do?), will not come with a bit of new technology (then how can it survive?), and will not employ people (robot age has not come, man)? Certainly, foreigners will not come to open a jute mill. So, what those nicely worded conditions aimed at? Jyoti Basu always put stress on technology transfer: but 'must upgrade the Indian economy technologically' does not necessarily mean technology transfer.

These changes created excessive enthusiasm. First, some of the comrades thought any investment coming for any industrial projects was part of the socialist agenda, and started inviting all sorts of investment, giving a few chosen industrialists a bouquet of concessions and subsidies. This denoted end of Leftism, particularly in Bengal. It did not affect Kerala that way as the Chief Minister VS Achuthanandan did not follow this path there. Secondly, it gave up ideological position of opposing things which were against the interest of the people, and brought in reformism, i.e., changing things slightly to make them less painful and pass them as acceptable.

As soon as the aforesaid document was passed, Bhattacharya went berserk with his neoliberal ideas. It seemed that the Party congress had allowed perestroika and glasnost in the party. Emboldened by the new approach, during a foreign trip in the last week of August 2005, Bhattacharya said in an interview with *The Jakarta Post* : *"Globalization is a must. Nobody can stop it. And we have to admit it."* He went for inviting private parties to develop new airports in Calcutta and being asked whether it would be ratified by the party, Deng Xiao Ping of Bengal answered that party's line was whatever he said. It seemed that the document had sanctioned whatever Manmohan Singh, the PM was doing. But the party did not acknowledge that globalization was a 'must', it only acknowledged that globalization was 'inevitable'. Well, that too showed defeatist attitude. The recent economic crisis in the world has clarified that it is not even 'inevitable'. It shows that Achuthanandan or Pandhe was not really 'old haggard' as believed by one politburo member of the party. After facing stiff resistance from Pandhe, the party did not allow Bhattacharya to go for inviting private parties to build new airports in Calcutta. However, the party could not stop him either from doling out huge concessions (from taxpayers money) to Tata Motors.

Bhattacharya was doing everything openly. It was not that he was giving interview to a newspaper of Jakarta only. After his huge victory (in terms of seats, not vote percentage) in the assembly election of 2006, in an interview with *CNN-IBN* (14 October 2006) Bhattacharya said:

> "We did commit some mistakes in the early 60s and the early 70s in the name of the trade unions and I am trying my best to erase that image of West Bengal.... I am trying to portray West

> Bengal as an investment-friendly government and also I am trying my best to persuade the trade union leaders to behave.... I want a harmonious relation between the management and the labour. In the 60s, when we were in the opposition, we encouraged some irresponsible agitation in different industries that does not help us."

While we are free to criticize as we wish the mainstream Left for their militant trade unionism, many leaders of the party felt what Bhattacharya was doing was improper. He was not criticizing his past—he was criticizing the role of those who built the party in 60s and 70s, thanks to whom he was the CM of Bengal. They also pointed out that political decency was not expected from him. After all, he left Jyoti Basu's cabinet in 1993 because he did not want to be a part of the 'cabinet of thieves', and then rejoined it. It was Karat who was instrumental in bringing him back a couple of years later.

***

After Bhattacharya and Yechury went ahead with their neoliberal plans and cornered Karat, the only option before Karat was to assert himself on the political front.

He asserted himself at the right moment to withdraw support and started taking control of the party. But to complicate the matter for Karat, though he withdrew support on a high moral ground of national interest, there were no ripples among the vast majority of the population. And Karat had no one to blame except himself for it.

We had noticed that in the autumn of 2008 there was merriment in the air, but that air was restricted to the abodes of the elite, in the cities and in some towns. If Karat had taken on the elite (As VP Singh did once, by implementing Mandal Commission report and thereby ensuring reservation in jobs for the intermediate castes), there would have been jubilance among the mass. But that was missing.

Quite expectedly, for Karat never raised poor people's issues.

True, they insisted on historic decisions like hundred days employment guarantee scheme, or the rights of the tribesmen on the forest land and products (the implementation of which was inordinately delayed by the government even after the Bill was passed). But, throughout these four years, their tone was conciliatory, except when they stalled the disinvestment process of some important public sector companies. They lacked the zeal of the communists of yesteryears, and always took caution to not to break the rule of the game—if you support a government, be courteous to it, otherwise the elite community would label you as spoilsport. By following this rule, the Leftists tried to appease the elite and also the growing middle class who is under its influence. But finally they landed themselves nowhere. The elites were initially pleased, and then branded them as betrayers. Ironically, the man on the street did not bother for them, for they never said that they would withdraw support if price of essential commodities soared up. The man who was an outcast in a city, a construction worker or a domestic help, had no feelings for them, for they never demanded a better life for them as the price of their support to the government. They never said that they would withdraw support if food was not available for the whole population. They did not threaten to withdraw support if proteins and vitamins remained unavailable to half of the children of India. They did not announce that the government would face dire consequences if the government was not honest to reach out to the whole population with effective social security network. They did not demand setting up of a Hunger Commission (like Women or Minority Commission) that would constantly monitor if people everywhere had enough food. They did not demand statutory measures for punishing the corrupt officials who siphon off the money the government allotted for the poor.

These four years showed clearly that the Left was also a part of the elite. They did not raise novel demands in the changed time for they were cut-off from the masses. Like the leaders of the Congress or the BJP, the Left leaders too did not understand the condition of the people. How could they? They do not travel in an ordinary train, or even in a bus while they are in the cities, they do not stand in the queue for acquiring their ration from a public distribution system shop, they do not spend hours without a fan in a dingy room during power cut on a hot summer afternoon, they do not have to wait for hours for their pension from the banks or post offices in the last years of their lives. The Nuke Deal, an issue of concern for the anti-American segment of the elites, and worrisome if seen against the theoretical possibility of the US taking refuge in Hyde Act, is at the end of the day an elitist issue. Their hardened stand on this issue surely won them applause from the Leftist elites—professors, researchers, university students and other intellectuals who constitute their secondary support base—but had failed to cut any ice with the common man.

It was bound to be so, as in these four years they failed to raise the issues of those who travel by buses in the cities, by second class or unreserved compartments of the train, or those who do not even dare to board a train. They did not raise issues relating to the invisible people of the country, except for once when they threw their weight behind the demand for right to forest for forest dwellers.

We may assume they did not raise those demands as they were not acquainted with the lives of those people. But, they did not even raise their voice to demand more positive discriminations for the unprivileged. The data of 2009 shows that of all the students who appeared for IIT entrance examination only 1 per cent belonged to the Scheduled Castes and much less than 1 per cent belonged to the Scheduled Tribes. Thus, the people who consist one-fifth of population came down to less than 1.5 per cent as far as appearance in entrance examination for IIT was concerned. Does not the country need more positive discrimination to end this inexplicably unjust system? Social divisions all over the world—including the West—gets reflected in politics and gives birth to political parties who fights for a particular population. It helps to raise demands against socio-economic injustice. VP Singh brought in qualitative change in the polity by consolidating the backwards and opening up new opportunities for them. But during the days when they were most powerful, the Left forgot why they were in politics.

The gap between the Left and the common man, and the total failure of the Left in understanding and interpreting social reality alienated the Left parties from the people. It was mainly applicable to the CPI(M), but no other Left party associated with it was any exception. They all clung on with the big brother through everything. None of them came out of the Government of West Bengal. In fact, it is the major reason for which we will mention them at times, but will not study them separately. They have no separate identity at all. Curiously, after the defeat of assembly by-elections in 10 seats, the CPI general secretary AB Bardhan said that the CPI(M) should take the onus of this debacle and the CM would do better to resign.[11] Probably, Bardhan's statement would have carried a little more weight had they come out of the government after Nandigram firing. Probably, Bardhan's words sounded hollow now.

***

In these four years, the CPI(M) and the Left proved that they had no willingness to think in new terms to eradicate poverty and end social insecurity of the people. On the other hand, the attitude of Prakash Karat, initially the *de facto* and then *de jure* general secretary for the whole period of 2004–08, was cynical. Quite a few times, he told me, *"What do you expect from this government? They will follow our policies? They will follow their policies."*

It had never been clear why did they extend support to the UPA government then.

And just juxtapose this attitude to what Surjeet wrote after 2002 Party congress (and also take note of the fact that here Surjeet is narrating Party congress' attitude on the United Front, where the party had aligned with another party to fight the election and then supporting the ally's government):

> "The review sums up the shortcomings in our united front with bourgeois parties: Firstly, a self-critical examination shows that at various times we have failed to demarcate from the bourgeois parties with whom we ally. Secondly, when we enter into electoral alliances with bourgeois parties we continue to maintain the unity or alliance with these parties even when they run state governments and there has been a lag in asserting our independent stand and launching

> struggles in defence of the people's interests. Thirdly, the United Front tactics have been mainly confined to electoral alliances and sufficient attention has not been paid to united platforms for mass struggles and campaigns. Fourthly, failure to conduct independent activities and assert our independent political and ideological positions vis a vis the bourgeois allies leads to blurring of our identity and at times tailing behind them. All these shortcomings have resulted in our being unable to gain access to the masses following the bourgeois parties and initiating a process of winning over sections of them towards us. At the level of the PB and CC also we have failed to intervene at the appropriate time to check such shortcomings due to our pre-occupation with keeping such allies with us."[12]

This was in relation to the alliance with bigger state parties, about which we have studied earlier also. However, comrades may not care to read what has been written in a party document. But, it is expected they read what the general secretary wrote. Curiously, with the Congress they had no pre-electoral understanding, except for in Andhra Pradesh, and yet their attitude after the government was formed reflected the same attitude that was discussed in 2002 when the country was ruled by BJP-led National Democratic Alliance.

So, the autumn of 2008 left Karat deserted and disarmed, and his badly-divided party in disarray. It was so not because they had withdrawn support from the government. That was irrelevant. It was so because they failed to have any impact on the lives of the people either by supporting the government or by withdrawal of support. They behaved like any other party and that doomed their future.

Truly, it was autumn for the Indian Left. Whether they would ever again speak the language of those outcasts, of the silent majority living a wretched life, was not known.

It is not known even today. But it is sure that if they do not speak the language of the poor, it will be winter forever for them. They will become an irrelevant force, just like any other party representing the Indian elite, without any particular space left for them.

It all depends on one man, Prakash Karat. Not so because he was a hardliner, not so because he has any great concern for the poor of this country. It is so because he is the general secretary of the party. It all depends on him whether he would fight and corner Bhattacharya, whether he would fight and corner Yechury. It all depends on him whether he will try to bring Leftism back as the agenda of the party. Muttering the mantra of socialism does not make one a Leftist. One's acts and motives decide whether one is.

So, let us focus on him now and see what his rise means for the party and the Indian polity as such. He is important not for what he did in 2004 onwards, which is the most inglorious period for him, but what he stood for before 2004. He committed mistakes, even blunders like not allowing Jyoti Basu to lead a Third Front government. His faith in Stalinist organization has blinded his vision even in 2009, as reflected in his attempt to rid the party of VS. But yet, once-upon-a-time he stood for Leftist ideas, and many in the party still have faith in him. They still believe under him the party will be able to correct its course in near future.

And by forcing the party to withdraw support, though on an elitist issue, he has proved again that he is not yet finished.

References

1. Basu now works in the central party office and thus have acquired knowledge about Kerala too.
2. "Let me tell you that the resistance that we have seen is half of what I had expected..." Mukesh Ambani told *NDTV 24×7* in January 2008. It was a joint interview of Mukesh and his wife Nita Ambani.
3. The SEZ Act was passed in 2005 and the Commerce Ministry notified the SEZ law in February 2006.
4. The *Financial Express*, 22 September 2006.
5. The *Business Outlook*, 5 October 2006.
6. The *Times of India*, Delhi edition, 9 September 2008.
7. The *Hindustan Times*, 17 September 2007.
8. 'On Certain Policy Matters', adopted in central committee meeting held on 3–5 June 2005, in Calcutta.

9. 'On Certain Policy Matters', adopted in central committee meeting held on 3–5 June 2005, in Calcutta.
10. 'On Certain Policy Matters', adopted in central committee meeting held on 3–5 June 2005, in Calcutta.
11. 14 November, 2009.
12. 14 November, 2009.

Five

Prakash Karat: Return of Hardliner

THERE WOULD have been no need of this chapter had there been no withdrawal of support. There would have been no need of this chapter had there been no Karat to fight against India becoming victim of the US hegemony.

Then it could have been assumed that the CPI(M) has decided in favour of perpetual surrender and would go on supporting everything with some proposals of amendments, most of which would not be accepted. It could have been assumed that they would support the Congress for all time to come, and would embrace oblivion. It could have been assumed that everybody in the party was happy to copy what the CPI did in the 1970s (for years they supported the government of Indira Gandhi and whatever base they had just vanished in those days). It could have been assumed that during the polls they would say tall words if only the Congress forgave that, and afterwards would play the role of a loyal attendant of the largest 'bourgeois' party.

But that was not the case. The party tried to re-establish an identity of its own, and all this was due to Prakash Karat, who was known as a hardliner. It was strange that he agreed to provide direct support to a Congress-led government, but we can only speculate on the reason: maybe under duress, maybe he was trapped, maybe he himself was willing. We will never know the real reason. But, we may say after four years of surrender to the neoliberal camp of the party, he planned ways to assert himself.

However, before we start that discussion, I must tell you that I assume Karat is a Leftist. The assumption lies in what he did till 2003. I also assume that he failed to resist the onslaught of the neoliberals because, as discussed in the previous chapter, for the neoliberals were in majority. But, here I must mention, many people do not think these two assumptions are correct. Some of them argue Karat is not a communist. I am not interested in that as no one knows who is a communist as all shades of people—from anarchists to staunch neoliberals—claim themselves as communists. I am not trying to assess who is a communist. My sole point of reference is to Leftism and not a vague concept of communism. What do I mean by 'Left' is there in the *Terminology*. Again, I must mention that some also think that Karat is an opportunist. He allowed the neoliberals to have their way as a part of experimentation. Had it succeeded electorally, he would have sailed along. On this argument, I have no comment to offer, because I simply do not know.

Karat was relatively less known in the political arena than all his predecessors. Karat's immediate predecessor was Harkishan Singh Surjeet, a nice frank man who had close and warm relation with many leaders of the Congress, the Samajwadi Party and many other parties. Though among the puritans he was a suspect, his followers regarded him as a great pragmatist. Before him the party secretary was EMS Namboodiripad, a legendary communist leader and the first communist chief minister in an Indian state. He had succeeded P Sundarayya, who was another legendary leader and who gave up the party position as he felt real organizational work that would create the structure of a future revolutionary party was being neglected. I am not going beyond that as that was undivided party about which we will discuss later in detail.

While Sundarayya was a hardliner to the core, Namboodiripad was a moderate with a rabid anti-Congress mentality. Surjeet was comfortable with the Congress and he succeeded to bring an anti-Congress party at the door of the Congress after reversing the Namboodiripad regime's twin-danger theory.[1] Thus, through time, from Sundarayya to Surjeet, the CPI(M) had walked a long way and had come closer to the Congress. However all the three had the background of leading mass movements, going to jail and sticking to their commitments even during the dark times the party had faced earlier.

Karat is a younger man (born in 1948) and without much experience of mass movement. But that is not a disadvantage for him in the party, for the leaders of his age-group, those between 55 and 65 from Bengal or Kerala or any other state do not have any big record of participating in a meaningful way in any mass movement either. During the Emergency almost all these leaders went underground, and Karat was no exception. Since 1977, Indian democracy has moved through a calmer phase and has not given much chance to have a chequered career of a revolutionary to any of the mainstream communists. Since and after that period, the mainstream communists have not fought the system. The communist who still play that role are known as the Maoists, who are nowadays considered by the establishment as terrorists. Thus contrary to many people's beliefs—who in their minds unwittingly compare Karat with the past stalwarts and wonder how he became general secretary of the party—Karat is genuinely one of the most deserving candidate for the post. Again, some others refer to him as JNU-bred communist. I do not know what it means, because almost all the younger leaders have come up from universities or colleges. Apart from student politics, there is hardly any route now to come up the ladder to the positions of high-level leaders. In earlier times, trade union was an important area that made many brilliant Leftists, but the CPI(M) has successfully killed its trade union over the years, and discredited it in last few years. It is not likely that in future anyone will rise to the leadership of mainstream Left from the trade union wing.

So, Karat is not suffering from any disadvantage vis a vis his colleagues. However, the whole party is suffering from disconnect with the people like any other elitist party.

But that is not all. Karat has earned this post.

He was initiated in Marxism by Victor Kiernan, his professor in Edinburgh, and was a hardliner from the very beginning. He was a leader of the Students Federation of India (SFI) and then secretary of Delhi party. He entered the politburo in 1991, and within a few years became the representative of the hardcore communists. He utilized the vacuum in the party that was created by demise and absence of leaders like BT Randive, EMS Namboodiripad and, more relevantly, P Sundarayya. A large number of the district level or state level leaders of the party believed HS Surjeet and Jyoti Basu were soft on the Congress and were eager to compromise with the ruling elite. They respected these leaders for their capabilities, but believed they should be kept in check by a strong group of hardliners. And, in Karat they found their man in politburo.

Karat also started looking after the organization since mid-90s. It was a laborious job, and he took it to his heart. By 1996, he proved himself to be the leader of the majority group in the party, and yet showed magnanimity to ask Surjeet to continue in the post of general secretary. It was he who led the majority faction to reject the proposal that came from the then Third Front leaders to make Jyoti Basu Prime Minister in 1996. When it was deliberated upon in Calcutta Party congress in 1999 (whether 1996 decision was right) he led the discussion defending the decision and garnered the support of two-third majority. He rose to the top post of the party because the majority of the politburo, the central committee and the delegates of the Party congress desired so.

Karat had come to the top post because there was no alternative. Nobody else had the three qualifications he had: (i) command over party organization, (ii) a national perspective, and (iii) the qualities of an ideologue. Some people still believe that like in old times there was no scope to oppose an official panel and that was how Karat had occupied the top slot. The argument is invalid because the question is who decided Karat should head the official panel. He had no hereditary claim on the post. If there was an alternative, the two stalwarts the party had—Jyoti Basu and HS Surjeet—would have thwarted his rise. Basu could have chosen his loyal man Sitaram Yechury for the post if he had the ability to install him. The reason for Basu–Surjeet's antagonism was simple: Karat and they belonged to opposite schools (Karat was a hardliner and the two veterans were moderates) and Karat had challenged them all through the late 1990s. Karat's opponents had fought bitterly against him on the question of judiciousness of the decision of rejection of the proposal of Basu's premiership that came from the Third Front, but had lost.

Thus Karat had, no doubt, earned his position.

That was, and still is, the secret of Karat's power in the party. He is the leader of the majority group and that is why he is the general secretary of the party.

But since he became party secretary he started making compromises, and most strikingly, even in matters related to economic issues. Naturally, this was quite unexpected, so to say unbelievable, from a party led by Karat. His argument against accepting premiership in 1996 was that the party would not be able to influence the policies of the government. Here, by policies of government he definitely alluded to stalling neoliberalism and opening the door for much more intervention by the state. Now, after their support to SEZ, one wonders what did Karat and his followers mean by 'policies'. And the question comes, what they gained as far as policy issues were concerned by supporting the Congress government for 50 months. If so many compromises were to be made, what was the harm in putting Basu at the helm of a government! He nullified his own logic, and his own past by his compromises. And so, naturally a question comes in mind: was there a personal angle too? Some people think that if instead of Basu the proposal came for EMS, Karat might have agreed.

In 2005, the situation was different. Neoliberalism was at its peak. The Left all over the world was searching for new paths. The CPI(M) leaders were confused. A section felt that they had become tremendously relevant in Indian politics and should adjust with the others to remain relevant. This was the neoliberal group. They did not understand that the elites were just using them and would not hesitate to throw the new converts away when the need would be over. The other section believed they should not sacrifice all their theoretical and practical understanding and obliterate their past.

The communists committed many mistakes in the past. They often apprehended the crux of the reality, but failed to understand it in totality and thus could not carry forward the propositions in a logical way. When they opposed computerization, they rightly pointed out that it would take away job opportunity of the people. But they failed to realize the new horizon it would open up, and they put things in such a narrow perspective that they are, still now, criticized for that blunder. Instead, had they raised the demand of alternative opportunities for the people who would be hit, that could have been much more relevant.

The trend continues. When they oppose privatization of public sector units, they dwell rightly on theoretical aspects. The global economic crisis has proved that they were on right track, particularly with their opposition of banking and insurance and related sectors. But they failed to see another aspect of it. They failed to see how job opportunities for the Dalits and the *Adivasis*, who could still get some jobs only in the government sector, is shrinking. So they failed to raise this additional point in favour of keeping the public sector character intact of those industrial or commercial units. And, they have not raised the issue of job reservation in private sector (no problem, rather better, if done by barring the creamy layer). It showed the detachment of the Leftists with the poorer and underprivileged section of the people. Herein lies the greatest drawback of Karat. If he has to fight the neoliberal section of his party, if he is willing to fight, he must have his feet deep in the ground. So far he has ruled from the party headquarters. But that is a closed place. The reality cannot be understood with information coming only through party channels. To get a feel of the lives of the poorer section, he should occasionally go back to them as he did many years ago as a young leader.

Karat could not check this onslaught of neoliberal thinking of his party for it was too widespread. In the Party congress (2005) majority of the party delegates, as ever, were from the middle class. Vast majority of those delegates had no experience of being with the people in their struggle for food, shelter or social security. So, they were gullible. They thought neoliberal path was the right path to garner votes. For them winning election was the most important thing. So they dumped their past, they forgot their ideology. Ironically, that did not bring them votes, but brought them rejection!

During Karat's time, it is total confusion about the path. Two governments (Kerala and Bengal) started walking in opposite directions. Karat presided over the total confusion, or may we call it total anarchy, in the party. It may be that Karat himself was totally confused and wanted to see where the neoliberals were taking the party.

When the neoliberals faced disaster, he stepped in. Police firing in Nandigram gave him the first opportunity. First, he bridled the Bengal party. Even that was not without giving concession. Bengal CM and the whole party cooked up so many bizarre theories of opposition, the Maoists and the CIA conspiracies. In short, they claimed that God and Devil had come together there to fight the CPI(M). Well, these arguments are part of their regular lie-campaign, and does not merit any comment.

Whatever, even while allowing the party propaganda at the state and at the national level, Karat also took measures against the Bengal party. He stopped them from forcible land acquisition.

Then he planned a detailed course of action to change the total environment that helped the neoliberals grow inside the party.

***

Before probing how Karat planned his retaliation, it must be mentioned that this neoliberalism is a total break from the past. It is often said that Jyoti Basu also belonged to this school. Wrong. It was 90-plus Jyoti Basu who had often supported these things. But he did not tread this path when he was active.

Basu had a long tradition of being with the people. I heard a story from my senior colleagues of Calcutta which is worth mentioning here. Once the journalists were travelling with Basu, who was the CM then, to a distant town. After a couple of hours, the convoy stopped at a level crossing. The journalists sent a request to the CM to stop at a tea shop for a while in the town they were about to enter. The convoy started again. Basu did not stop anywhere in the town. When the convoy crossed the limits of the town, the journalists told each other how rude the CM was to ignore their request like that. But after a couple of kilometres away from the city, the convoy suddenly stopped. There was a tea shop, with discoloured walls, its roof done with hay. A few wooden benches were everything it offered to sit. Basu got down and walked towards the shop. As the others followed him, they saw an old man stood silently with his hands folded at the shop. Basu went close to him and asked whether he had forgotten the old days and would not serve tea. Then everyone came to know that decades ago Basu was there for some time in that area, and used to come to this man for afternoon tea.

I wonder whether any top leader of the CPI(M) today has this experience of mingling with the people and feeling their pulse. All the leaders who now dominate over the party are, in the eyes of the people of Bengal and Kerala, representatives of the ruling elite. People do not share their actual feelings with these leaders. Till a few years ago, Basu could alert the state party about seats the party could lose in an election, and also could explain why. He had his own network. Other members of the state secretariat (as at the national level they have a politburo, at the state level they have state secretariat) were often taken aback by the retired old man's network of information.

It was thus not surprising that when journalists told him about the package of subsidy Tata Motors was to get, Basu's initial reaction was: '*E rakom abar hoy naki*' (things cannot be like that).

Probably that was what Karat's attitude should have been.

But Karat washed off his hands from this and kept a safe distance. After Nandigram firing he conceded to different people that it brought shame to his party. 2008 Party congress held under his leadership stated categorically that Nandigram was a political and administrative mistake (and yet the party is clueless about the reasons of debacle in Bengal!). But about Singur he had not been so categorical.

True he himself had not defended it passionately, but that does not absolve him.

It placed the party in a curious situation. The third alternative the party talked of—different from a Third Front, an entity that will develop through struggle for alternative policies—became redundant. The CPI(M) itself was without a proper alternative economic thinking. Yes to SEZ, yes to Indian companies in retail trade (the effect of which may take a decade or more to unfold), yes to Singur, and tall claims of being different is just ridiculous.

During Karat's regime, the party had also paid the price in terms of fast-falling credibility. When the Left fought half-heartedly, opposing foreign investors in retail trade and being silent about the Indian giants, rumours abounded in the corridor of power that they were doing so to favour the Reliance. And it was also true that Mukesh Ambani met Prakash Karat and Sitaram Yechury at the party headquarters in New Delhi quite secretively. While the CPI(M) leaders tried to keep it under carpet, the Reliance sources leaked it to the Press, and thus it became known. So a simple question came up: Why did they want to keep it secret? Again, another simple set of questions were being asked without being answered. Why Bengal government favoured Tata in an unprecedented way? Why selectively one group? Why the state should acquire land for them when hundreds of other corporate houses were buying land directly from the peasants? Thus, it is the CPI(M) leadership, who was responsible for downgrading their status. Once upon a time their record of probity was so high that no one dared to allege things like these. And it would not be easy for them to regain it.

If you add the strange case of Pinarayi Vijayan, the secretary of Kerala, who had made all attempts to stifle investigation against him in the infamous Lavalin case, you understand where Karat's the CPI(M) stands today. When the parliamentary election was taking place, Kerala government's attorney general opined that there was no case against Vijayan and the CBI should not be allowed to go ahead. These are all same stories, whether about Quattrochi, or Advani's inflammatory speech at Ayodhya before demolition of Babri mosque, or Vijayan. Thankfully, the governor of Kerala gave a go ahead without paying heed to it. Karat supported Vijayan to the hilt.

Altogether, whatever Karat had done in last five years had negated his position of either being a Leftist, or a leader of a party that is prepared to wage a relentless fight for uplift of the poor.

Though there are sufficient reasons to cast doubt on his real intentions, we may give him benefit of doubt and may assume that he made compromises to consolidate his position. Now, let us move over to the story of Karat's retaliation.

***

How Karat planned retaliation is a fascinating story.

It is interesting that Karat, Yechury, Bhattacharya and Vijayan belong to same age group. Karat belongs to Kerala, and he is a soft-spoken man, sober, determined and looks like a thinking being. Vijayan is rash, parochial and aggressive. Bhattacharya is vacillating, without any fixed point of conviction. Once known for his misbehaviour with people, he changed himself in recent years. But still he uses provocative language and apologizes regularly for different comments made. Yechury belongs to Andhra Pradesh, has a pleasing personality, and is over-friendly with the Press. Bengal party secretary Biman Bose too is of the same age group, and is not taken seriously by many of his comrades.

Here it should be noted that since the untimely demise of Anil Biswas, the then state party secretary in 2006, Buddhadeb Bhattacharya became the overall commander of the state party. The last time I met Biswas, he told me categorically that the 'support' is a mutual give and take between the two sides. By give and take he did not mean only clearance of state government's proposals. He meant political give and take. After his demise, this political content was lost in Bengal. There almost the whole party took by rote the concepts thrown up by the neoliberals.

But Kerala was different. Here party secretary Vijayan, had to fight a hard battle everyday with the veteran and hardliner VS Achuthanandan. Anti-Congress and anti-US plank were alive and kicking in Kerala. And in this, Vijayan too had a role.

So, Karat had inherited a party which had no conviction in Leftism. That limited his options. He could not take on the neoliberal mindset of the party. So he picked up the anti-US psychological build up of the traditional communist base. Karat had started working on this line for one-and-a-half years before the final call. His intention was to hit the Congress and the neoliberals of his party in one fell swoop.

Karat made his first attempt of assertion on the Indo-US Defence Deal. He wanted the party to withdraw support on that count. But the pro-Congress neoliberals somehow managed a rapprochement. But, even on the Defence Agreement he compelled the party to take note of certain points that he himself elaborated at a Left rally on 8 July 2005:

> "Can the Defence Minister and the UPA government explain whether this agreement is in consonance with this approach in the CMP?
>
> Indo-US Defence Agreement comes at a time when the US is actively working to contain China. It is pressurizing the European Union not to lift its embargo on supply of arms to China. Donald Rumsfield, the US Secretary of State, had recently in Singapore voiced concern about China's defence expenditure and acquisition of arms. The United States does not see China as a strategic partner but as a strategic rival. In contrast, the US approach manifested in this agreement is to prop up India as a counterweight.
>
> It is clear that India will be given concessions only if it plays the role the US has designated for it in its global and Asian strategy."

There was no doubt that what Karat said was right. America under George Bush turned into a dangerous imperialist force, bent upon destroying every population that resisted the US aggression. But, the moot point was whether containment of China was in our interest. While a large cross-section of concerned Indians feels that a powerful China is not in our interest, a small section (particularly the communists and the pacifists) feels there is no clash of interest between China and India. Karat's speech identified him as a China-lover in the eyes of the establishment.

Karat however did not hesitate to issue a threat to the government:

"The framework of the Indo-US defence relations should be rejected. Let it remain just a framework skeleton. It should not be fleshed out."

Note that he demanded that the Indo-US defence relations framework should be rejected. The government did not do that. And Karat also failed to retaliate as the party was not in favour of withdrawing support.

While Karat failed here, mainly because the agreement was signed before much was known about it, he could easily persuade the party to view the civil nuclear agreement with suspicion. That was not difficult in the wake of the Defence Deal. The leaders of the CPI(M) still call them 'communists' and that calls for a certain degree of anti-US approach. So Karat had no difficulty to persuade the party to question some points of the agreement and raise some doubts. Initially, he was not talking of withdrawal of support.

Just take a pause for a moment. After the party lost direction as far as economic matters were concerned, they decided not to object to the US capital. But curiously they still imagined they were fighting against the US hegemony and their documents still acknowledged that the strength of the US was sourced from its big business and finance capital for the benefit of which the whole system worked. We will not ask them why they never took the same critical approach about the USSR though its imperialist character was so clear in East Europe or in Afghanistan. But we must wonder if they were fighting the US then how could they welcome the US capital, or for that matter capital from anywhere of the developed world. After all, it would strengthen the capitalist world and the hegemony of the US. This is one of the many riddles that we do not expect the communists to answer, for there cannot be logical answer to these.

Coming back to our topic, initially Karat was just preparing the ground for a possible retaliation. Withdrawal of support was still not in his mind. Probably, he believed that the Left's threat would be enough to stop the government. He underestimated the strength of the Congress. And still he had his plan B ready: if the Congress went ahead he was ready to take it by its horns. When the party came out with a terse statement on 7 March 2006, hardly anyone could see through the plan:

> "The Indo-US Nuclear Deal signed during the recent visit of US President George W Bush to India is clearly part of a wider strategic partnership into which the US seeks to drag India. The CPI(M) has already noted that the present Government has regrettably allowed itself to be pushed into a slew of agreements in the areas of defence, agricultural research, science and technology, and infrastructure development which seriously damage India's interests and compromise Indian sovereignty. While the CPI(M) views the Nuclear Deal within this context, it is also important to take note of the specifics of the Deal itself."

But the statement left enough space for rapprochement. Once beaten, Karat was more cautious now, and agreed to give enough leeway to the neoliberals of his party.

I remember in those days I asked Karat whether he really believed the Nuke Deal and the Defence Relations Agreement, seen together, was dragging India into the US orbit. When he answered in affirmative, I further asked whether the Left could support such a government. He smiled his characteristic smile and said, *"Let us see."*

AB Bardhan, the general secretary of the smaller communist party, did not see much threat in the India-US proximity. When I asked him same set of questions, I gathered that he believed Nuke Deal was too technical and would have little impact on the lives of the common man. The CPI had earlier supported a Congress government led by Indira Gandhi in the 1970s. But, it was this party that started discussing an important theme: whether people's plight could be overlooked for achieving secular unity. The CPI(M) did not go into this debate.

Here it must be mentioned that a small Left party, the Revolutionary Socialist Party, having only 3 MPs in the last Parliament [the Forward Bloc too had 3, while the CPI had 10 and the CPI(M) 43] was the first to urge other Left parties to withdraw support from the government. Way back in 2005 it announced that the Left should review its support to a neoliberal government. The CPI(M) ignored the appeal, the CPI ridiculed it, and the Forward Bloc kept mum.

Back to our topic. Karat had founded the base of anti-imperial struggle during the run up to the Party congress held in 2005 (where he became the general secretary of the party) by raising the slogan that the US neoimperialism was the greatest danger before the world. During Iraq War, Lal Krishna Advani (the Deputy Prime Minister of the NDA government led by the BJP, the Hindu chauvinist party) was in favour of sending Indian Army to the death-fields, and AB Vajpayee was unsure of the situation. It was the Left that fought against it and, with the support of the Congress and other secular parties, was instrumental in passing a resolution against it in the Parliament. Karat used this precedence to force discussions in the Parliament on the Nuke Deal time and again (though, curiously, important treaties and agreements with other countries can bypass the Parliament in India). He succeeded in extracting promises from the PM to abide by certain guidelines.

However, after the US Congress passed the Hyde Act (India Specific Act for giving concession to India), Karat put down his feet. On 11 December 2006, just after the Hyde Act was passed, the CPI(M) despatched a Press release containing the heading 'US Legislation on Nuclear Deal not Acceptable'. Have a glimpse of its arguments:

> "Replying to the debate in the Rajya Sabha on 17th August 2006, with specific reference to the nine points of concern raised by the CPI(M), the Prime Minister had unambiguously stated that India cannot and will not accept any compromises on the following:

1. Full civilian nuclear cooperation: 'Removal of all restrictions on all aspects of cooperation and technology transfers.'
2. Principle of Reciprocity: 'India will accept only IAEA safeguards on nuclear facilities in a phased manner...only when all restrictions on India have been lifted.'
3. Annual certification by the US President: 'We have conveyed to the United States our opposition to these provisions, even if they are projected as non-binding on India, as being contrary to the letter and spirit of the July statement.'

4. India as a state possessing advanced nuclear technology: 'India's strategic programme is totally outside the purview of the July statement and we oppose any legislative provisions that mandate scrutiny of either our nuclear weapons programme or our unsafeguarded nuclear facilities.'
5. Safeguards agreement and fuel assurances: India seeks uninterrupted supply of fuel to reactors that would be placed under IAEA safeguards together with India's right to take corrective measures in the event the fuel supplies are interrupted. Further, 'There is no question of allowing American inspectors to roam around our nuclear facilities'.
6. Autonomy of decision making on future scientific research and development: 'We will not accept interference by other countries vis a vis the development of our strategic programme.'
7. Moratorium on production of fissile material: 'We are not willing to accept a moratorium on the production of fissile material.'
8. Global Nuclear Disarmament: While committed to the Rajiv Gandhi action plan, 'There is no question of India...accepting full scope safeguards as a requirement for nuclear supplies to India now or in the future.'
9. Cessation of Future cooperation: Responding to the US terms to cease cooperation in case India proceeds with further nuclear tests the PM had stated, 'India's position and development of nuclear weapons is an integral part of our national security. This will remain so.'

The final Act of the US legislation runs contrary to most of these assurances given by the Prime Minister. This includes provision of imposing restrictions and trade regimes barring access to dual use nuclear technology thus denying India its full nuclear fuel cycle. The annual good conduct certification by the US President remains. There are nine references to India's role being one of support and complicity with the US designs on Iran. The Act talks of India's foreign policy being 'congruent to that of the United States'. Instead of an India specific additional protocol with the IAEA, the US law calls for a modified additional protocol meant for non-nuclear weapon countries etc.

> Once again goalposts have been shifted. Two new provisions have been included concerning a) in case of the US cancelling its obligations it would help facilitating alternate fuel supplies from friendly countries of the Nuclear Suppliers Group, this is now restricted only under conditions of market failures and does not cover the deliberate US termination; b) It was agreed that the US would help build a strategic fuel reserve to ensure continuity of running our reactors for their lifetime. The final Act now explicitly bars any reserve other than normal operating reserves required to run our reactors.
>
> Under these circumstances, the argument that the country should wait for the final bilateral agreement is specious. Obviously, the US administration is bound by the provisions of its Act while negotiating this agreement. This cannot be accepted by India as it negates the most significant, if not all, assurances made by the Prime Minister to the Indian Parliament. Thus, further negotiations on this score must not proceed."

At this point, even Yechury was with Karat. Yechury is pro-Congress, but he is not pro-America. Rather like the vast majority of the party members, he too is anti-America. But, till then Yechury and other pro-Congress neoliberals were confident that a final clash would be averted. He had taken a lead role in the August debate in the Rajya Sabha, and he thought escape route would be available to please the hardliners without putting at peril the relation between the Congress and the CPI(M).

But, neither side budged. So from the statement issued in December of 2006 to the statement issued eight months later, on 18 August 2007, was just a logical step forward. This second statement said:

> "Given the widespread opposition to the agreement and the fact that a majority in the Parliament do not support the nuclear cooperation deal, the government should not proceed further with the agreement…. It is for the Congress leadership to decide on the matter which will have serious consequences for the Government and the country."

Thus Karat slowly nudged the party into a position from where there was no scope of a return. At this juncture, the neoliberals had to choose between anti-Americanism and pro-Congressism, and they chose the later. The neoliberal faction of Bengal and Sitaram Yechury then attempted to fool the reporters or editors, particularly of Bengal. They tried to build up pressure from below to encumber the path of Karat. But that was bound to end in a failure. Their attempt to negotiate and find a common ground was bound to end in a fiasco.

Karat played his game extremely well. And credit must be given to him for his steadfastness against what he felt the attempts of 'US imperialism' to drag India firmly into its orbit. For him it was a question of principle and he stood his ground, thanks to the strong anti-US sentiment prevalent in the Kerala party as well as everywhere else other than Bengal.

***

This victory was important for Karat for two reasons.

First, those who questioned 'Karat who' (he was and still is an enigma to politicians of all other parties, a large section of the middle class and the elites, including the business or industry barons, and even to the scribes) realized that Karat was the real boss and not Buddhadeb Bhattacharya or Sitaram Yechury.

The false notion that Bhattacharya and Yechury were the real bosses originated from and was actively stoked up by Bhattacharya and Yechury themselves. After their success in making the party 'pragmatic', they went berserk for propagating neoliberalism. Bhattacharya was ready for foreign investment, up to 100 per cent, almost everywhere. Yechury was ready to compromise with the government on every issue, even on Bills concerning banks, etc., which were the core areas of Leftist unions. Bhattacharya and Yechury tried to rally the party in support of new pension scheme that had to be earned by the employee (it might have been okay for a section of the Central Government employees, but surely was harsh on state government employees, particularly in states like Bengal, where the state employees were paid much less). Strangely, this happened when the trade unionists were fighting tooth and nail against the pension scheme. It looked like that Bhattacharya–Yechury duo was trying to finish off the party's trade union wing. It looked like they were calling the shots in the party. It looked like Karat was a puppet of the duo.

In those days, media, industry and government circle was abuzz with the phrase '*deal ho gaya*' (deal is done) on almost each and every issue on which dispute arose between the government and the Left. Everybody knew that the government struck these deals with Yechury–Bhattacharya duo. Bhattacharya's statements soon after the Party congress, like 'globalization is a must', or the party's view 'is what I say' not only strengthened the impression, but also thrilled the elite.[2]

It was another matter that the party compelled Bhattacharya in 2005 itself to eat his words on 100 per cent FDI for new airports that he proposed, but the elite hoped that someday Bhattacharya would be able to turn the party to his line and egged on him. Thus, the ultimate withdrawal of support showed finally Karat had taken over the party.

The victory was also important for Karat for a second reason: restoring some principled politics in the party. There are a very large number of people in the underdeveloped world and a sizable section in the developed world who are against America. They are not against American people. But they are against the globalization of American policies. For them globalization of policies such as abolition of subsidy for the poor, or globalization of investment or financial capital is not a must. They are for state intervention on behalf of the poor. They are for pursuance of independent policies. They are against the US militarism. By resisting the political-military part of US policies, Karat credited his party with an exclusive identity in Indian polity. At least one aspect of Left ideology was restored.

At the end of the day, we all know might is right as far as the US is concerned. In simple terms, those were for the Deal who had faith in the US. Again, those were for the Deal who felt, like the Indian PM, that Indian people loved George Bush. And also those were for the Deal who believed closer relationship with the US was in India's interest. Many others were against the Deal. It was a question of faith. It was a question of ideology.

It was true that Manmohan Singh's insistence on passing the Deal during George Bush's regime gave Karat an opportunity to absolve himself from the allegation of being rash. The Prime Minister behaved in a way as though Bush regime was the last opportunity to sign the Deal. Surely, it was not worth risking a government that promised to be focussed on eradication of poverty, for with this poverty in its backyard India can never expect real respect from the outside world.

But despite his success on these two counts—showing who is the real boss of the Left and re-establishing a line of principled politics—Karat lost another battle. When the CPI(M) woke up from the grossly erroneous notion that Sonia Gandhi would not risk division among the secular forces for the sake of an international deal, it was too late. That too was a turning point in Karat's political life. He must have understood that the Left, at the end of the day, will have to fight alone, have to fend for itself.

In an overall scenario, during the autumn of 2008, one could say that Karat had started acting according to a plan. He achieved certain things: (i) withdrew support and broke Congress–Left ties, (ii) stalled the brutal Rightist onslaught on the people of Bengal, and (iii) won the Kerala units support. On the first two counts his achievement was based on principled politics, on the third point it was unprincipled.

But the main task remains yet to be started. A Left party cannot follow neoliberalism. Curiously, a large part of the CPI(M) has not understood how and when it became Rightist. But, surely Karat knows it. However, as things stand now, in November 2009, he has not found any means to fight the neoliberals of his party. On the question of confronting neoliberal ideas, he is still in minority. And, many people also nurture the doubt whether he had willingly acquiesced with the neoliberals.

No doubt, it is the autumn of the Left. What will be interesting to probe is whether they will be doomed in the winter—by doom I mean bidding goodbye to their old commitments to the downtrodden, the poor, the toiling mass—or whether the neoliberal click will be contained and the party will see the Spring again. It has nothing to do with how many seats they win, for if they are bereft of their exclusivity that earned them respectability, they are just another party, just one among 10 or maybe 100s of parties of India.

So Karat had just won a battle in 2008. The war was yet to be fought.

References

1. The Congress and the BJP are equally dangerous for India's future.
2. *The Telegraph* of Calcutta reported how Bhattacharya stunned the veteran reporters touring with him in Singapore in 2005 by saying that he was working for 100 per cent FDI in ports and airports. During those days, the trade union wing of the party was fighting tooth and nail against privatization bid of the government of airports. When the journalists asked him whether the party would endorse it, Bhattacharya showed a bulldozing attitude and said, *"It (the party's view) is what I say. I consciously said what I had said about airport privatization yesterday."* His comment surprised the reporter from *The Telegraph*, who had reported on the Left for many years and was considered quite a knowledgeable person.

Six

A Regional National Party

IT WAS early 1990s. Jyoti Basu, the most widely known communist leader of India, faced an unusual request from his younger colleagues, mainly Prakash Karat and Sitaram Yechury. Both of them were newly inducted in the politburo, while Basu had to his credit four consecutive victories in Bengal. Karat and Yechury and a few others requested him to shift to Delhi and fill up the vacuum that had been created after the death of some senior leaders and virtual retirement of EMS Namboodiripad (who relinquished the post of party general secretary in 1991). But Basu declined.

Just a few years later, before the parliamentary elections of 1996, VP Singh, the former Prime Minister, foresaw an opportunity to form a Third Front government and felt Jyoti Basu would be the right person to lead it.[1] Basu phoo-phooed the proposal and commented that whenever the leaders of the Third Front saw a problem they sought support of the communists. After election, the Third Front mooted a proposal to have Basu as their Prime Minister, but the party rejected it. Months later, Basu described the refusal as 'a historic blunder'.

Historic or not, many people felt it was a blunder. It would have given them an opportunity to showcase what they stood for and what they would like to do if in power at the central level. A lot had been written about it, and in those days we found Prakash Karat at fault. It was a question of mindset, and we believed Karat's and the party's conservative and isolationist mindset was responsible for the blunder.

But, more than a decade later, now I wonder whether we were right to blame Karat. True, Karat led the majority faction and he initiated the debate against accepting the proposal. He stuck to it and in Calcutta Party congress got it endorsed by two-third majority. But was he alone responsible for the conservative mindset of the party?

The question is what role Basu played in the party. We must try to understand it in perspective. Basu later described it as a historic blunder because he wanted to change the mindset of the party. In a changed scenario, after one-year rule by the BJP, Karat was ready to have Basu as the PM if only Sonia Gandhi agreed to support him in 1999.[2] This cannot be ascertained from the party documents since it was an informal decision. But it happened. It may be argued that Basu's utterances and the consequential flutter in the party changed the mindset of the party. It can also be argued that not Basu, but the BJP's ascendance to power and its rule for 13 months changed the mindset.

But it is certain that what Basu could achieve after his open criticism of the party, he failed to achieve in 1996 when the real opportunity knocked at his door. Was it not true that he himself could not foresee what was going to happen after the elections of 1996? The great pragmatist, as he was described by everybody, suffered from serious lack of vision as far as the national scenario was concerned. He failed to see it coming, and discarded the possibility when VP Singh floated his name months before it actually came up in the meeting of the United Front.[3] If he could foresee it, he could have started a debate in the party, or on his behalf Surjeet could do it. Then it would not have come as a bolt from the blue to the central committee members.

Actually, when Basu rejected what VP proposed (surely VP was trying to put things in place in advance), he showed that he was the victim of the same mindset. He too treated the business of government formation as something alien to them. Then as a veteran politician at the last moment he realized the significance of the opportunity that came. But he could not expect that the conservative members of his central committee, having much less capability to understand and analyse the situation, would change in a day. Thus though Karat was directly responsible for it, Basu and Surjeet were to be blamed equally.

But why Basu, described as a great pragmatist, failed in 1996? Or, even more pertinent question is, how Surjeet failed to see what was coming. He worked for a repeat situation in 1999, but failed to convince Sonia Gandhi. However, he had little initiative in 1996 prior to the meeting of the United Front.

Basu failed to see the future because he had no national vision. He was a pragmatic leader true, but his pragmatism was limited to Bengal. He heard about national developments from other leaders and formed his opinion on that. His political world was limited to Calcutta. He had personal relation with Indira Gandhi, but that had never grown in him a broad interest in the national politics. As far as Surjeet was concerned, it seemed that initially he was not interested. He did not realize that his party had acquired such a prestigious place in Indian polity—particularly after the weakening of the erstwhile Janata Dal which was the leading 'Third Force' on earlier occasion—that it would be asked to lead. He could not realize that a real 'Third Front' was emerging for the first time in 1996.[4] None in the party understood the significance of the changed scenario that was going to give birth to a real Third Front (it was really third and really a front). So no one could prepare the party for this new situation. The failure was, in a true sense, collective. You do not expect a team of conservative communists to suddenly walk out of their cocoons and grab the opportunity that destiny had presented them.

Once again, this happened because they were an exceptional force in Indian polity. The CPI(M) is the only party that despite its recognition as a national party [it had off and on governed three states, Bengal, Kerala and Tripura (a tiny north-eastern state)] is actually a confederation of some state units. It was not so about the CPI. But as the pro-Chinese section (who claimed their faith in revolution) came out of the CPI in 1964, and gradually got confined in three states by the 1980s, they lost their pan-India outlook. Go and ask any worker of the Congress party anywhere and you will find that he or she is conscious about their party being a national party. If he is a real political worker, he will be able to argue with you on why they claim themselves to be a national party. It is same with a BJP worker. But I have found even the regional-level leaders of the communist party in Bengal or in Kerala limiting their knowledge to their states only. A party worker of the CPI(M) in Bengal feels Bengal party is everything.

Basu also failed to imagine what could happen in near future for he was preoccupied with Bengal. And yet he was much better than the others whose world started and ended in Bengal. This mentality almost split the party in 1996: when the central committee decided to reject the proposal for making Jyoti Basu the leader of the United Front and thereby the Prime Minister, most of the Bengal leaders were found in a foul mood. They seriously discussed the plausibility of a split, but Basu vetoed it and Anil Biswas convinced them of the risks of adopting such a course.

It only increased bitterness and, more dangerously, created a sentiment in Bengal against Karat and his faction. In Bengal, the issue became that of a Bengali being denied the opportunity to become the PM. Some party leaders actively stoked this feeling, and it was Anil Biswas who fought against it and could douse the fire before it engulfed the state party. However, gradually the whole party in Bengal became an antithesis to central leadership.

***

It shows that this party is just a confederation of state units.

It was always so. But the state units had some respect for the central leadership. Pramode Dasgupta, the builder of the party in Bengal, was a tough man and he used to say that the central leadership could run the party because Bengal provided the money. But he never revolted against the central leadership. He was a part of it and during the split he was eager to have Namboodiripad and Jyoti Basu (both of them fence-sitters for sometime) in the party. Dasgupta had respect for the non-Bengal leaders and they had respect for him. Now, with that respect part increasingly missing, it will be increasingly difficult for Karat to manage such a party.

Similarly, I have heard from some other journalists that Vijayan and his people privately questioned the authority of Karat to intervene in Kerala. Most of the Bengal leaders too share this mentality. This can be overlooked in a study as an expression of disappointment or frustration. But this shows the ugly trend that had raised its head in last about 12 years, and has now reached a situation where the state units feel the central leadership is superfluous. The regional satraps want complete autonomy. It is not so in other parties like Sonia-led Congress or the leaderless BJP or even Mayawati's BSP.

This has happened with the CPI(M) because the experience of the two state units which are the mainstay of the party has varied widely. With no other major state unit having anything to share or add with this experience, it has created this peculiar situation where both the state units feel they should have full autonomy. From another angle, we can say this is only natural because the party is limited only in two major states which are geographically, culturally, linguistically and politically very different.

First, let us look at these two bastions of the Left and their political experiences. First time a communist government (also the first non-Congress government) came to power (in 1957) was in Kerala. It was led by EMS Namboodiripad, the legendary communist leader who was a practical politician, an ideologue and a scholar. It was also the first democratically elected communist government in the world. Then off and on the Left had ruled the state. In Bengal, the Left came to power for the first time in 1967. A rebel Congress leader Ajoy Mukherjee became the chief minister and Jyoti Basu was the deputy CM in the government. But none of these governments in Bengal or in Kerala were allowed to run for the full term, as in those days the Congress turned the art of dissolving state governments almost into an industry. So, during the 1960s or

1970s the experiences of Bengal and Kerala was the same and the party was not divided. The first rift came in July 1979, when the question of dual membership split the ruling Janata Party. In those days, the present BJP was inside the Janata Party and they kept their membership of the RSS intact. A section of the party rebelled against it and Morarji Desai's government fell. The Bengal unit was eager to overlook the question of dual membership (as the BJP was no force in Bengal) and feared that toppling of the government would clear the path for return of the Congress to power. But Kerala (where the RSS was active) was in favour of withdrawing support, though there also the main political competitor was the Congress. The national party supported Kerala, and that was on ideological ground.

It is strange that now the arguments of the two state units have swapped their positions. But that is mere political expediency.

Since then the two state units started drifting away. In Bengal, the Left returned to power in 1977 and have not lost it till now, creating a record of sorts. Namboodiripad introduced land reforms and educational reforms in 1957. Bengal implemented such measures from 1977. But in Bengal, the Congress failed to challenge the Left till Mamata Banerjee rose to a significant height in the 1990s. Since then Bengal Left had always been eager to side with the Congress at the central level showing the spectre of the BJP. A promising leader Saifuddin Chowdhury (also a neoliberal) advocated this line steadfastly and was punished for that by being dropped from the central committee in 1996. Later, he left the party. But curiously the party adopted his line.

In recent years, while Bengal had embraced SEZ most ravenously, Kerala rejected it, thanks to its hardliner CM. When Kerala had observed *bundhs*, Bengal refrained from that. When Kerala launched movement against Coke–Pepsi, Bengal looked the other way. While in Kerala the US imperialism and the CIA stand as enemies and are referred to in politics, Bengal party has almost forgotten these terminologies. We will not discuss whether that is good or bad, prudent or not. We are just taking note of the differences. Kerala had followed this different line because there it had to fight the Congress regularly, and also the RSS in certain parts of the state. They needed a distinct identity, and a rebellious one, if only to convince the people that Marxism is not a lost case. In Bengal, very few care for Marxism anymore.

And there is another major difference that we have already referred to. While in Bengal the neoliberal mindset had engulfed the whole party (barring a section at the grassroots without having representation at the upper echelon of the party), in Kerala an acute confrontation between the neoliberalist and the hardliners is on. No one knows what will be the outcome of this confrontation. The octogenarian leader Achuthanandan may leave the party and float a new one. A large chunk of hardliners may leave the party with or without Achuthanandan. Or, the neoliberalists may be reigned in by pressure from below and a compromise formula may save the party from a split or a major damage. Or else, the Leftists will lose out gradually, and the difference between Bengal party and Kerala party will be mitigated.

The question is why such resistance to the neoliberals came up in Kerala but not in Bengal? Why Bengal took a line of ruthless inhuman capitalism, but Kerala abhorred it? Maybe, because 30 years of governance has made the Left a bankrupt force in Bengal (power corrupts, and absolute power corrupts absolutely), or may be because of some other factor. In Kerala, the Congress was strong and to fight it the Left had to put forward a different package to the people. That package was Marxism. In Bengal, there was almost no political opponent for first 20 years. In this vacuum, the different ideological package of the Left lost its relevance. Afterwards Mamata Banerjee came up, but she did not challenge them ideologically. For many years she did not offer even an alternative programmatic package, forget about ideology. In this scenario, growth and development became a major issue. The Bengal communists took the easiest path to convince people about their ability to deliver: they put the entire stress on wooing big private investment that cannot solve the problem of unemployment. Thus, maybe, a political void has sucked in Leftism of the mainstream Left in Bengal.

There are also cultural differences of the two states. We must keep it in mind that Kerala was and is more educated, more multicultural, and is far ahead of Bengal in socio-economic indicators of development. Bengal has failed to improve social indicators to put itself in a leading position in India despite more than three-decade long Left rule. Thus the incidence of hunger, poverty and semi-poverty is more acute in Bengal. That probably explains the rejection of the new Left. But, with a history of renaissance in previous centuries, Bengal had less of communal or caste tension, and is almost free from social violence. That hemmed in the BJP's prospect of growth. Strangely in Bengal, the Left tried to use the spectre of this non-existent BJP. People have rejected that too.

These differences have now brought Kerala and West Bengal at two different junctures.

This centrifugal tendency in the party is likely to be strengthened in coming years. Will it lead to a split? It depends on two factors; the geographical division and the ideological division. Let us first study briefly the present position in these two states and see the extent of these divisions. Then we will look at the role the central leadership had played in past and may play in the future.

***

First, over to Kerala. It would be better if we first focus on VS Achuthanandan.

The month of May, 2007, was a historic one for the CPI(M). The politburo of the Communist Party of India (Marxist) decided to suspend VS Achuthanandan and Pinarayi Vijayan from the membership of politburo for indefinite period. It concluded that open criticism against each other aired by the two veteran leaders from Kerala had 'violated the norms of the party'. However, both of them were to continue to 'discharge all their other party responsibilities'.

In other words, 84-year-old Achuthanandan continued to be the Chief Minister and 63-year-old Vijayan performed as the state secretary of the party. Significantly, the politburo also appreciated the work done by the Achuthanandan-led Left Democratic Front government which had completed the first year on May 18. The politburo underlined as its major achievements the revival of several public sector units, measures to tackle price rise, reaching an agreement on the Smart City project in Kochi and the then ongoing firm action against encroachment of government land in the hill resort and tea plantation town of Munnar. Massive portions of land allegedly grabbed over the years by resort owners and multinational companies were recovered. Later, the demolition team landed in the city of Kochi, and other cities in Kerala and recovered huge parts of land.

The suspension of the two top leaders from politburo was historic. But there was also a catch. First, despite the huge age-gap between the two leaders both of them were meted out the same punishment. This was generally not done by the communists in earlier times who revered the aged. Surely the person who deserved higher degree of punishment was the younger man, if Indian or communistic tradition was to be adhered to. Secondly, it was Vijayan who saw threats in different measures of the Left Democratic Front government, including action against encroachment. But politburo sat as helpless prisoner of the state secretary, because he had the organization with him. This was an example of the party's faith in Stalinist structure of operation, and lack of faith in wider mass. This same politburo had decided earlier, under pressure from Vijayan, that Achuthanandan would not contest in election! When the mass base of the party revolted against it and flooded the central party office with text messages and e-mails and letters, the top body of the party backed out.

Kerala had never seen earlier what it was witnessing then. The Congress was always fragmented with the factions openly quarrelling. K Karunakaran and AK Antony fought over the years, nay decades. Other players like Vayalar Ravi and Oommen Chandy are also involved in groupism. Like them, Kerala CPI(M) was also divided. Namboodiripad was an undisputed leader. But, even during his time there were various lobbies. EK Nayanar and VS Achuthanandan headed two main rival groups. The differences between the two leaders were somewhat similar to the differences between Pramode Dasgupta and Jyoti Basu. Both Basu and Nayanar were born in affluent families. They became communists, and the Leftists would like to believe they were de-classed, though in reality one can hardly de-class oneself. Both Nayanar and VS were among 32 members of the CPI's national council who walked out from the party and thus were members of the central committee of the CPI(M) from 1964. Nayanar was elected to the politburo at the 14th congress in 1992. He served as the secretary of the Kerala state committee of the CPI(M) from 1972–1980 and again from 1992–1996.

Achuthanandan too was the state secretary from 1980–1992. He became a politburo member in 1985. However, he could not become CM in 1991 as the Left Democratic Front lost the election that time, and in 1996 he lost the election thanks to alleged sabotage by Pinarayi Vijayan.

Thus, there was no comparison between Achuthanandan and Vijayan, either by stature or by the yardstick of popularity. Both could not be treated in the same way. But the politburo, apart from its organization-dependent mentality essential to muzzle the opposition, was a victim of neoliberal mindset. Achuthanandan was and still is a hardliner of an extreme sort. He is more Leftist than Karat. He is a traditional Marxist leader who has a mass following in the red strongholds in central Kerala. He opposed Microsoft learning programmes in Kerala schools, did not want foreign capital flow in the state, and had vehemently fought against projects such as the Dubai Smart City. The veteran leader had also opposed signing an agreement with ADB for a Rs 1.6 billion loan for the state in January 2007. The agreement for the loan was signed by Local Self-Government Minister Paloli Mohammed Kutty, without the knowledge of the CM. In fact, Kutty was the man whom Vijayan thought of making the CM. Politburo, or the central leadership had decided to ignore all such developments.

On 13 November 2008, when the meltdown had started, Achuthanandan said, *"Our Prime Minister Manmohan Singh has agreed that globalization is the reason for the economic crisis. He is now aware of the danger of the pro-American economic policies. Some people from our side also supported the neo-liberalized policies. Those who justified the ADB loan for the state are speechless now."*

This was too much not only for Vijayan camp, but also for the national leadership.

It is quite evident that such a man is a misfit in the present CPI(M). He alone was challenging the wise decisions all the politburo members (except Pandhe) were taking. He has his guts. He was born in a poor family and at a young age took up the job of helping his elder brother in a tailoring shop. Later, he started working in a coir factory. After his being CM, the *Indian Express* wrote:

> "VS's entire past is paraded as an allegory for his present and future. As a child who lost his mother when he was only four, his father at 11, he dropped out of school when he was in Class 7. End of education. Recalls a senior colleague at *Deshabhimani*, the party paper: 'I once asked him why he, who loves to read so much, dropped out so early. He said he could have continued even without buying books but just didn't have the strength to starve in school every day.'"

Things would be more evident if we probe a little deeper into his activities.

Let us look back at 1996. Under his initiative an anti-reclamation stir was launched by the Kerala State Karshaka Thozhilali Union (KSKTU) at Mancombu in 1996–97 against filling up of paddy-fields for purposes other than cultivation. The anti-reclamation stir had earned widespread criticism following the violent methods resorted to by the KSKTU cadre. It was Achuthanandan himself who had inaugurated the agitation in 1996–97. The first victim of the stir was a farmer at Mancombu who had planted coconut and other crops in his reclaimed paddy-field. The KSKTU workers destroyed the crops completely. That was followed by destruction of crops in a four-acre plot by the side of Alappuzha–Changanassery Road. The stir, later, spread to other parts of Alappuzha District, which included Charumood, Veetikkode and Nooranad. The KSKTU cadres planted the party flag at a plot, which was levelled by its owner for forming an industrial unit. The industrialist had to revoke his plan following the fierce agitation by the KSKTU men. Violence and forceful occupation of the filled up paddy-field was the main feature of the KSKTU stir then. The CPI(M) did not interfere in it. It was alleged that the whole movement was planned to cut the influence of the CITU lobby then led by E Balanandan and others. However gradually it lost momentum and finally in June 2005, Achuthanandan (then opposition leader) announced at a KSKTU meeting at Mancombu that destruction of crops will not be carried out in future as a part of the agitation for protection of paddy cultivation.

It showed that the man, who in 1946 participated in the Punnapra–Vayalar Struggle[5] had changed little.

He is not going to be intimidated by threats. On 28 February 2009, he said, *"The ocean called Soviet Union became empty because of certain Gorbachevs. In Kerala politics also, there are Gorbachevs. Such leaders have created a parallel economy. And if the sun was going to rise in the middle of the night, all can see the faces of certain leaders who stand neck deep in corruption."*

The party is fortunate that this man has not opened his mouth about the Bengal CM's policies.

Thus, very clearly, this man is too much for present disposition of the party or the elite in general. A large section of media is hoping for quite some time that this man will be kicked out from the post of chief minister. Curiously, the media was speculating on his being sacked when Vijayan was struggling with corruption charges. However it will not be surprising if the CPI(M) finally does so, for in these days probity in public life is irrelevant. A true communist leader, like a true Gandhian, is an extinct species. Maybe, in future, like the true Gandhians the true communists will also have to involve themselves only in social work!

Whatever, after the Lok Sabha election the junior comrades of the party decided to punish VS further, and this time they dropped only him from the politburo while retaining Vijayan. Karat tried to remove him also from the post of chief minister. Clearly, Karat tried to secure his position in the party by siding with Vijayan, the undisputable leader of the organization. However Karat's attempt was resisted by four politburo members—Yechury (the second most-influential member), Manik Sarkar (the CM of Tripura), MK Pandhe (CITU president) and Brinda Karat (most prominent woman leader who happens to be the wife of Prakash Karat). That is how Achuthanandan is still in his office.

Before concluding this, I must mention one charge against Achuthanandan. His daughter VV Asha landed him in a controversy with her receiving a grant of Rs 35 lakh under the Marine Biotechnology Research Programme of the Kerala Biotechnology Mission (KBC) of which the CM was the president. The money was granted to her for a research project but the decision to give the money to her drew flak from several quarters as, allegedly, she had no prior expertise in the area of marine biotechnology.

***

Now let us move over to the leader of the 'official faction', that is Vijayan, supposedly the future of the CPI(M) in Kerala.

Vijayan too has a mass following, especially in North Kerala, and he is seen as the modern face of the Marxists. He travels abroad, his son studied in London, he wants private investment, and he is a dynamic person. Like Buddhadeb Bhattacharya he has risen through the middle class route, from student politics. He served as a minister between 1996 and 1998. He then became the state party secretary. But that small stint of his in the ministry is still haunting him. The state secretary is an accused in the Lavalin case and has done everything to stall enquiry against himself. Vijayan, as electricity minister in 1998, renegotiated a deal with SNC Lavalin, a Canadian firm, for the renovation of three hydel projects. He moved upwards the money the Canadian firm would get, and sealed a deal that ultimately caused a Rs 86.25 crore loss to the state exchequer. In 2006, state's vigilance and anti-corruption department registered a case. On 16 January 2007, Kerala High Court ordered a CBI enquiry into the case. On 21 January 2009, the CBI filed a progress report on the investigation in the Kerala High Court. Pinarayi Vijayan was named as the 9th accused in the case. The CPM backed Vijayan saying that the CBI move was 'politically motivated'. Chief Minister VS Achuthanandan, however, stated that the culprits in this case would be punished. But the state party differed with him and wanted him to be sacked for fighting the comrade. The central party resisted the move.

It was reported that the contract was awarded after the company promised an investment of Rs 98.3 crore to set up the Malabar Cancer Centre in Tellichery in North Kerala. That could have given the Deal at least some moral credibility had it been true. However, the money that was actually paid on this count was only Rs 12 crore. However, SNC Lavalin later posted on its website its version of the story:

> "At that time because of our long-term relationship with India, the company of its own goodwill agreed to the repeated requests from the government of Kerala to build a hospital and to sign a memorandum of understanding (MOU) accordingly."

The company then claimed that numerous attempts from their side 'to enter into a formal agreement were ignored by the government and the MOU was finally allowed to expire' in 2001. Well, it is up to the CPI(M) to answer. They have defended Lavalin so far (defending Vijayan and Lavalin is synonymous here) and now they should explain this statement.

As per the reports, the CBI charge sheet has accused Vijayan of entering into a criminal conspiracy to award the contract without floating a global tender. It was stated by some leaders that it was a case of political vendetta after the CPI(M) withdrew support from the Central Government. However, we can look at it from a slightly different angle. It shows the advantage of being with the Central Government: you can divide the opposition in Bengal and thereby can hope to win more seats despite your rapidly declining support in the state; and you can hush up the allegations and cases of corruption against you mainly coming to surface from Kerala. Withdrawal of support was really costly!

However, Lavalin is not the only allegation against Vijayan. It had also come to light that as the head of the 'organizing committee' of the Nayanar Memorial football tournament he received money from Pharis Aboobacker, a controversial business man described by the CM as a 'hated figure'.

But Vijayan is a great comrade who behaves in a way as if he is full of revolutionary fire. He is somewhere caught carrying with him cartridges of a revolver. He threatens the media if it goes to expose him. The Editors Guild of India once strongly condemned the threats issued to K Gopalakrishnan, Editor, *Mathrubhumi*. The Guild demanded an immediate end to the arm-twisting tactics against *Mathrubhumi* and called upon the Government of Kerala to ensure that there is full protection to Gopalakrishnan and journalists of *Mathrubhumi*.

With this man Vijayan at the helm of the party, it is natural that the ideological obstinacy of the octogenarian CM, popularly called VS, will be stonewalled. The CM had proposed (on 22 November 2007) that the time was ripe for second round of land reforms in his state, and said that 'if there was at least one communist left in Kerala government', the state would go ahead with another round of land reforms. It was aimed at recovering land (illegally occupied by the others or forcibly taken away from the peasants) and distributing it among the landless. The state committee led by Pinarayi Vijayan rejected the proposal and said that the second land reforms proposed by 'certain extremist groups' was mere blather that would divide the society. Before the electoral debacle, it seemed certain that SEZs would appear in Kerala very soon. The veteran Chief Minister of the state was always sceptical about the real estate interest of the developers of the SEZs: he fought within the party when central leadership gave their nod to SEZ. He overruled his own industry minister, Elamaram Kareem, who cherished a fond desire to have these enclaves in the state. But then it seemed that curtains would be down soon in Kerala also, for the CM was reduced to a microscopic minority in the party, and in the goverment. However, the rout in the Lok Sabha polls has put a stop on such designs.

The two groups had clashed so many times, and had publicly abused each other in such nasty ways, that they have made themselves butt of ridicule in the public eye. Both sides were equally responsible on this count. The adjectives they used against each other are reminiscent of the adjectives the two section of the CPI used against each other in the early

1960s. That time it resulted in a split. It is a wonder that this time they still belong to the same party.

In Bengal, even such last wall of resistance like VS does not exist. And in Kerala, where the CPI(M) is the most disordered unit of any party in any state, after VS everything would be in the hands of the neoliberals.

Now it is time to move over to West Bengal, but before that just one observation.

It is widely believed that concerned papers of the Lavalin Deal was handed over to an interested journalist by E Balanandan. The point is debated though and the late trade union leader can no more confirm or deny it. But as I knew this man Balanandan, he was an unrelenting fighter against moribund values and was quite likely to do so. But I have no personal knowledge on this particular incident and so it is better to leave it as disputed, particularly when party politburo said that they never received a letter against this Deal from the veteran leaders. We all know sensitive letters and papers are very slippery things and often they go missing. It happens all over the world. We should leave it at that.

***

It is time to move over to Bengal. Bengal saw a lot of things that Kerala did not. Kerala had not seen firing on peasants by the police of a communist government, had not seen large-scale forcible eviction of peasants, and had not seen attempts to justify such efforts by spreading lies. All the rust that could gather from a continuous rule over three decades, a penchant for blindly following the barbaric regime of China, and a love for the Congress mark the communists of Bengal. Here the BJP is an imaginary threat, for there is no killing field like that of Tellichery (Kannur district of Malabar region in Kerala) where the BJP–RSS has been fighting the CPI(M) cadre for years and decades. In Bengal, the BJP is alluded to only to further political gain.

Kerala is an instance of fight between radicals and neoliberalists. Both sides there are failing to cope with the reality: one side failing to change and the other side failing to understand the relevance of the party.

Bengal is a case of unanimity to disown the legacy and move towards obsolescence. Just when I was going through the draft of this book, I heard Subhash Chakrabarty on TV. It was 34 hours to go before the last phase of poll. The interviewer and a commentator discussed between them the policies of Bengal government being decided in an air-conditioned room in Delhi by those who had not participated in popular election. I will not comment on the journalist or the expert, for I have heard many of them discussing this without ever mentioning the case of Manmohan Singh, who had never in his life won even a Panchayat election. Let us ignore this convenient forgetfulness. I must mention that I too strongly believe that the decision making should be done by the elected representatives. That is however not my point here. I saw Chakrabarty enjoying the debate and laughing indulgently. This showed his utter disrespect for the leaders of his own party, whom he himself had accepted as leaders by being in the party.

More interestingly, Chakrabarty then questioned the decision of going along with Naveen Patnaik who was with the BJP earlier. I wondered how he so conveniently forgot his leader (the only one whom he acknowledged as a leader) Jyoti Basu once held the hands of VP Singh raised high while the Janata leader's other hand, similarly raised, was held by Atal Bihari Vajpayee. That was in 1989. Forget that. This man openly advocated that Left should ally with the Congress forever and grow by doing so. Do not expect to get any answer for such questions as to why the Congress will allow it to grow when under Rahul Gandhi's initiative the party itself is trying to recover its lost grounds. Chakrabarty stated in that interview that if in India a fight has to be fought against the imperialist forces then the Left should join hands with the leading anti-imperialist force of the country, the Congress.

We will not comment on Chakrabarty, because he is no more. But many comrades of Bengal has this sort of understanding about national and international situation. Chakrabarty was a state secretariat member. I will not go further to probe another very senior leader Binoy Konar. It will suffice to mention that he put forward such bizarre understanding of following capitalism that Prabhat Patnaik had to write an article to counter that from a proper theoretical perspective. It all shows the pathetic limitations of Bengal leaders as far as theoretical understanding is concerned.

Naturally so. Bengal had never known any ideological debate, for there was no Namboodiripad there. Never expect a debate in Bengal about whether Abdul Nasser Madhani (accused of being with the terrorists and later released for lack of evidence) can be a friend or not. That debate in Kerala, I believe, is a continuation of a debate that started from the thesis Namboodiripad put forward in the last years of his life, in which he wanted to differentiate between communal parties and parties based on religious identities. The line was not accepted then by the Kerala party or the national party, and that stand was thereafter ratified by the Party congress. As far I remember MA Baby and others fought, theoretically, against Namoodiripad in those days. Baby is a sharp person with penchant for such debates, and as I recollect, he explained to me the Bengal party's eagerness to have Jyoti Basu as PM by attributing it to sub-nationalism. I accepted his arguments in those days when we discussed it sitting in his flat in VP House in Delhi; but now I differ from him and feel it was sheer Bengali chauvinism. I reached this conclusion some years ago, and it was reinforced in recent weeks when I heard Buddhadeb Bhattacharya saying in a TV interview that 'it is not proper that Pranab Mukherjee will not be made Prime Minister only because he is a Bengali'. For record's sake, he said this in an interview with *Star Ananda*, a Bengali channel, and the interview was aired during the run-up to the Lok Sabha polls. So, it does not matter who is referred to, Basu or Mukherjee, communist or congressman, Bengali chauvinism will always keep Bengali communists engrossed. Again for record's sake, when the CPI(M) leaders (Yechury and others) studied the causes of the USSR's fall, two of the major reasons they identified were following a Rightist path and giving indulgence to chauvinism. Remember, that was about the erstwhile USSR, and not about the Bengal party.

Now you find out who stopped Pranabbabu from becoming the Prime Minister because he is a Bengali! You thought, like me, that Mukherjee could not rise up to the hot seat because he was not as trusted lieutenant of Sonia Gandhi as Manmohan Singh. But see, how much more the communists of Bengal know.

I want to add now that the CPI(M) in Bengal was never interested in anything theoretical. After the split of the party in 1964, Pramode Dasgupta thought of a 'partisan war', and feigned that he was preparing the underground cell of the party. Leaders got pseudo names so that they would not be identified when they would work underground. In reality what they did was not at all different from what the CPI did, and in 1967 they joined hands with the CPI to form governments in Bengal and elsewhere. Jyoti Basu had no interest in theoretical work. He accepted 'bourgeois democracy' as *fait accompli* and worked only in the practical field.

Thus Bengal CPI(M) was always a party of the middle class without any strong ideological conviction. It had never produced a Namboodiripad, or even a Prakash Karat. Thus when the leaders take a U-turn there, the cadre follow without raising questions. This is a major difference between the party elsewhere and the Bengal party.

***

The younger correspondents who cover the Left, as well my friends, often ask me why I feel there cannot be any turn around for the party in Bengal before the 2011 assembly elections. Let me answer it. A turn around is a function of people accepting the changed intentions of the leaders. The intentions depend on the mindset. Otherwise whatever one says or claims, ultimately one gets exposed.

The mindset becomes obvious whenever the leaders of the CPI(M) speak in Bengal.

Tata Motors has left Bengal. But Buddhadeb Bhattacharya said during election campaign that there will be an industry in Singur on the same land, and not an acre of that about 400 acres whose owners did not accept compensation will be given back. He himself made Singur—where one thousand acres of very fertile agricultural land (that the government passed as mono-crop land citing records which the government forgot to update for decades) was acquired for setting up a factory of Tata Motors—a symbol of industrialization, leaving hundreds of other projects that were coming to Bengal and were being implemented. Thus it was he who helped to send the message that Bengal was still not a safe place to invest. He made it a personal (and maybe partisan) issue and even now is not ready to settle the dispute. On record he has said that the majority of people accepted compensation, and so the minority was bound to accept it. I repeat again: the minority will have to accept it because the majority has accepted it. Probably, Bhattacharya knows that is democracy.

This is the mindset. This is sheer majoritism. He and his colleagues betray this quite so often. I will not comment on this, but will quote a few sentences from a textbook in political science (*Democratic Politics—II by NCERT*) that my son reads in class X. It reads (PAGE 6):

> "Imposing the will of majority community over others may look like an attractive option in the short run, but in the long run it undermines the unity of the nation. Tyranny of the majority is not just oppressive for the minority; it often brings ruin to the majority as well.... A democratic rule involves sharing of power with those affected by its exercise, and who have to live with its effects."

Well, you yourself judge.

Now, Bhattacharya is probably on notice. There are chances that he will be replaced by Nirupam Sen a few months before the assembly election. So let us examine Sen's statements.

The industry minister appears nowadays as being a very powerful leader in Bengal. In an interview to a Bengali channel on April 15 he defended use of plastic citing the reason that it was the trend of time. The pliable interviewer commented that we could not walk backward. Pardon the ignorance of the journalists: most of them know very little about the global crises, about environment or about anything larger than 'this has happened today'. But, another correspondent present in the programme asked Sen why he could not think of banning plastic carry bags. And then Sen (who a minute before was referring to plastic lobby pressurized the Central Government for reducing the mandatory quota of jute packaging for use in bulk carriage of food like rice, paddy, sugar) unmasked himself and asked, then what would happen to the petrochem industries coming up in the state.

We can assume that being a responsible minister of a state Sen was not so ignorant that he did not know that Delhi government had banned plastic carry bags months before that day. We can assume that being an educated man he is not so naïve that he does not know why and how plastic is dangerous for environment and for the future generations who have not yet come on this planet. Then why was he publicly behaving like a lobbyist working for the plastic industry? I leave it to your imagination.

On that evening I found Sen was discarding all suggestions against land acquisition by the private parties or state's interventionist role with the same phrase that these were against the spirit of liberalization. I wondered whether it was a communist speaking. That was not all. He said at the beginning and at the end that when people's individual interest is hurt, they lose sight of the greater perspective. He said, the opposition was stoking up that narrow interest of people, but this politics would fail. Well, that clarifies everything. If the peasants do not want to give up their land to have industry where a miniscule section of them would at best be a third class worker earning a couple of thousands of rupees per month, that is narrow interest. And the perspective they are missing is that of urban middle class people earning high salary from those industries, and of course, they should be accused for depriving prosperity of others.

Forgive my diversion for a minute. But sincerely I want to share with you one of my secret thoughts. I often wonder why ministers do not leave their narrow interest of becoming and remaining a minister and serve the country as social workers. I believe the day I will get answer to this question I will also understand why poor peasants resist the greater good of the society for their narrow interest.

Back to the topic. Well, you have got glimpses of the new classless society the Left now propagate in Bengal. I will not deal here with the past and the link it has with the present. Here my point is simple: with this mindset with which the communist leaders roam about in Bengal clueless about the reasons of defeat, they cannot win over people again. Do not think I am joking as I tell you that weeks after the defeat the state secretary of Bengal found the reason for victory of the Trinamool Congress: they bought voters with money!

There is little chance that the present Left will make a turn around in Bengal within few years, because their credibility is at the bottom. Because, their imaginative power is nil. Because, they are stuck in a maze. They cannot present before people anything to enthuse them. The polity has changed. People see through the guiles of cosmetic and lip services.

After SS Ray's excesses (1971–77) in Bengal, the Congress (or Mamata Banerjee's party that belong to the same clan) is all set to regain power in Bengal after 35 years. I do not know how long it will take the Left to stage a comeback to power.

But why and how they entered this blind alley?

***

I have said that that the CPI(M) was always a middle class party. By that I refer to the leadership at central and state levels, and also to the majority of those at district level in West Bengal or Kerala.

But half-a-century ago the middle class was much more close to the soil, closer to the poor. They possessed less wealth, less gadgets, less of self-centrism. Forty years ago, a fixed land line telephone connection meant the family was upper middle class. Thus not only the gap between the middle class and the poor was much less, in those days middle class people often took the cudgel for the poor. It was the middle class leadership of the CPI(M) that worked with the poor and fought against the system. This fight brought not only the party to power, but also secured an honourable life for the poor. Mostly it was social, a dignified social life, and an economic dimension was added to it after the Left came to power. This right to dignified social life was later copied to a large extent by Laloo Prasad (the work done by the Naxalites, particularly Liberation group and the then MCC, helped him in this regard in Bihar) and even afterwards by Mayawati in Uttar Pradesh.

This social respectability and empowerment (reinforced by the Panchayati system that was so fascinatingly implemented in Bengal) was a major boost for the poor and lower caste–*Adivasi*–Muslim population of Bengal. When Left Front came to power three more 'revolutionary' steps were added to this. Operation Barga (registration of sharecropper's name to ensure his right over the land) brought a sort of security in life to the vast number of sharecroppers. Ensuring minimum wages brought light, however dim it might be, to the lives of the millions of agricultural labour. 'Food for work' programme (probably first introduced by the Left in modern India) supported the most wretched population and also other segments during distress, particularly in the aftermath of a flood or during a drought. This two-pronged attack on socio-economic backwardness of the majority of the population led to successive victories, maybe in first elections held in first 15 years of the governance.

Then started a critical period. Stagnation started eating away their base.

Another 15 years later, the party is standing upside down. The leaders who led in winning over the poor like Harekrishna Konar, Binoy Chowdhury and so many others are dead now. Pramode Dasgupta, the commander, died in the early 80s. The man who could appreciate the value of such work despite his elitist viewpoints—Jyoti Basu—is also gone. That generation is gone. Their great contribution stopped by late 80s. Despite efforts, the government failed in revolutionizing the health system, in spread of quality education, in providing routes for further development of rural population (like cooperative farming, agro-based industries and marketing initiatives through cooperatives). Those who had come up the ladder to lead now, have no vision. They decided a course of development (the same model that was being followed by all the states of India since Independence) and when the poor resented their plans, they unleashed repression.

Now, many people feel what Bhattacharya tried was an earnest and honest effort to develop the state. I differ with them. The first question is whose development? Industrialization is a process that is unfolding in India for more than a century. Does it solve the problem of unemployment? Does the Government of West Bengal know what is the degree of underemployment? Does the Chief Minister understand why for the peasants his piece of land is so important? He often says, the son of the peasant does not want to become a peasant, implying that was why he went for industrialization. But if he had lived with the poor peasants he would have known that for over a century the boys from poor rural families had migrated to the cities and worked in the secondary or tertiary sectors. A farmer having four sons sent two to the city and the other two looked after the land. A poorer farmer used to go and still today goes for other jobs in seasons when agriculture cannot provide him with job. Had the CM or his party known this they would have understood the importance of NREGA and would have not failed in its implementation. Then they could have understood that the land is the last line of defence for agriculturalist families: if something happens (like a Great Depression), if the factories or shops close down, the whole family will be back in the village and will not starve, thanks to the small plot of land that is otherwise uneconomic.

Now, let us see why industrialization contributes only to a limited extent in eradication of poverty. From 1973–2003, industrial output in the country increased by 8 times, but employment in this sector went up by 2.5 times only. Of course, the growth in secondary sector also contributes to the tertiary sector growth. But again, while the tertiary sector grew by 11 times, employment growth in it was less than 3 times. Together these two sectors had 55 per cent share in GDP in 1973 and more than 75 per cent in 2003. But they employed about 25 per cent of people in 1973 and less than 40 per cent in 2003, though in these 30 years production of goods and services from these two sectors increased from about Rs 17,000 crore to Rs 160,000 crore. Due to technological advance, the employment potential of the industrial sector will shrink continuously. Even today less than 10 per cent of the workforce is engaged in the organized sector. The rest are left to their luck and live in total insecurity. So a government's claim that by industrialization it will solve employment problem smacks of dishonesty. The political motive of misleading people was too clear. Thus it had faced debacle in cities and rural areas alike.

It does not mean that industrialization is not needed. Industry is an important part of our life and civilization. But it is not panacea for unemployment. For solving the problem of unemployment a host of measures in rural areas are a must. Initiatives targeted at manifold increase of storage facilities, marketing facilities, agro-based industries, local crafts, local tourism can provide gainful employment to a very large number of people. Initiatives in spreading educational and health facilities will go a long way to change the face of rural India: it will improve social indicators while providing employment to many people. In short, development by urbanizing all rural areas is impossible. Rural areas should be developed as rural areas.

Whatever, total lack of vision and knowledge led the Leftists of Bengal to hoodwink people by selling an impossible dream. They had done it earlier too. They pledged blood to build the Bakreshwar Power Station. They had won election by selling the dream of Haldia as panacea of all woes of Bengal. On earlier occasion, people believed them for their credibility was intact. Now that credibility is washed off, people voted heavily against them.

And still, there was an exception: the people of western part of the southern Bengal. This is the region where development is still eluding the people. And in this region challenge has come from the Marxists. Here the protest was against the atrocities of the police and the cadre, Lalgarh falls in this region, and this area was liberated without the Maoists firing a single shot. It was liberated by the locals, and then the Maoists took advantage of the situation. In absence of any other political force standing by them, people of the area have accepted the Maoists as their friends. We know Maoists believe in anarchy, but are also winning hearts of the people robbed of their dignity. Probably, Lalgarh is more significant than the rest of Bengal in identifying the alienation of the Left, both from Leftism and from the people.

***

Thus, there is hardly any commonality of interest or perspective between Bengal and Kerala. Again, Andhra party had also lost its old vigour and now aligns with any of the two opposing forces in the state, the Congress or the Telugu Desam Party. We have earlier seen what they themselves discussed about it in their state party conference some years ago. But, nothing has changed. Thus in Andhra Pradesh it has no ideological overtone in its decisions and the only motivating force seems to be winning a few seats. Upset this time for failing to win any seat, Andhra party has turned somewhat pro-Congress, but they are still essentially against neoliberalism. Tamil Nadu party vacillates between different Dravidian parties and the Congress is not a factor for them, but opposition to neoliberalism matters. The party has made fantastic growth in Rajasthan, all by its own, and is hurtling towards a situation when in the Sikar–Churu Belt they will be able to win a parliamentary seat in future, provided they grow at this rate. They have won two assembly seats there, without aligning with anyone. This advancement is due to tooth and nail opposition of neoliberalism, and more importantly, fight for eradicating farmer's plight, particularly in distribution of water. Rajasthan party fights against both the Congress and the BJP, and if there is any indication of a brighter future for the party, it is out there, in Rajasthan. Interestingly, Bihar party has also come out of its dependence on Laloo Prasad, the OBC leader whose party was acting, till before this election process started, as a branch of the Congress.

Thus the party has become a looser confederation in these days. Curiously, this cannot nullify the need of a central leadership. It has a national aspiration. It always had a national aspiration, but of a different kind. In the past, it sought to intervene in the political set-up to ensure a more socialistic system and benefit of the poor. Now, many of its leaders, particularly almost the whole lot of Bengal, want to intervene to share power and glory of the Central Government. It does not matter for many of them whether they will be able to influence the policy of the government in favour of the poor. They just want share of central power and all that go with it. In this way, they will be with the Central Government after few more years irrespective of who leads it. Whatever, even for this a central leadership is needed.

And they have this concept of a strong central leadership from the beginning. It was needed for two reasons.

Firstly, the communists of yore could not exert themselves unless their modes of work had a solid theoretical base. So, leaders who could interpret the reality were needed. That was why the politburo, which later became the central secretariat in the undivided CPI, and again assumed the old name in the CPI(M) after its formation in 1964, was always filled up with people who had this intellectual capability to interpret the world and Indian situation. After formation of the CPI(M), for a few years the politburo functioned from Calcutta. But that was due to logistical reasons. Then it shifted to Delhi and carried on its work. This central leadership had provided very important inputs for the party. When Gorkhaland movement first started in the 1980s (here we are ignoring the fact that the Gorkhas demanded an independent state—they demanded independence, I repeat—just after Independence, and the local communists were involved in making the demand), Bengal leaders were too eager to dub it as 'anti-national'. That coinage was in vogue then as it was often used against the Khalistanis, the Sikh extremists who dreamed of carving out an independent state. The national leadership stopped the Bengal leadership from using the term 'anti-national' as Gorkhaland was a demand for a separate state within India. Thus they saved the day, as otherwise the CPI(M) could have looked like a fool when three more states were created in the recent past. The compromise formula they worked out is being followed till now. They are opposed to formation of a new state for logic best known to them (the old states were drawn on the basis of language and so, if they want to cling to that, they cannot oppose formation of Gorkhaland as the Gorkhas speaks different language).

Now to our second point. The Leftists always hankered for playing a significant intervening role in the functioning of parliamentary democracy. That was congenital, for they worked for changing the system and unless they could intervene at the central level, they stood no chance of traversing a meaningful distance. Thus, they were different from the likes of a Deve Gowda or a Chandrababu Naidu.

This tradition is being continued. Though the party has always been influenced by the needs of the day, and learned from the compulsions of practical politics of Bengal, it still had a clear national outlook. Its constituent units were powerful (mainly West Bengal and Kerala), but their interest was taken note of only in perspective of development of the state. The national perspective was decided keeping in mind the relevance of the Left and its power to intervene in the system.

Karat's initiative to stall the Nuke Deal and withdrawal of support was a continuation of this old line of national perspective. But now West Bengal wants to impose its interest on the national party. In other words, instead of being a subsidiary unit of the national party, Bengal now wants to make the national party its subsidiary. The Bengal party does not require any theoretical exposition: it is rather scared of it. Post Achuthanandan, it will be same with Kerala. And as for power to intervene, Bengal party can do that if it wins enough seats Bengal party wants to make the CPI(M) like any other party like Mayawati's BSP (where Uttar Pradesh's interest is supreme) or Sharad Pawar's NCP (in which Nagaland unit can be sacrificed for Maharashtra unit).

On earlier occasion, such irreconcilable difference had led to split.

And like this time at the core of it was love for the Congress.

Let us move over to that.

References

1. One of my friends and I came to know of the development and reported it, and the paper I worked for tried to obtain a reaction from the veteran leader.
2. After ruling for 13 months' Vajpayee government was defeated by one vote. Sonia Gandhi could not show majority support as the Samajwadi Party and two small Left parties, the Revolutionary Socialist Party (RSP) and the Forward Bloc, did not support her. But these parties were prepared to support Basu. If only Sonia agreed there could have been an alternative government.
3. The formal name of the then Third Front.

4. In 1977, Janata Party was the second force, a rival to the Congress; in 1989, Janata Party was the second largest force supported both by the Rightist BJP and the Left.
5. Over a thousand people were killed during the movement in which the communists armed themselves with bamboo spikes, machetes, sticks and stones, and the Army met them with rifles and machine guns.

PART III

Present in Perspective of the Past

Seven

Curious Case of Love for Congress

THE PARLIAMENTARY election of 2009 was destined to be a turning point in Indian political history even before it was fought. Even two months before the election, everyone in the know of the things guessed that none of the two major alliances that had ruled the country for a decade would be able to cobble up a straight majority. So attention was on the Third Front, for it seemed they will be the balancing force. The Left had worked for a Third Front, a combination that would neither be with the Congress nor with the BJP, and even before the election it was clear that presence of this Front had marred the chances of any of the two major combination winning the poles conclusively.

What nobody could see was the fact that if the Congress could go close to the halfway mark, there will be a rat race to satisfy it by offering unconditional support. And of course nobody expected or apprehended that the Congress would win more than 175 seats.

Thus the election was being fought in the dark. Previously, the Congress had ruled the country for decades securing majority on its own. But since 1989, the mandate had become too fractured and Third Front governments had begun to fill the vacuum, first by seeking support both from the Left and the BJP, as in 1989, and then with the Congress support, as in 1996. Then, since 1998, a BJP-led coalition ruled the country for six years, and thereafter an anti-BJP combination led by the Congress and supported by the Left was firmly in saddle. But this strong 'secular' combination was torn apart by the obstinacy of Manmohan Singh, the Prime Minister, to go ahead with the Nuke Deal.

But six months later, when the election was being fought amidst high temperatures and frayed tempers, the Nuke Deal was a forgotten chapter. The Congress leaders, except Rahul Gandhi, hardly mentioned of this Deal that was presented before the nation as a revolutionary one. That was natural. The Congress leaders and the elite of the country who claimed that this Deal would raise India's status in the world and usher in a new age of what not, had proved that either they knew very little about India and the world or they were just bluffing. The Left led by the CPI(M) too had shown their lack of understanding as the Deal itself could not make India subservient to the US. Conclusively, it was a case of overreach by both the sides, and thus it was conveniently forgotten during the campaign.

But, one thing was evident. Manmohan Singh wanted to free himself from the dependence on the Left, for he believed till they would be around he would not be able pursue his favourite path of limitless liberalization. He (and the Indian elite as well) was peeved with the Left because they had not allowed the government to introduce hire and fire policy that would bring more prosperity for the rich and more insecurity for the poor and the lower middle class. He was angry with the Left for stopping him from privatizing the insurance and banking sectors, and for preventing a free run of foreign investment in all sectors. That was why he was happy after shaking off the Left from his shoulder. Left leaders, mainly those like their general secretary Prakash Karat who understood his game, were eager to pay him back in the same coin. That was why they were prepared to walk extra miles to woo Mayawati, and everyone else. They had earlier persuaded Chandrababu Naidu of the Telugu Desam Party (Andhra Pradesh) and Jayalalitha of the AIADMK (Tamil Nadu) to shake off the BJP from riding their piggyback, and during the run-up to the election they were happy to see Navin Patnaik, the Biju Janata Dal chief and Chief Minister of Orissa, dumping the BJP and switching over to their side. Thus, they were wrecking havoc with the BJP combination, but the Congress was nervous to see another secular front emerging.

It was all hard politics, frayed tempers and uncertainty looming large during the run-up to the polls. Everything was going as it should have.

Suddenly, Manmohan Singh turned melodramatic. A day before the first phase of the most unpredictable parliamentary election of recent times began on 16 April 2009, Indian Prime Minister made a surprising effort to appease the Left. Curiously, it came from him just a few days after his scathing remarks that the Left was always on the wrong side of history. Forgetting everything he had said during the Nuke Deal conflict and during the campaign, he praised the integrity of the Left and said he had no problem with the Left while running the government with their support. *"An alliance with Left parties is possible only after the elections,"* Manmohan Singh said at an interaction with members of the Editors' Guild and added, *"circumstances will decide if we go with the Left"*. He even said that he regretted parting ties with the Left over the Indo–US Nuclear Deal.

One wondered which statement of Singh was true. The latest one (he did not have any problem working with the Left), or the one stated more than six months ago (that the Left wanted him to behave like a bonded slave). The elite media did not raise this question either, for Singh was their icon, their best bet. However, as far as Singh was concerned, this was not unexpected from him. It is common knowledge that he has no fixed point except having faith in certain outlandish conceptions like Indians love American Presidents. Evidently, he had his eyes set on the PM's chair and he was trying to woo the Left.

This brought in a new dimension and sparked off something that again was only expected: a rift in the CPI(M) showing once again.

***

Karat's immediate reaction to Manmohan Singh's statement was amply clear. *"We will not support a Congress-led government,"* he told whoever contacted him for reaction. He continued with that line and a few days later I heard him categorically saying in a TV interview with a Calcutta-based channel that in the formation of a Congress-led government, the CPI(M) would have no role. He expanded it further and added that in case of a Congress-led government installed at the Centre, his party would sit in the opposition. Party leaders of Kerala and other states dittoed it. That is only expected in any disciplined party.

But like in the BJP, in the CPI(M) too 'discipline' is a word that was only relevant in the past and not to be found in the dictionary of the present. While Karat was categorically denying any understanding with the Congress, Buddhadeb Bhattacharya continuously indicated that the option of working with the Congress was not closed. Bengal media reported it day after day. Biman Bose, followed Bhattacharya like a disciplined soldier.

Then Bhattacharya became bolder and after Karat clarified the confusion once more on April 23 at the party headquarters, the West Bengal CM told *CNN-IBN*: *"We are not committing anything"*. He was asked about the possibility of supporting the Congress to prevent the BJP from coming to power, and he added that after the election they will decide according to concrete situation. When reminded that he was contradicting Karat, he remained unruffled. Without amending his statement he just expressed optimism, using the cliché that 'history does not repeat itself', that there would not be a repeat of 2004. Biman Bose came up to explain that the party had not decided about the post-poll scenario, and added 'no decision can be taken before the election about the scenario that will emerge after the election.' Both Bhattacharya and Bose, without any clue of the ground reality of the state their predecessors had ruled for decades, were dreaming of golden days of the Congress–Left collaboration once again.

It seemed in those days that Karat and Bhattacharya belonged to two different parties. However it was great amusement for the people of Bengal, for they had seen over the decades the growth of this party through rabid and often irrational opposition to the Congress (the communists painted the walls there depicting Indira Gandhi as a witch, and then scribbling slogans that said Rajiv Gandhi was a 'thief' who had pocketed the Bofors bribe). Now having a communist chief minister courting Sonia Gandhi (Indira Gandhi's daughter-in-law) and Manmohan Singh (dubbed by the communists a decade ago a world bank agent) was great fun.

Though many people have written angry words against the Left for many years, I believe what is unfolding before us is a tragic end of a spirited resistance-movement against the onslaught of mindless capitalism that has kept more than half of the population (that is more than half a billion) at the subhuman level. No sane person can deny the role of the Left in the past in protecting the interest of this poorer segment.

Whatever, the two views, one expressed by Karat (the party will in no case support a Congress government) and the other expressed by Bhattacharya (we will decide after the elections) would have come up before the politburo had there been a real hung Parliament and if the Left could have won more seats. That could have exposed the divisions of the party badly.

***

But this debate on the Congress is as old as the party itself.

When I was first trying to understand the communist parties in the early-90s, one CPI leader gave me a very valuable clue. He, Pratul Lahiri, was a man who loved to read and analyse. He told me that since their inception communists were in a dilemma to fix their relation with the Congress. In the meanwhile, the Congress came down from 400-plus seats to a situation where they had lost power (till then) twice. But the communists were still debating their relationship with the Congress.

When Narsimha Rao became the Prime Minister of a minority government, the Left decided not to topple him. It was primarily because of the BJP's ongoing crusade against an age-old structure called Babri mosque. LK Advani, who had made many flip-flops in his long political career was up in arms to establish a Ram temple just at the site of the mosque. His was a case of brazen mixing of religion with politics and ultimately it resulted in not only the razing of the structure, but also the deaths of hundreds. To prevent him from further rise, the Left thought of keeping Rao in power and forcing him to fight the communal agenda of the BJP.

The Left was proved wrong in its assessment. Rao never fought the communal agenda of the BJP. But the Left kept on supplying oxygen to him. Probably, there was no alternative to it. After the demolition of the mosque that continued for hours with the Central Government sitting tight without initiating any action, the Leftists were eager to have joint campaign with the Congress. Rao cold-shouldered that too. Finally, the Left brought no-confidence motion against it and Rao won over a section of the opposition with money and influence to save his government.

In later days, relation with the Congress became more complicated issue. In 1997, the Left was with the United Front government supported by the Congress. Sonia Gandhi was still not in politics and after Rao's defeat the party president was Sitaram Kesri. He flexed his muscle and compelled the Front to change its Prime Minister. It was thought that the Left would not succumb to such pressure. But even they agreed and Deve Gowda was replaced by lightweight semi-politician IK Gujral. In fact, Gujral was the first PM who had no control over his party or the front and was not the political head of the government. Manmohan Singh was the second such man.

In last 20 years, the Congress had gone through tough times. It shrunk and, at a time, was almost on oxygen. Now it had more or less returned to resemble what it was 20 years ago. But the debate in the Left has not ended. The Left has failed abysmally to take advantage of the situation of last 20 years, either in terms of its own gain, or in terms of creating a third pole in politics that would revolve around it. It had squandered away a great opportunity. And now with no firm understanding, the party secretary of Bengal saw a wave in favour of the Congress. For the time being, the Congress does not need them. So there will be no way out, except adopting anti-Congressism.

But the debate will resurface since the history of the communist movement is besmirched with this debate. This is a historical burden on them that had doomed them. From pre-Independence day they remained confused as to what line they would follow vis a vis the Congress, and vacillated to extreme opposites. PC Joshi favoured a line where the communists would be able to guide the Congress and SA Dange took it forward by aligning with the Congress. These leaders failed to realize that the Left had its future hidden in its militancy, and not in capitulation before the Congress. On the other hand, BT Randive believed in fast track militancy and that damaged the party in many ways.

***

The debate was there from the very beginning because the Communist Party consisted of three distinct flow: one came from the Congress, another from different revolutionary organizations, and the third was of unattached men and women.

From SA Dange, Singaravelu M Chettiar, AK Gopalan, EMS Namboodiripad, P Sundarayya, to HS Surjeet, a lot of people who had been prominent leaders in the communist movement till the end of last century were from the Congress. Then there were people from revolutionary organizations such as Anushilan Samiti and Yugantar (MN Roy, Virendranath Chattopadhyay and Bhupendranath Dutta) and the Ghadar Party (Bhagat Singh, Ratan Singh and Santokh Singh). Ajoy Ghosh (general secretary of the undivided CPI after BT Randive) too was from Bhagat Singh's group. Then Surya Sen's comrades also joined the party. Apart from them there were the third loose group who were either active in national cause in other ways (like Muzaffar Ahmed or Ghulam Hussain, a professor from Peshawar who became a trade unionist), or directly joined the party leaving the beacon of brighter career (Jyoti Basu, Indrajit Gupta and many others).

In the 1920s, inspired by Lenin's writings, in various countries, people were dreaming of a socialist world. Indian communists from four major industrial cities of Calcutta, Bombay, Madras and Lahore came together and the first conference of the CPI was held in Kanpur on 25–28 October 1925.[1] It was initiated mainly by the industrial city leaders involved in trade unionism who were trying to organize people in view of what they felt betrayal by Gandhi by calling off the Non-Cooperation Movement. They set out to achieve twin goals of earning freedom and bringing social change. It was not strange that many cases were registered against them by the British. A series of conspiracy cases starting with the name of cities like Peshawar, Kanpur, Meerut were launched. But trade union movement gained strength in the industrial cities.

To circumvent the British tactic of repression, the communists carried on their activities under the umbrella of the Workers' and Peasants' Party (WPP) which mainly belonged to the Left forces within the Congress. It had different names in different provinces. This was the first instance (in the late 1920s) of the communists taking shelter under the Congress tree. The Congress had its influence on them and some believed that the communist movement was being diluted by this.

Well, that was the first debate on relationship with the Congress. The CPI came out of this experiment in 1929, because international communist movement did not favour such proximity to the bourgeois organization. Now the communists started abusing the Congress, including the Leftists of the Congress like Jawaharlal Nehru or Subhas Chandra Bose. But it hardly helped them to grow among the mass. Unlike what happened in China, the Indian communists could not reach the peasants and evolve a mass struggle. Their strength grew only among the industrial workers. From those days a very strong wing of the Communist Party, established in 1920, AITUC (labour wing of the CPI) started growing. It will sound unrealistic today if we remind ourselves that the communist trade unions were strong in almost every industrial city of India (including today's Pakistan).

But again, under the behest of international communist thoughts reflected in those days through Comintern (Communist International), the communists changed tack and started another chapter of mingling with the Congress. This was second case of proximity after the late 1920s. It started from 1935, and again the communists started joining the Congress and the Congress Socialist Party (CSP) (which was a Bloc within the Congress), contested for provincial assemblies and won some seats. According to Namboodiripad, some serious discussions took place between the leaders of the CSP and the Communist Party and 'the results of these discussions were spelt out' in the Meerut Thesis adopted in second national conference of the CSP (1936):

> "The Congress Socialist Party grew out of the experiences of the last two national struggles. It was formed at the end of the last CD (civil disobedience) movement by such congressmen who came to believe that a new orientation of the national movement had become necessary; a redefinition of its objectives and a revision of its methods. The initiative in this direction could be taken only by those who had theoretical grasp of the forces of our present society. These naturally were those congressmen who had come under the influence of, and had accepted, Marxism socialism. It was natural, therefore, that the organization that sprang up to meet the needs of the situation took the description: 'socialist'. The word 'Congress' prefixed to 'socialist' only signified the organic relationship—past, present and future—of the organization with the national movement.
>
> The socialist forces that were already in existence in the country were completely out of touch with Congress and had no influence on the national movement. Therefore, there did not take place, as otherwise there would have, a fusion of the emerging Congress Socialist Party with the groups previously existing. With the adoption of correct and sensible tactics by all the parties concerned, there is every-likelihood of such a fusion-taking place at a later stage.
>
> The immediate task before us is to develop the national movement into a real anti-imperialist movement-a movement aiming at freedom from the foreign power and the native system of exploitation. For this it is necessary to do away with the present bourgeois leadership and to bring them under the leadership of revolutionary socialism. This task can be accomplished only if there is within the Congress an organized body of Marxian socialists. In other words, our party alone can, in the present conditions, perform this task. The strengthening and clarification of the anti-imperialist

> forces in the Congress depends largely on the strength and activity of our party. For fulfilling the party's task it will also be necessary to coordinate all other anti-imperialist forces in the country.
>
> Consistent with its task, the party should take only an anti-imperialist stand on congress platforms. We should not in this connection make the mistake of placing a full socialist programme before the Congress. An anti-imperialist programme should be evolved for this purpose suiting the needs of workers, peasants and the lower middle classes.
>
> It being the task of the party to bring the anti-imperialist elements under its ideological influence, it is necessary for us to be as tactful as possible. We should on no account alienate these elements by intolerance and impatience. The Congress constructive programme should not be obstructed or interfered with. It should, be scientifically criticized and exposed.
>
> In Congress elections, we should not show keenness to 'capture' committees and offices nor should we form alliances with politically undesirable groups for the purpose.
>
> This does not mean that the party shall not carry on socialist propaganda from its own platform. It must continue to do so—and do it more systematically and vigorously.
>
> It follows that the party's own programme must be a Marxist one: otherwise, the party will not be able to fulfil its task and leadership. Marxism alone can guide the anti-imperialist forces to their ultimate destiny. Party members must, therefore, fully understand the technique of revolution, the theory and practice of the class struggle the nature of the state and the processes leading the socialist society."

By then the CSP was being led by Jayaprakash Narayan (JP) as the general secretary and the CPI was being led by Puran Chand (PC) Joshi and together they were instrumental in writing (at the third conference, Fasipur, 1937):

> "It is the Congress that we must take as the basis and starting point, and we must attempt to make it an all-embracing United Front against imperialism. The Congress has already succeeded to a extent in uniting wide forces in the Indian people for the national struggle and remains today the principal existing mass organizations of diverse elements seeking national liberation.... While the Congress is a mass organization, its leadership is predominantly bourgeois. This leadership is unable to develop, while the framework of its conception and interests, the struggle of the masses to a higher level. At the same time it should be kept in view that the Congress leadership is no longer undivided. Recently, a conscious Left has been forming within the Congress and this development is reflecting itself in the leadership also.... Our task within the Congress is not only to wean away the anti-imperialist elements from the bourgeois leadership but also to develop and broaden the Congress so as to transform it into a powerful anti-imperialist front."

About the consequences of this agreement of these two parties, EMS Namboodiripad wrote:

> "The agreement between the newly formed Congress Socialist Party and the reorganized all-India leadership of the CPI, however united not only these two parties but a large number of anti imperialist throughout the country. The top leaders of the Left in the Congress, like Jawaharlal Nehru and Subhas Chandra Bose, were in broad agreement with them. The pronouncements of Nehru as Congress President for two years and Bose reflected the views of not only these two individual leaders but of the entire Left inside the Congress as well as outside....
>
> The work of developing a powerful anti-imperialist front, however, was not smooth or easy. The struggle was hard, since the differences among the various parties and groups were wide and sharp. This was particularly true of the difference between the communists and other Leftists, including the Congress Socialists, and the mass of Left congressmen, on the other.

> The Congress Socialist Party, as its very name implies was an organization of congressmen, with commitment to socialism being an extension of the congressmen's commitment to the the Gandhian, Nehruite and other ideologies of the Congress party. For them and Left congressmen, socialism was a development from the resolution of the Lahore and Karachi sessions of the Congress."[2]

But the split between these two forces soon became imminent. Let us take a small break from the main question of relation between the Congress and the communists, and have a glimpse of the breakdown of relationship of the CSP and the communists.

Here it should be mentioned that the communists who came from the Congress Socialist Party blamed the break up of the tie-up on changed attitude of JP. EMS wrote:

> "The situation, however, radically changed in the latter half of the 1930s. The Moscow trials against the Trotskyites, including several top officers of the Red Army, made liberal socialist like Jaya Prakash indignant. They began to doubt whether all that Masani and company were saying against the Soviet Union and the communists were as baseless as they had thought earlier. These doubts became enormously strengthened when the Soviet leaders signed the non-aggression treaty with Nazi Germany.
>
> These developments in the world brought JP closer to such rabid anti-communists among the leaders of the CSP as Masani, Ashok Mehta Patwardhan and so on. However, a large number of young congressmen and women who had joined and worked in the CSP on the line laid down in the Meerut and Faizpur theses did not join JP in moving away from the earlier pro-soviet and anti-fascist to the new anti-communist line. They thought that in the then world situation, the Soviet Union, which was the most dependable bastion of the anti-fascist forces in the world, had to defend itself against enemy agents. They therefore gave wholehearted support to the leadership of the Soviet Union and the communist international.
>
> As for the Soviet–German agreement, it undoubtedly understood, that when imperialism was using every diplomatic and political means

> to isolate and weaken the Soviet Union, the leaders of the latter were obliged to do everything possible to get out of the isolation into which their country was being forced. Subsequent developments in the world situation—the perfidious Nazi attack on and the heroic resistance put up to it by the Soviet people, culminating in the final defeat of fascism—proved the correctness of the positions adopted by the Soviet leadership.[3]

EMS also explained that he had no prior contact with the communists. It was during his time in the CSP that he came in contact with Sundarayya, and when there was breakdown of the arrangement he joined the Communist Party. In fact, the whole Kerala unit of the CSP turned into the Communist Party. Once again, over to EMS:

> "I was elected one of the four Joint Secretaries of the All-India Congress Socialist Party along with Masani, Goray and Gautam at the very first conference in October 1934.
>
> None of the delegates who attended the Bombay Conference from Kerala (including Krishna Pillai, AK Gopalan and myself) had, in fact, any earlier contacts with the Communist Party at that time. No question therefore arises of 'EMS, a communist, being permitted to infiltrate into the CSP'.
>
> It was a year after the Bombay Conference of the CSP that the late Krishna Pillai and I had the first contact with the Communist Party of India through Sundarayya. It took almost two more years after this first contact in 1937 to form the first unit of the Communist Party of India in Kerala.
>
> During this whole period, the CSP leaders of Kerala worked as honest and loyal workers in the cause of socialism, to develop the trade unions, Kisan Sabha and other organizations as well as to develop the Congress as a radical anti-imperialist organization in Kerala. It was this solid work in the urban and rural areas of the state and not the mercy of Masani and Co., that made us leaders of the trade union and the peasant movement, members of the AICC, etc., making me the

Secretary of the Kerala Provincial Congress committee and a member of the then Provincial Legislative Assembly of Madras.

Krishna Pillai, AKG and I, in other words were Congress Socialist leaders in our own right and not because JP or somebody else 'put us in charge' as the anti-communist 'historians' want the people to believe. Why, then, did the Congress Socialist of Kerala join the Communist Party en bloc? Because they were tremendously impressed by the gigantic strides taken by the Soviet Union in its (First) Five Year Plan. They naturally came to the conclusion that the socialist revolution in Russia showed the revolutionaries of India, as the revolutionaries of other countries fighting for freedom, the path forward. They, therefore, joined the very first group of congressmen who declared socialism to be their final objective, the group headed by JP, Masani, etc.

"It may be added here, that, if in fact the founders of the CSP in Kerala had come into contact with the then illegal CPI before the formation of the All-India CSP, they might have probably plumped for that party. For, unlike Masani and Co., that did not have the background of the British Labour Party whose 'socialism'; was infected with anti-communist, anti-soviet prejudices.

Naturally, therefore, the moment they got the first opportunity to contact the then illegal CPI, the Congress Socialists of Kerala entered into serious and businesslike discussion with them, and on weighing the merits and demerits of the policies laid down by the leaders of the CPI, on the one hand, Masani and Co., on the other, they found the former more correct. Their change over from Congress socialism to communism was thus as natural as the earlier transition of Gandhite or Nehrite Congressmen into Congress Socialists....

If Socialism provided the more effective method of winning Independence, as JP pointed out in why Socialism, the socialists cannot afford to join the chorus of anti-sovietism and anti-communism. JP, too, in the first years the CSP refused to toe the line of Masani and Co., though subsequently he succumbed to it. May others, including the entire CSP of Kerala and of some other areas in the country, refused to follow JP into the anti-communist camp."[4]

EMS had also argued that despite their stand during 1942, it was proved a decade later in the elections that people had more faith in the communists than any other opposition parties.

***

We have seen how the communists worked with the Congress Socialist Party and then broke away from them. Now once again we come back to the relation between the Congress as a whole and the communists.

As World War II spread, the Congress initially took a conciliatory approach and tried to extract as much concessions from the British, probably hoping that the British will free India under such pressure. The communists on the other hand planned to launch a struggle against the British utilizing the war crisis and criticized Gandhian line of conciliation. Communist members of AICC like Somnath Lahiri tried to steer the Congress towards launching a movement, but failed. The communists tried for uprisings in Malabar, Madras, Telangana and Bengal and were successful in creating isolated but strong bases.

But the communists were suffering from lack of confidence as the movement was not led by the Congress. Party statements of late 1930s show that the leadership believed a real national movement could develop only when the Congress would join and lead it. Curiously they believed in 'proletarian hegemony' and yet thought that it could be achieved only by a movement led by the Congress.

But then, as the USSR was attacked by Hitler, the CPI suddenly found merit in supporting the war effort of the allied powers. It presupposed suspension of agitation against the British in India. Thus, suddenly the whole approach changed, once again at the direction of the USSR. The Indian communists proved that for them the USSR was more important than India. That was not surprising if we keep in mind the infantile disorder that communists suffered from in their political thinking in those days. But because of that decision when the Congress launched the famous Quit India Movement, they opposed it. They thought they were so important that they should hold their might instead of the British making compromises for the sake of winning the war. They thought all responsibilities of defeating Hitler were on their shoulder!

You can draw your inference here comparing with the present day situation. They feel the responsibility of defeating the 'communal BJP' rests on their shoulder though they have no strength to fight it on ground in its strongholds scattered all over India. The party that really fights it on ground, that is the Congress, shows no concern for the communists on that account: for the Congress it is only political expediency.

It shows the communists never take lessons from the mistakes committed in the past.

Whatever, the notorious stand of the Left against Quit India Movement is well known and had been condemned from all quarters, even by themselves at a later stage. But here it must be mentioned, that whatever be their weaknesses, their intention was genuine. They believed sincerely that social injustice should end, though they did not know how to proceed. Even a large section of the party favoured a line of fighting the British to achieve freedom so that Indian people could stand meaningfully by the people of the USSR. The then general secretary of the party PC Joshi, Namboodiripad, Sundarayya belonged to the camp that sought to make a combination of two tasks: defeating the imperialist power in India and supporting the USSR ideologically. But SA Dange and BT Randive opposed this and called for truce against the British to support the 'People's War' launched against the fascist powers. The debate ended by 1941 and 'People's War' line was accepted.

Here note three things. First, despite their penchant for theorization and ideology, they chose a wrong path then, and even in recent past. And ultimately, despite their choicest epithets against the Congress, that party carried the day then and even today. In 1942, the Congress launched Quit India Movement and that accelerated India's freedom. In 2009, the Congress launched a political campaign against the BJP and emerged as the strongest force.

Second, because of their inferiority complex the communists did not try to solidify the base of the party either in the late 1930s and early 1940s when the Congress was dithering and not fighting the British, or any time in last 15 years when the Congress did not fight the communal agenda of the BJP. Thus, they lost all their battles at each juncture in history. The second Party congress held in 1948 confessed: "*...total underestimation of the role of imperialism in the period of People's War made us lose sight of the task of exposing imperialism and fighting it within the framework of support for anti-fascist war*". We have to wait to see whether similar confession come in next or next-to-next Party congress of the CPI(M). But, the similarity is striking: it was then anti-fascism getting priority over anti-imperialism when both should have been fought to create an alternative space. And, in recent past, it was anti-communalism getting priority over anti-neoliberalism.

Third, note how SA Dange and BT Randive joined hands in 1941, under instructions from their bosses from Moscow. From there Randive went to an extreme Leftist position after Independence. Probably, he was inspired by the sporadic uprisings in Telangana, in Punnapra–Vayalar, or by the Tebhaga movement. SA Dange, on the other hand, gradually shifted to total dependence on the Congress, taking the CPI to the doorstep of that party. He supported Emergency and was finally expelled from the party after the electoral debacle of 1977.

The overall leadership till 1948 Party congress was banking on the Congress party to create the infrastructure basing on which they would start their revolutionary factory. During the regime of PC Joshi (1935–1947), party's membership rose from almost scratch to 90,000. The party headquarters was shifted from Calcutta to Bombay, where provincial government of the Congress would allow it to function overground. That helped the party grow. And yet it waited for the events to take their own shape so that afterwards they could take advantage of the situation. In simple terms, it was not the people who failed the party, but the party who failed the people due to their total lack of capacity to understand the reality or interpret it positively, their lack of confidence and childlike dependence on the USSR.

Thus, PC Joshi period was one of close proximity to the Congress and Joshi never wavered in his faith that communist movement should grow by keeping proximity with the progressive section of the Congress.

He was ousted from his post and for a while expelled from the party by BT Randive, who belonged to the extreme opposite position.

You may draw a conclusion that in today's perspective Yechury follows Joshi line and Karat follows Randive line. But there is a risk of simplification in it. Thus for a better understanding let us have a glimpse of the contradictory positions of those two most important stalwarts of communist movement in India.

***

The perpetual dilemma of the Left over the Congress was best demonstrated just after Independence in the clash between PC Joshi and BT Randive. Both were great leaders and tried in their own ways to ensure a bright future for the Communist Party. But, they lived in positions poles apart.

Joshi propagated a line of compromise with the progressive section of the Congress. He believed that by working with progressive congressmen the communists would be able to build a just and fair society and polity in India. He believed that otherwise the communists would be marginalized and will not find their root in the national soil. At that juncture, after Independence, this meant that Nehru should be supported, though the communists should continuously mount pressure for reforms in government and in society. This theory, known as Joshi line, presupposed three things: (i) there were two broad groups within the Congress: a progressive group and a reactionary group, (ii) the progressive group would try to free the party from the reactionary group, and (iii) for that it would need the support of the communists. The first two presuppositions were not wrong. Nehru and SC Bose and some others belonged to the 'Left group' within the Congress, and we know—the knowledge stems from, along with other sources, Nehru's own writings—that on issues of abolition of zamindari and several other things they faced stiff resistance from those leaders who had, or were connected with, interests in land or capital. It was also true that Nehru and the socialists were trying hard to establish their line of mixed economy in India. So what the Joshi line advocated was that the communists should mount pressure for such positive change by joining hands and thereby strengthening the position of the 'progressive' elements within the Congress. Joshi advocated a national front based on the Congress–Communist unity.

But the third presupposition was wrong. It is said that Joshi was fond of saying that the communists should be the mahouts of the Congress elephant. This is an example of infantile disorder in political thinking. His line is still being propagated in different forms by intellectuals of different sorts and a section of the partymen. To be honest, till a few years ago I too believed that the communists can advance by aligning with the Congress. But then, as I crossed 40, I realized politics was not a game where one leaves space for another. That is the fallacy of Joshi line. The progressive section of the Congress (in today's context we may say Sonia Gandhi belongs to that section for she wants the party to cater to the poor) will not leave any space for the Left. On the contrary, it will try to finish off the Left so that it can occupy that space. This is politics. In past, Indira Gandhi did it. At present, Sonia Gandhi (and apparently her son also) is trying to do it.

What Joshi failed to understand was the simple fact that an elephant would allow a mahout to guide it only when it was tamed. To tame an elephant you need to be more powerful than the elephant. Those who still support the basics of this line probably suffer from self-delusion, like Joshi, that they are more powerful and superior to the Congress.

But we must remind ourselves two facts. First, Joshi became party secretary at the age of 28! At the age of 22 he served penal deportation to Andaman being accused in Meerut Conspiracy Case, and had become a figure to be recognized. The foreign communists who guided and controlled the Indian communists saw in him a great potential of successfully executing their diktats. And then, he was deposed from his post when he was 41. But despite being under constant guidance of those foreign experts (who knew nothing about India, particularly about the caste reality), he tried continuously to evaluate the situation in his own way and find the true path. He was not willing to toe the line of 'People's War', but was compelled to do so. He was all praise for Nehru and missed the genius of Gandhi, the greatest philosopher-politician the world ever had. Again, those who dictated line from Britain suffered from this myopia and Joshi reflected that. It must also be mentioned that through time his outlook changed. He called Bapu 'Father of the Nation', but still categorized Gandhi as one who had many reactionary traits.

Second, Joshi adhered to the basics of his position that he expounded before 40 for the rest of his life. It should also be mentioned that the basic was not as simple as we have stated here due to lack of space: we have just taken note of the things in a nutshell. At times he was so critical of the Congress that it would seem he was just like any other anti-Congress leader of the party. His was no case of surrender before the Congress. As late as 1951–52, he criticized the Congress for misguiding Indian people, for propagating the ideology of 'bourgeois' nationalism, for covering up its 'imperialist alliances', and for its 'sell-out to foreign capital' by indulging in 'freedom demagogy'. He proposed a front of all Left parties and progressive individuals.

How the international movement in those days pressurized and compelled the leaders would be evident from one example. When Joshi became general secretary, the dominant view among the foreign guardians of Indian communists was that the progressive section led by Nehru should be encouraged to take more positive steps and change backward-looking principles and policies of Gandhi. It came from Dutt–Bradley thesis. From this Joshi developed his 'national front' theory. Then the World War II started, and initially the leaders of the USSR and all the communists of the world believed it was a war between two imperialist camps. Then the USSR had a no-aggression pact with Germany. So, in the changed context, England was to be blamed for the War and need for fighting against Britain became all the more necessary. Accordingly, the CPI started criticizing Gandhi for not launching a massive struggle against the imperialist power. But then Germany attacked the USSR. So the War became a People's War and USSR's friend Britain was not to be disturbed at all. Unfortunately for them, thereafter Gandhi launched Quit India Movement and the CPI stood isolated and exposed. Still, it had to propagate the view that by disturbing the British the Congress was committing a grave mistake, that by joining hands with the Japanese forces Subhas Chandra Bose was acting as a dog of Tojo (the Japanese PM). All this happened during the era of Joshi, but blaming him would be wrong. The whole set of communist leadership were puppets in the hands of foreign communists who were ignorant about India and yet had the brazen audacity of directing Indian communists. Rather, here it must be mentioned that Joshi never gave up on his theory of national front even in his later life. It also should be mentioned that as general secretary, when he was freed from the diktats of Comintern, he once again tried to push a nationalist line, essentially aimed at strengthening Nehru against Gandhi, and from that point of view he urged the communists to celebrate India's Independence. Eminent historian Bipan Chandra has written:

> "PC Joshi's great merit was that, once he was freed from the Comintern's dominant influence, he began to understand the nature and character of the freedom struggle at least from 1945, if not earlier. He was virtually alone in this endeavour and also perhaps the endeavour was too late. He was alone in this endeavour because as the General Secretary of the Party, he had played a predominant role in inculcating the dominant view among the leaders and members of the Party. After all, the Party rules had assured that the dominant Party line was publicly propagated through his voice and his pen.
>
> Consequently, when he attempted to change the course of the Party, he was isolated and then unceremoniously thrown out from the Party and almost the entire Party he had assiduously built up turned against him."

That happened because the party felt, again under foreign direction, that the Independence earned by the Congress was bound to be fake. At a much later stage, Joshi himself wrote about how the Stalinist dogma blinded the leaders and restricted their development in understanding and interpreting Indian reality. Whatever, before concluding this section we must have glimpses of other facets of the leader: because those facets are important and at times studded with real gems.

It was not surprising that Joshi favoured entry of intellectuals in the party's leading rank and had a penchant for scoring theoretical points. His imagination on 'national front' was an intellectual exercise and he encouraged debates on such points. He founded the Progressive Writers' Association (PWA), All India Students' Federation (AISF), All India Kisan Sabha (AIKS), All India Trade Union Congress (AITUC) and later in 1943 the Indian People's Theatre Association (IPTA). The secular cultural renaissance through PWA and IPTA was one of the most glorious chapter of the Left movement. According to Bipan Chandra:

> "Never was Gramsci's concept of hegemony regarding the role of intellectuals applied so well. Gramsci argued that in democratic or semi-democratic conditions it is necessary for the Communist Party to occupy all intellectual ground from political parties and the Press to education, gender relations, and all cultural and intellectual activity. The Joshi period witnessed giant steps forward by the communist movement in this direction."[5]

The great organizer that he was, it was quite natural that Joshi would be able to lead on many counts. But like his theory of a front with the Congress that would usher in socio-political-economic changes, his dependence on intellectuals was probably at the cost of real working class leadership. Like all 'bourgeois' parties, the leaders of communist parties in India came from the upper echelon of the society or from the middle class. It might be so that it had something to do with the intellectual mindset of Joshi. It is also true that he derived his position due to the thoughts of international communist movement that dictated party line for different countries. For India, Dutt–Bradley thesis of 1935 argued for the United Front with national anti-fascist forces.

Again, it must be mentioned that he was a colourful man. During his regime in the party, peasants struggle in Kayyur (Malabar) became history and Joshi actively encouraged it. It is claimed that he was involved in preparation for Telangana movement too. He was not a man who would dance to the tune of Comintern or its next avatar Cominform. He was suspended (January 1949) and then expelled (December 1949) from the party by Randive. But his answer to that is one of the most glorious examples of a communist mind: *"But try however much, you will not succeed in provoking me to repeat the crimes of your own youth, that is, try to split the party and start a rival racket.*" If that stuns you, then I will offer you one more instance of his camaraderie. Randive himself was removed and replaced by Rajeshwara Rao in 1950 and then by Ajoy Ghosh. While they were trying to finish off Randive, Joshi regretfully felt that 'Ajoy Ghosh and SA Dange were trying to do to Ranadive and those loyal to him and his line what he had done to me and others...'

Whatever be his views, right or wrong, culturally he was a great Leftist. A Leftist should have a great and democratic heart. Very few in the movement had so great and democratic a heart as Joshi had. He was a democrat and a nationalist. He believed Independence of India was a great turning point and should be celebrated by all, including the communists. For this he was condemned. After the infamous 1948 Party congress, he was isolated from the others. He had to carry his luggage to the station alone as younger comrades were told not to help him.

The new leadership did not hesitate to betray the brazen sectarian and inhuman face of the communists that had come as their nemesis, be that in the USSR, Western Europe or now in Bengal and Kerala. The CPI(M) inherited both Randive and this mindset. Joshi was its antithesis. After being reinstated in the party a couple of years later, he declined to join Ajoy Ghosh or Rajeswar Rao, who earlier worked as his close assistants, only because he thought they were doing the same thing to Randive and his men what the latter did to him. Had the communists tried to follow such cultural magnanimity instead of following dogmatic and inhuman Stalinist line, they would have been in a far better position today.

After his reinstatement in the party, Joshi never came back to lead it. Only in Palghat Congress of 1956, Nehru's government had taken Leftward turn by promoting genuine mixed economic pattern reflected in the 2nd plan, pursuance of Non-Alignment and Panchsheel, and growing proximity to Soviet Union, Joshi argued that while pursuing people's democratic revolution the party should change its attitude towards Nehru's government and should support it. He felt that Nehru government was curbing feudalism, helping development of indigenous capitalism and opposing imperialist countries.[6] At the same time, he offered resistance to Nehru's 'anti-people' policies. One-third of the delegates supported him. The party did not exactly endorse his line of supporting Nehru, but decided to support government's progressive policies and oppose its negative policies.

Afterwards, he returned to party headquarters to edit the party organ, a responsibility that he later regretted taking up. He had earlier also worked as an independent journalist. During the split in the party, he proposed to remove Dange and make the issue ideology-based rather than personality-based. His last political effort was to warn the party against aligning and forming SVD governments at various states along with the Hindu chauvinist Jan Sangh in 1967. For this he was removed from the national council of the party. With his deteriorating health, he retired from politics and shifted to JNU to write a history of the communists.

In brief, despite his romantic dream of guiding the progressive section of the Congress by aligning with them, he was a leader that the communist movement in India had not seen again. His political line was not wavering. His nationalism and anti-communalism was as solid as rock and was thereby invincible. I again reiterate, had the communists been not followers of Stalin, had they been not blinded by a desire to intervene in national politics in whatever manner possible, had they been not political opportunists, they could have grown immensely by following the principles on which Joshi based his life and work.

***

Now we move over to the proponent of the other extreme, to BT Ranadive. Joshi was thrown out of the leadership in 1948 as a revisionist by Ranadive and his followers. After two years Ranadive met the same fate, accused of being a Left adventurist.

BT Ranadive (BTR) completed his studies in 1927, obtained a MA degree with distinction and next year joined the underground Communist Party of India. He was active with the Girini Kamgar Union of the textile workers in Bombay and with the struggles of the railway workers. He became the secretary of the Great Indian Peninsular Railwaymen's Union. In 1943, he was elected to the central committee of the party. In February 1946, he played an important role in organizing a general strike in support of the Naval revolt. He replaced Joshi, and at the 2nd Party congress held in Calcutta in February (1948), his elevation to the post of general secretary was confirmed. In 1950, he was denounced by the party as a 'Left adventurist' and was sent back to work at the local level. He came back to central committee in 1956, was jailed during the days of Indo-China border conflict in 1962, and was a founder politburo member of the CPI(M) that was born in 1964. When CITU was formed in May 1970, he became its first president.

Ranadive was a Stalinist.

Stalin, 'the gardener of happiness' ushered in a happy period in Russia by killing and banishing not only his opponents, but also those who he felt was more popular than him. He was one of the most dreaded characters history has ever produced. Between 1937 and 1938, he was successful to kill at least 700,000 people of his country (total in his regime, it is claimed, at least 3 million) for the real or imagined offence of opposing him. For this great act he won admiration of the communists all over the world. After World War II, when he turned one after another country into satellites of the USSR (a great tradition that continued till their invasion of Afghanistan), and when he unleashed repression if the people of any of these countries revolted, communists all over the world clapped in applause. They believed all such things done by Stalin were furthering the cause of Marxian socialism, and thereby they themselves proved they believed in a Satanic dogma.

Stalin and Stalinists believed that any number of people could be killed for conspiring against the communists. It presupposed that communistic version of socialism is the ultimate truth, and for upholding it innumerable human lives could be sacrificed. This was not very far from Hitler's belief that Aryan race was supreme and any other population could be sacrificed for keeping that supremacy intact. In Hitler's case it was race that gave licence to kill, and in Stalin's case it was dogma. So it was not surprising that all over the world the Stalinists would do the same thing when in power, or while striving to gain power. From this it could easily be deduced that they would refuse to accept any positive work of anyone else. That was why Ranadive wanted to nullify the gains of Independence.[7] It is a mindset that essentially wants to establish itself by eliminating all competition. Essentially, it proves that the people having this mindset know they will be defeated if they have to face competition. At the end of the day, we know from the history of the USSR and East Europe, it only promotes mediocrity and stifles all genius. Ultimately, people have broken open those brutal systems. If China has survived till date, that is through barbaric repression and passing capitalism as socialism. Whatever, when Khrushchev ascended to power, Russia was de-Stalinized.[8] Khrushchev, however had no control over the minds of many a communist, and thus Stalinism thrived in many communist parties.

Thus, it was only natural that Ranadive would have a narrow sectarian viewpoint. He felt that the Independence that had not come under the guidance of the communists (as though it would have ever come that way) was a fake. He discovered in Joshi the suitable enemy, and so he and his colleagues heckled Joshi as far as possible. The new avatar of centre of international communism, the Communist Information Bureau (Cominform), fully endorsed him. Blinded by Stalin's influence, those international pundits felt that Joshi's regards for Nehru and Gandhi and role of the Congress was condemnable. The communists, affected by childish romanticism, thought they were the representatives of the proletariat who was ready for a revolution. It was fated to be disastrous for the communists did not have with them the support of even 10 per cent of the working class and peasants. It is as true today, because they concentrate on organized labour, though 90 per cent of the workforce is in unorganized sector. Thus, they were not true representatives of the proletariat, and did not have the ability to be so. I doubt whether at any given point their politburo or state secretariats had more than a couple of members who actually toiled as non-white collar labour. People like Achuthanandan are only exceptions in this party and destined to be heckled.

Ranadive brought in disaster. The party was banned and all revolts were repressed by the government. Reportedly, party membership came down from 90,000 to 9,000. Bipan Chandra wrote:

> "In the Ranadive period, the intelligentsia felt stifled and their individuality threatened. Writers in particular left the Party in hordes under the Stalinist stewardship of Dr Ram Bilas Sharma as the General Secretary of the Progressive Writers Association. The entire hegemonic project has never been revived by the Left since 1948."[9]

And this loss was not compensated by any surge in support for the party from the working class. The party was almost to be wound up. Immaturity of leadership caused unnecessary confrontation, and brought in hardship for the remaining cadre. Finally, Stalin and his cohorts realized that antagonistic attitude towards the Congress leadership and Nehru would not benefit the USSR. So, international masters of the Indian communists changed tack. Ranadive was thrown away and the leadership went back to persons close to Joshi. Now let us see what Ranadive's closest admirers have to say about it. One of them is MK Pandhe, the octogenarian CITU president. He wrote a booklet on Ranadive and there he stated:

> "As a result of valiant struggle of Indian people, British Imperialist had to hand over the power to Indian leaders but the country was divided into India and Pakistan. There had been severe outbreak of communal riots and the Communist Party was active in defending unity of the people and prevent riots. An interim Govt was formed in the country and on 15th August 1947, the country got Independence. In this period the Communist Party committed certain reformist mistakes of tailing behind the bourgeois parties. Ranadive realized these mistakes, analysed their nature and played important role in unifying the Party against those errors.
>
> BTR played an important role in criticizing the reformist policies of the CPI. In 1948 in the second congress of the party at Calcutta

> Ranadive was elected as the General Secretary of the Party. The Congress Government banned the CPI and detained 25,000 of its activities. BTR went underground and remained till 1950. However, the party policy went to the other extreme and sectarian mistakes were committed. It had its impact on trade union movement too. Periodic call for strikes were given which could not succeed. Adventurist struggles of detenues in jail were conducted which resulted in loss of life of several valuable comrades. Unjust disciplinary actions were taken against several party leaders. At the intervention of Communist Information Bureau (Coinform) the mistakes were corrected. Ranadive was removed from the post of General Secretary of the Party and membership of the Central Committee. He, however, admitted his mistakes and commenced his activities in Bombay as an ordinary party member.
>
> In this period he wrote 2 important books—*'India's Five Year Plan–What it offers?'* and *'Crisis of Indian Economy'*, which received wide acclaim. He soon became secretary of the Maharashtra State Committee of the party in 1955.
>
> BTR's intellectual calibre and his deep knowledge of Marxist Leninist principles were recognized by the Party and he was soon acknowledged as a national leader by the CPI. He was elected as a member of the Central Committee in the Fourth Congress of the Party. He shifted to Delhi and functioned from the Party centre. He was working as editor of New Age monthly, theoretical journal of the party."[10]

BTR was active in the party once again and during the confrontation of two sections in the party that was known as a clash between the 'Rightist' and the 'Leftist' wings of the party, he played an important role. He presented an alternative document on behalf of 21 members of national council in the sixth congress held in Vijaywada (1961). That document clearly marked the differences in attitude towards the path and the means of advancement between the two opposing groups. He was one of the main architects of the split along with people like Pramode Dasgupta, M Basavapunniah, P Sundarayya and so on. We will not go into justification of the split here. We will study that briefly in the next chapter. But of course relationship with the Congress was the core factor. Those few mentioned above who were the real architect of formation of the CPI(M) believed that preparation for revolution, a journey they believed would go through a stage called people's democracy, was urgently needed. And unlike Joshi, they were prepared to sacrifice national interest for international communism which was a hoax (not only because it was bound to fail, but more than that, because it was an instrument to serve the interest of a particular country, either Russia or China). They all bore the same mindset as of BTR, who even questioned the logic of McMohan line[11] in his bid to show that China was not an aggressor in 1962. For BTR and his co-travellers, the logic was simple: Nehru or Congress had a rotten capitalist character that was collaborating with imperialism, and so they had to be blamed if they clashed with the God-like communists of China.

But even his co-travellers had suspicion in their minds about BTR. Some of them felt that he was trying to steer the party towards an anarchic ultra-Left position. When P Sundarayya left the post of (first) general secretary of the CPI(M), he accused BTR of following a line of paralysing the country with industrial strikes to facilitate take-over by the communists. Sundarayya dubbed this a continuation of Ranadive's old anarchic line. The Naxalites, who broke away from the CPI(M) in 1967, were actually, by their mindset, very close to BTR, though he did not support them in any way. Of course, unlike the Naxalites of 1960s, BTR always put stress on mass movement.

BTR, who always remained a trade unionist, was also instrumental in splitting the trade union wing AITUC. It was again the reflection of same mentality, the same sectarian mindset: the desire to grab and control everything, the romantic dream of being able to achieve great fiat, and the inability to recognize the value and significance of works undertaken by the others. However, the BTRists have their own argument and that must be recorded. Once again from Pandhe:

> "Despite split in the Communist Party in 1964 BTR advocated unity of the TU movement and work inside the AITUC. In the

conference of the AITUC in 1966 he strongly advocated a platform of TU unity and stressed the need to work together on the basis of the programme. However, Dange felt that the leadership of CPI(M) would remain in AITUC to capture its leadership and he was opposing all efforts for unity. BTR was elected as a member of General Council of AITUC in the Bombay conference. During the meetings of the General Council he always emphasized the need for strengthening the class struggle and building TU unity. However, Dange and AITUC leadership wanted to sideline Marxist leaders in TU and began to form rival unions to CPI(M) led unions all over India. More than 300 unions led by CPI(M) were denied affiliation to AITUC while rival unions were formed in over 200 establishments. After consistently fighting for 4 years to build united nationwide struggles and Dange leadership's consistent opposition to these struggles while advocating class collaborationist line the dissidents in the AITUC found it impossible to work together. Dange also desired that the CPI(M) leadership should leave AITUC so that his unhindered control over the AITUC would be maintained. Thus the split in the AITUC became inevitable.

Thirty-two members of the General Council who walked out the meeting in 1970 decided to call a convention of members of the General Council and State Councils and Committees to hold a National Convention on 9–10 April 1970 at Goa to chalk out further course of action. BT Ranadive presided over the convention and guided its deliberations. A resolution adopted by the convention stated, 'Repeated efforts made by the class conscious workers and those who wanted to carry forward the line of class struggle to put an end to this disruption and unite trade unions were frustrated by the dominant leadership. The leadership refused to implement even the principle that had long ago been accepted by the AITUC itself of unity of the trade unions on the basis of democratic elections with proportionate representation and democratic decision by the workers and their elected organs on all questions affecting the workers.'"

Till his last days BTR remained the same. He and his comrades were not been able to live with those communists who were soft towards the

Congress. So it is understandable how anti-Congress he was. He was a radical who believed that the Left can grow only by depending on its own strength. But ironically, the split he and his colleagues engineered to preserve the puritan ideas also spelled doom for the party.

BTR's sectarian attitude dominated the mindset of the CPI(M) from day one. It is as dominant today as it was ever. If corruption cases come up against their opponents they will make unprecedented shout, but if it comes against them they will shout '*sab jhut hai*' (all lies). When the allegations were made against Rajiv Gandhi on Bofors case, red bastions were abuzz with the slogan: '*gali gali me shor hai, Rajiv Gandhi chor hai.*' But if corruption cases come up against a politburo member, then it is politically motivated, then they will try their best to nip it in the bud. They, the accused, will take up the role of the judge! If a case of killing a girl (presumably after raping her) comes up against a zonal committee member, then it is all bullshit. Then, the CBI is politically motivated. If the CBI indicts people from non-friendly parties, they are right. If they indict the CPI(M) leaders, they are politically motivated, corrupt. Even if court finds the CPI(M) leaders guilty, then the judges are sold out. This is their outlook.

But BTR too was great, for he was uncompromising on the point of safeguarding the interest of the poor people. He and Joshi lived in two opposite poles, but none of them could have supported SEZ had they been alive today. They differed on the path of achieving the goal. One was liberal, the other was sectarian. Joshi could see the future and interpret things through his genius. That was why he was one who condemned Soviet Union's intervention and arrest of Dubcek (who was trying to built a democratic foundation in Czechoslovakia). BTR was not such a genius, but he had his contribution in building a party free from foreign control. That was out of compulsion (as the Chinese supported the Naxalites who broke out from the party), but it helped the party in later days.

Ranadive was an honest communist and his contribution and guidance, if delinked from his Stalinist mindset, can help the Leftists even today.

***

It was unfortunate that in communist movement no one could follow up and combine the positive sides of Joshi and Ranadive. But that was urgently required: a combination of free liberal mind, analytical power and nationalistic odour of Joshi and confidence, endless effort and line of independent growth of Ranadive. But as these two extremes remained extremes and no synthesis was made of the contradictory positions, Left movement in India actually shrunk and stagnated for a long time, and is now dying.

It is time we conclude this section. A split occurred in 1964 in the Communist Party and that too had something to do with the relationship with the Congress. We will study it in greater detail in the next chapter. Here we can just take note of the fact that the split was between the pro-Congress and anti-Congress sections of the Communist Party. Most of the CPI leaders had faith in basic proposition of Joshi, and they believed they could wean away the progressive section of the Congress from the reactionary elements. By 'progressive section' they supposed leaders who had some faith in Leftism and by 'reactionary element' they meant those who believed in more Rightist ways. After the split, both the CPI and the CPI(M) supported the SVD governments in the states in 1967 and the CPI went to the extent of participating in governments along with the Jan Sangh. PC Joshi, the hardcore anti-communal, wrote a letter to the leaders against this decision. Soon afterwards, the CPI took a U-turn and in 1969 sided with Indira Gandhi, the daughter of Nehru. With them by her side, Indira engineered a split in the party and got rid of 'reactionary' elements like Morarji Desai, Sanjeeva Reddy, Prafulla Sen and so on. Enthused by this new progressive Indira Congress, SA Dange and Rajeshwar Rao led the CPI so close to it that the original Communist Party became a satellite of Indira Gandhi's party. They supported Emergency and talked of consolidating the 'gains' of that repressive authoritarian days. They faced a threat of extinction after the general election of 1977 and the larger section of the party revolted against Dange and threw him out of the party. Then they came back to the Left fold led by the CPI(M).

On the other hand, the CPI(M) carried a staunch anti-Congress line. They too were enthused by the Leftist line of Indira Gandhi, and had with her a sort of clandestine understanding: but that was short-lived. Thereafter, at least openly, they persuaded an anti-Congress line. That brought them to join hands with the Janata Party sponsored by Jay Prakash Narayan, Rashtriya Swayamsevak Sangh (RSS) and the 'reactionary' section of the Congress known as Congress(O). Socialists and a section of Indira Congress also joined it.

Thus both the party vacillated and could not fix their positions. They misinterpreted a situation and reacted according to the immediate need. They lost sight of the whole, and of the future. They failed to expand the organization and turned over-dependent on their ability to intervene in the system. They became obsessed with their interventionist capability and forgot the basics (that a force that had scanty space to stand on cannot afford to do that).

The rise of the BJP, in fact, put them in a tight corner. Meanwhile communism collapsed almost all over the world. That left the mainstream Left in our country orphaned, particularly the CPI. But it shook the CPI(M) too as it was ideologically the end of the road. This along with the rise of the BJP strengthened the Rightist intellectuals to assert them. Some extreme Rightist intellectuals also came up with their bizarre theories. Anyway, the rise of moderate Rightist intellectuals made Leftist intellectuals defensive. Now there was talk of inevitability of globalization. People, particularly the Leftists, forgot that events and developments swing between extremes and nothing is permanent. A section of Leftists started arguing that PSUs had to be divested, and the thought of developing new PSUs became a sin. The intellectual paucity of the Left leaders finally crushed all their convictions. In the eyes of a section of the leaders fight against imperialism became redundant, pro-poor policies became unnecessary, and the new mantra became market, investment, globalization.

Joshi and Ranadive faded into insignificance: both of them firmly believed in Leftism. Achuthanandan and Pandhe carried on the last of their battles knowing fully well that they were destined to lose. Prakash Karat kept on playing his balancing game like a political gymnast, while a very large chunk of the party turned against everything they stood for in the past.

***

At the end of this chapter we should take note of a document called the party programme. The CPI(M) claims that it is the polestar for them. A small discussion on it will show that this document leaves no scope for holding the hand of the Congress. Probably, that was why that the leaders had to invent a sudden danger (of communalism) in the BJP's rise.

This document is also important because it elucidates the concept of people's democracy, which is a fascinating concept if only treated as an end. The CPI(M) however treats it as a transit point from where its journey towards anti-democracy will commence. The party programme reflects the thoughts of Ranadive, who dreamed of accelerating the process of coming to power by imagining an intermediate stage between capitalism and socialism. This stage was invented by some Soviet pundits only to fulfil the need of the time to serve the USSR's interest and was called 'people's democratic revolution'.

It is different from the common concept of democracy that the communists call 'bourgeois' democracy. They believe that the 'bourgeoisie' is the ruling class in our society and thus they have absolute control over the state and its democracy. They want to change it, ultimately, with 'proletarian' democracy, where the toiling mass will have absolute control over the state and the system. But, it calls for a revolution to move directly to proletarian democracy from bourgeois democracy. Then how to pacify the communists of the Third World and convince them that socialism can be attained through peaceful means: that was the headache of the Russian leaders. But they had had to control the communists to keep the 'bourgeois' governments of these countries with them. So, an intermediate step was to be thought of as immediate goal attainable through election. For them, 'people's democracy' is an intermediate stage between 'bourgeois' and 'proletarian' democracy.

However, their proletarian democracy in reality is neither by the proletariat, nor a democracy. In the name of the proletariat, a group of elites who control the Communist Party comes to power, and then unleashes totalitarian regime. Thus proletarian democracy is, in reality, dictatorship of the communist elites and as heinous as any other form of dictatorship. Once they are in power, if the communist elites have sympathy for the underprivileged and poor, they will take measures to ameliorate their conditions (keep in mind the regimes of Jyoti Basu in Bengal or EMS in Kerala): if their sympathy vanishes and they turn Rightist, barbaric repression may come down on the population (keep in mind Bengal under Buddhadeb Bhattacharya in 2007–08). As the CPI(M) operates in 'bourgeois' democracy, people have the right to remove it from power. People have started exercising it. Thus, 'bourgeoisie' type of democracy is much, much safer system than the 'proletarian' democracy.

Seen in this perspective, 'people's democracy' is a dangerous zone. For Ranadive and his colleagues, it was to be the launch-pad stage for proletarian democracy. However, this very stage could be conceived as 'bourgeois' democracy gives space to all sorts of opinion. The communists want to take advantage of the liberal nature of 'bourgeois' democracy to destroy it. They do not allow other parties or opinions to exist in a communist country. But they want to operate in a democratic country and use all its advantages so that they can they can ultimately kill the feeder system, i.e., liberal democracy. With this in their mind, Ranadive and his colleagues accepted the idea of 'people's democracy'. The goal was simple: come to power through democratic means, then take pro-people measures and prepare yourself for an armed struggle, and when through this insidious design you have become quite powerful, overturn the system. In later pages, we will see how their faith in this sort of strategy remained intact till the 1980s.

Once again I reiterate, seen from this perspective 'people's democracy' is a dangerous proposition fraught with evil consequences.

However, the concept itself can be very useful if put and implemented in a different context. Instead of seeing it as a transitional phase between 'bourgeois' democracy and socialism, it can be seen as an end in itself.

Forget the terms like 'bourgeoisie' or socialist. Our democracy, i.e., the democracy we see all over the world, is an elitist democracy. It is a system over which the elites have absolute control. How? Here, winning an election demands a lot of money for campaigning. Otherwise people will not even know a candidate's name or symbol. To float a party and popularize it you need huge money. To become a Barack Obama, apart from your other great qualities, you also need great resources. This money comes from the rich, no doubt. But, only the rich do not have monopoly over power. The elite segment includes not only big or small or medium bourgeoisie, but a plethora of other different sets of people. Anyone who has come up the ladder and can influence the system—maybe a backward or a Dalit politician, maybe a filmmaker, an economist, a journalist, a professor, even a 20-20 cricket organizer—all are parts of this elite. Many of them may not be rich. What is important is not their wealth, but the authority with which they can intervene in the system. A not-so-rich economist may inspire the system to take much more Rightist or Leftist turn, and may play a role much more important than the big bourgeoisie. An honest (thereby not rich) politician can contemplate great future through a particular path and can change the course of history.

But the common people in general cannot influence the system. Among them there can be rich people too. However, the overwhelming majority of the people belonging to non-elite class are surely poor. If these people become conscious of their rights, if they understand the value of their vote, if they can be organized, a different system may grow up. In that system, decision-making power will at least be partially transferred from the elite to the mass. It is not an abstract idea. The way Congress is shifting to a Centre–Left position now shows that conscious mass can really bring in change. Through such a continuous process, a real people's democracy can emerge and can help to end crude exploitation of the moneyed class and indifference of the state machinery. Over time, the system can be perfected further. This is of course a 'reformist' idea, but it is revolutionary in the sense that it is dependent on consciousness and assertion of the mass.

However, Ranadive's or Karat's people's democracy is politically different as it is not the ultimate aim for them. But the programme they have announced for this stage is very similar to what we have discussed in the above paragraph.

Ranadive probably dreamed of reaching this stage through uprising here and there which would spread and scare the Congress leadership compelling it to have adjustments with the Left. Or, this might, he thought bring the communists to power. But, as we have seen, despite his path being wrong, his intentions or the goal were always sincere. He knew communistic socialism (when the party will be the sole holder of state power, and when something called working class, which is euphemism for the party leaders, will exercise all power) was a far cry. So, he and those sharing his ideas tried to enthuse people by putting forward a programme that till then seemed achievable. It did not presuppose a bloody revolution to achieve this goal. It could be achieved by winning seats in the Parliament. Thus the programme reflected a genuine mindset, though based on false hopes. The dedication to social change, to side with the millions of underprivileged, was genuine and sincere.

Let us have some idea of the programmes of this people's democratic revolution. Theoretical discussion will bring in more confusion. It is better to see what the CPI(M) says about things to be done if it comes to power to complete people's democratic revolution. In 2000, they updated the programme, and committed that if they come to power on their own strength operating through the system like the Nepalese Maoists, they will do these things for the peasantry:

i. Abolish landlordism by implementing radical land reforms, giving land free of cost to the agricultural labourers and poor peasants.
ii. Cancel debts of poor peasants, agricultural workers and small artisans to moneylenders and landlords.
iii. Develop a State-led marketing system to protect the peasantry from big traders and MNCs and sharp fluctuation in prices. Ensure long term and cheap credit for the peasants, artisans and agricultural workers and fair prices for agricultural produce.

iv. Maximize irrigation and power facilities and their proper and equitable utilization; promote indigenous research and development in the agricultural sector; assist the peasants to improve methods of farming by the use of better seeds and modern technology for increasing productivity.

v. Ensure adequate wages, social security measures and living conditions for agricultural workers.

vi. Promote cooperatives of peasants and artisans on a voluntary basis for farming and other services.

vii. A comprehensive public distribution system to supply food grains and other essential commodities cheaply to the people shall be introduced.

We do not know what prevented them to carry out a major part of this agenda while working under the present system in the states ruled by them, particularly in Bengal. Next, let us see the steps that such a government [which should be led by the CPI(M)] will take for industry and labour:

i. Take steps to eliminate Indian and foreign monopolies in different sectors of industry, finance, trade and services through suitable measures including State take-over of their assets.

ii. Strengthen public sector industries through modernization, democratization, freeing from bureaucratic controls and corruption, fixing strict accountability, ensure workers' participation in management and making it competitive so that it can occupy commanding position in the economy.

iii. Allow foreign direct investment in selected sectors for acquiring advanced technology and upgrading productive capacities; regulate finance capital flows in the interests of the overall economy.

iv. Assist the small and medium industries by providing them credit, raw materials at reasonable prices and by helping them in regard to marketing facilities.

v. Regulate and co-ordinate various sectors of the economy and the market in order to achieve balanced and planned economic development of the country; regulate foreign trade.

vi. Improve radically the living standards of workers by: a) fixing a living wage, b) progressive reduction of working hours, c) social insurance against every kind of disability and unemployment, d) provision of housing for workers, e) recognition of trade unions by secret ballot and their rights of collective bargaining as well as right to strike, and f) abolition of child labour.

vii. Provide maximum relief from taxation to workers, peasants and artisans; introduce graded tax in agriculture, industry and trade; and effectively implement a price policy in the interest of the common people.[12]

We have now a clear understanding of what people's democracy means. It is, even for the CPI(M), a stage when democracy will exist, but they will be in power and will have absolute control over power. They will dictate policies.

***

It is quite amusing to study such contradictions between following the road to 'people's democracy' and supporting a Congress government that according to its characterization represents the big 'bourgeoisie'. It will amuse you more if you read some other sentences of the programme:

> "The central social contradiction therefore remains that between imperialism and socialism for the epoch. The contradiction between the imperialist countries and the Third World countries rapidly intensifies under the neoliberal global offensive and it is coming to the forefront....
>
> The working class and its parties have to equip themselves ideologically, politically and organizationally to wage a relentless struggle against imperialism and its exploitative order. The unity of the Left, democratic and progressive forces around the world must be forged to fight against imperialism and defeat the ruling classes who seek to sustain and perpetuate the present unjust global order."

So, the principal task is to fight the ruling classes, and probably no Marxist is needed to tell us that the Congress party is the main and most credible representative of the ruling class in India. The BJP is far behind as only a small segment of top elites (including whom the communists would like to dub as top 'bourgeoisie') have faith in them. So the programme in no way can allow a joint political venture with the Congress. Now read this:

> "The big 'bourgeoisie', which earlier favoured State intervention to build infrastructure for capitalist development due to its weak capital base, accumulated sufficient capital over the decades and fattened itself on State assisted development and subsidies. By mid-eighties the big 'bourgeoisie' was prepared to enter the core sector reserved for the State, take over the public sector and expand to new areas in collaboration with foreign capital. This accompanied by the crisis in the State sponsored capitalist path formed the internal base for liberalization. Externally, the collapse of the Soviet Union hastened the process of shift in policies and the acceptance of the IMF and World Bank dictates.
>
> The pressure to open up and liberalize the economy brought about a shift in the economic policies from the mid-eighties during the Rajiv Gandhi regime. Import liberalization and growing short-term borrowings led to huge fiscal deficits. This along with the changed international scene led to a situation where the Congress government in 1991 accepted the IMF-World Bank conditionalities for getting a structural adjustment loan. The policies of liberalization were pushed further forward by the BJP when it came to power. The liberalization and structural adjustment policies pursued by successive governments since 1991 have led to the opening up of the economy to foreign capital, the process of dismantling the public sector and liberalization of imports. The areas of operation so long reserved for the State/public sector have been opened up to foreign and Indian monopoly capital. With a view to liquidating the public sector, the shares of public sector units are disinvested and sold out cheaply to private monopolies. Through reduction of import duties, indigenous products are displaced by foreign goods resulting in large-scale closures and throwing out tens of thousands of workers from their jobs. International finance capital has exerted relentless pressure for

opening up the financial sector. The privatization process in the banking industry and the opening up of the insurance sector have been given priority. The signing of the GATT agreement in 1994 led to India having to accept the WTO regime. Changes in the Patents Act and the opening up of the services sector, serve the interests of imperialist capital. All these developments have led to the erosion of economic sovereignty."

The particular mention of patent act is significant, for the Left supported the government to pass acts related to this during the period when it supported the Congress-led government. But, apart from that, the party itself stated that the government led by Narasimha Rao (in which Manmohan Singh was the finance minister) started satisfying the aggrandisement of Indian 'big bourgeoisie' and then started liberalization that the CPI(M) hated and that had 'enormously benefitted the big bourgeoisie'. The question is how they could act as a direct prop to the government of a party which was according to them, responsible for the following:

"The path of liberalization and privatization has enormously benefited the big 'bourgeoisie'. Its ranks have been expanded by the entry of new business houses. The assets of the top 22 monopoly houses shot up from Rs. 312.63 crores in 1957 to Rs. 1,58,004.72 crores in 1997 which is a five hundred-fold increase. Under liberalization, major concessions have been given to the big business houses and the affluent sections by the reduction in the rates of income tax and the abolition of other taxes such as wealth tax. Such policies have enormously enriched the affluent classes and expanded the market for luxury goods for their consumption. To meet this demand, goods are produced domestically in collaboration with foreign capital, or, are imported. The indiscriminate entry of foreign capital is affecting vital sectors of domestic industry. Multinational companies are buying up Indian companies. Even though some sections of the non-big 'bourgeoisie' appear willing to collaborate with foreign capital, large sections of the medium and small capitalists are badly hit by liberalization."

When you go against what you have written so carefully, that shows it was no act of sudden impulsive decision or over-reaction after the defeat of the BJP. In fact, they were ready to support a Congress-led government even in 1999, when they were drafting this updated programme. It was a well thought-out plan and was aimed at refreshing the leaders with share of some glory associated with power. The lure was too much.

Before concluding this discussion I shall quote a few lines from Lenin, written before Russian Revolution, and I hope this quote will not be out of place in this context:

> "Any worker who is at all class-conscious knows fully well that the people struggling against the autocracy consist of the 'bourgeoisie' and the proletariat. The 'bourgeoisie' is very keen on freedom, it is making a great stir about it, writing in the Press, and addressing meetings against the autocracy. Yet is there a person so naive who does not understand that the 'bourgeoisie' will never give up private ownership of the land and of capital, but, on the contrary, will fight to the last ditch to retain it against the encroachment of the workers? For the worker to abandon differences on questions of principles with the 'bourgeoisie', along with which he is fighting the autocracy, is tantamount to abandoning socialism, to abandoning the idea of socialism and the preparatory work for socialism. For the worker, in short, it means abandoning the idea of his economic emancipation, the emancipation of the working people from poverty and oppression. All over the world, the 'bourgeoisie' struggled for freedom, which it won largely with the hands of the workers, only thereafter to launch a furious struggle against socialism. Therefore the appeal to sink differences (that is to adopt the path of class collaboration-Ed) is a bourgeois appeal"[13]

***

So, we have seen how the historic legacy of vacillating between anti-Congressism and pro-Congressism had finally gobbled the CPI(M).

The same was the case with the CPI. But they set their party programme in such a way that they cannot be accused of opportunism, even if they support the Congress. In their case, contradiction of supporting the Congress and the party programme is not acute. Thus, while the CPI(M) could in no way justify their proximity to the Congress in the context of their party programme, the CPI's case was different. Though now they toe everything that the big brother does, actually their attitude to the system and to governance is different. Entirely different. It often strayed from mainline Leftism, as during the days of their support to Indira Gandhi. But it allowed them to join the Third Front governments during 1996–98.

See what their programme says at the beginning:

> "Before Independence, the Communist Party of India characterized the Indian revolution as a two stage process in which the current anti-imperialist, anti-feudal stage (a national-democratic stage) would be followed by the anti-capitalist (the socialist) stage. The party broadly followed the strategy of national democratic front of the working class, peasantry, the middle classes and the national 'bourgeoisie'.
>
> Achievement of Indian Independence in 1947 ushered in a new epoch, a historic event for India and the world. This was the result of an unprecedented mass upsurge in India and the new correlation of forces in the world."

Its document of the 1950s is still relevant as its guide. In 1948, under BT Ranadive the party adopted a programme for 'democratic revolution'. But in 1951, the CPI substituted the slogan of 'people's democracy' by 'national democracy'.

> "This signified victory for the national revolution though the course of events had developed differently than the CPI had conceived or anticipated. It was also accompanied by Partition, with its dire consequences. Nevertheless, it opened great opportunities for Indian people to march forward to consolidate political independence and national sovereignty and work for economic independence. Our people were called upon to carry forward the revolution to a new stage, the stage of completion of the anti-imperialist, anti-feudal tasks of rejuvenating and building a self-reliant, democratic and vibrant

> economy, of ensuring better living standards for our people and enlarging and enriching the field of democracy, building democratic institution and ensuring individual rights and democratic liberties and rapid cultural advance."

They were talking of national democratic revolution. Basically it means they are ready to work, unlike the CPI(M), with the big 'bourgeoisie' (like Ratan Tata or the Congress) to strengthen the democracy and to steer it towards left of centre position. While the CPI(M) believed India was ruled by big 'bourgeoisie' (in alliance with the big landowners, and compromising with imperialism), the CPI stated in 1951 and reiterated afterwards in its programme that:

> "The state in India is the organ of the class rule of the national 'bourgeoisie' as a whole, in which the big 'bourgeoisie' holds powerful influences."

So, according to the CPI, big 'bourgeoisie' is not in the seat of the driver of the country though it has powerful influence over the not-big 'bourgeoisie'. Definitely, it was written keeping in mind Nehru and his people and reiterated (in 1968) keeping in mind Indira Gandhi. See its weakness towards the Congress while identifying the areas where it should criticize and exert pressure:

> "'The main aim of Congress legislation has been to replace semi-feudal relations and forms of production in agriculture by capitalist relations and capitalist forms of production.' This does not explain why 'despite the legal abolition of statutory landlordism, some of the worst forms of semi-feudal exploitation, such as subletting or leasing at exorbitant rents and sharecropping, are still widely prevalent in the erstwhile statutory zamindary areas.'"

Thus the CPI did not pledge to fight the 'bourgeoisie' in the way 1964 document of the CPI(M) did. Now we have the CPI(M) programme of 2000 and so not referring to the old one which was more aggressive and crude in nature. While the CPI(M) programme stands as a barrier between the party and the representatives of big 'bourgeoisie' (the Congress party), the CPI programme made room for such adjustments long back. Thus the CPI remained in its position when it supported Indira Gandhi's government or when it supported Manmohan Singh's. However, the consequences of supporting the Congress on both occasions had affected the party very badly and now it is fighting the threat of extinction.

Supporting the Congress was just an example of a few people setting in motion a car by pushing it from behind so that its engine starts. The engine has started and the car has gone, leaving the pushers scathed and deserted. Nothing else was expected. Nine out of 10 times a big and powerful party will exert more pressure on a small and marginally significant party if both come in contact. It is common sense. Only in some very extraordinary situation an exception can be found. Year 2004 had no such exceptional development in it.

We have seen how love for the Congress has damaged the communists of India. Now, let us move over to see the whole experience of the CPI(M) to see their journey through time and the compromises they were compelled to make. I have told you about the compromises they willingly and gleefully made in recent times. That was evidence of their ideological delinquency. But before that they made many other compromises that they were compelled to make.

The following chapter will explain another facet of Left's present state. Now, some people from within the CPI(M) argue that they will have to change themselves or else will be doomed. That reflects lack of sense of history. The CPI(M) was constantly changing for last 30 years. It is true that you cannot follow the socialist path in a bourgeois democracy. But, it was the CPI(M)'s strength on the ground that had put them in power in three states. So, out of compulsion they started adjusting with the system. They started changing. This constant process of change gave them scope to be leading lights in India. But their failure to bring in remarkable improve in the social indicators of development, their bad management, and their tactic of silencing all criticisms through force or by throwing up fudged data ultimately landed them in a quagmire. They realized that they were ideologically defeated and out of shock just got on the path that was not Centre–Right, but more Right than that. In

Bengal, they did it not with a sense of shame, but with sense of pride! They thought people will clap for this socio-political gymnastics. It happens everywhere. After recent failure of Labour in the European Parliament election (June 2009), the adamant Prime Minister was almost ousted from his post. Gordon Brown too was a Rightist in Labour, a man for privatizing public services and for financial capitalism, a man who did not care for the poor. He survived the ouster effort by reorganizing things, but his foreign secretary, the younger David Miliband made things clear in an interview with the *Guardian*: *'We have a responsibility to make sure that, come the election, [voters] know what Labour stands for. We were not being listened to, people felt that they had been forgotten, we neither inspired nor reassured.'* However, people believe that for denying its mass base that also included people dependent on state schools and public transport, no Miliband or no one else will be able to revive the Labour in next 10 years. Ditto for the Left.

Some people, who are of surface and not of substance, think that by going for short term immediate gains they can survive a long battle. They do not realize that a short gain maybe a trap, maybe bait for trapping. Maybe the leaders of New Labour of Britain or the new Left (they themselves called it 'better Left') of India belong to this category. That was why the Bengal comrades ignored the process of change that unfolded for decades and went on trumpeting the slogan of change, putting forward hundred year old theories of capitalism.

A peculiar problem of the Leftists is that they cannot see what is obvious. They invent things that are not real. You cannot show them what reality is. That is why they have to admit so many mistakes. But for us the study of reality is important. Let us move on to study the process of change that the party went through for decades.

References

1. "CPI" in exile was formed in Russia in 1920–21, but that was just that.
2. *The Marxist*, January–March, 1984.

3. *The Marxist*, January–March, 1984.
4. *The Marxist*, January–March, 1984.
5. *Mainstream*, 22 December 2007.
6. Only the bourgeois countries were imperialist according to them; they could never see that the USSR too had imperialist designs.
7. It is precisely for this mindset that even 50 years later the communists do not allow any NGO or voluntary organizations to work freely in areas under their control. It is as true about the CPI(M) as about the Maoists.
8. Now nay decades later, when the atrocities have gone under many lairs of consciousness, Russians are again accepting Stalin as a great national hero. But that is because of his role in saving the fatherland from the Nazis first, and the US then.
9. *Mainstream*, Vol xlvi, No. 1, 2007.
10. From the booklet on BTR written by MK Pandhe.
11. BTR said that it was not a 'customary and traditional' border.
12. The whole document, 'People's Democracy and its Programmes' (the sixth chapter of the party programme), is available at *www.cpim.org*.
13. *Lenin Collected Works*, Vol.5, pp. 503.

Eight

A Compelling Journey Through Time

LONG YEARS back, when they grew, the Leftists could easily catch people's imagination. The world at large could inspire them, and they could inspire the people. Within the country, they were under attack, and that filled them with fury. But then, everything started changing. The attackers stopped attacking them. The world started changing too. Inspiration evaporated. Those who martyred for the cause were lucky. It is so hard to live in a world with the fire in the heart intact when the cause cannot be advanced an inch, when it is only a saga of reversal that one sees all about. The CPI(M) veterans know it. They know how even the wildest fire extinguishes, and how it pains when the next generation they handed their torch to gradually capitulates before the 'enemy'. The Rightists may encourage them on record, and laugh at them on their back. The Leftists may criticize them for abandoning their pro-poor attitude. But the fact is, the story of the CPI(M) is a tragic story of broken dreams, of frustration, of trying to grow up to an image that itself was false.

It was not so that their leaders were all opportunists or prone to make compromises. But they had to make compromises. They abandoned the dream of an armed struggle by the 1970s, and that was the right thing to do, though by doing so they then negated their recent past, for the split in the party was partially on this ground too. So, the only difference that persisted with it and the CPI (if like me you too decide to ignore the differences in the party programme that ultimately bore no meaning) was on the approach towards the Congress.

The first bold action by the anti-Congress faction was their splitting the undivided Communist Party (CPI). They broke away from the CPI on certain questions, which came to a boiling point during and after the Sino-Indian War of 1962. But, in reality, when the pro-Chinese section refused to label China as an aggressor and embraced repression unleashed by Jawaharlal Nehru, they were actually fighting the other section of the communists who were later to stay in the CPI. The moot point was whether for pleasing the USSR Indian communists would give up their independent thinking and their understanding of Marxism. Nehru was gradually siding with the USSR and his Non-Alignment Movement was helping the junior superpower greatly. In exchange, Soviet party insisted on moderating the criticism of Nehru government and proposed sort of cooperation with it.

While a section of the party led by SA Dange was ready to carry out the wishes of Soviet party, another section rebelled against such attitude. Another question for them was whether they would adhere to the principles forwarded by the USSR that talked of 'peaceful transition to power' (that is the communists would concentrate on parliamentary means to come to power in countries like India), or they should have faith in the alternative means, mainly in the armed struggle. These questions and the debate got accentuated after the Congress dismissed the government led by EMS in Kerala. It got a further boost when an emerging alternative centre of socialist ideology came forward to accuse Soviet party of 'revisionism'.

This alternative centre was China. Earlier, we have seen how the foreign bosses controlled and dictated the party line. But after Stalin's death, the communist world started changing. China started identifying Nikita Khrushchev regime as a reactionary one and directly contested the position of the Soviet party. It had its root both in ideology as well as national interest. Khrushchev began de-Stalinization both internally and externally, and to win over more friends (like Nehru) the Soviet party asked the communist parties to play according to the rules of the game. Coming out of narrow sectarian view of Stalin era, Soviet party took more pragmatic approach, and it must be noted that though Khrushchev was removed for his reforms in 1964, another 25 years later most communist parties all over the world accepted many components of his line. Who knows, if Khrushchev was not replaced by a hardliner Brezhnev, Soviet Union could have evaded the fate it embraced. But surely, if Khrushchev line was followed and developed gradually, Soviet Union would have been a different country than what it was behind the iron curtains.

The CPI accepted the changes proposed by Khrushchev era and by late 1950s turned itself into a democratic and nationalistic communist party free from Stalinist ideas of organization, unilateralism and totalitarianism. It elevated itself above the cancerous mindset of 'we know the truth'.

Meanwhile, the propagation of Soviet line and China's defiance to it divided the world of the communists. As the big brother was not aiding its nuclear programme, China was peeved with it. Under Mao Zedong it still believed in supporting the revolutionary zeal in other countries, at least ideologically. Now, they played it against the Soviet party that was promoting theories of peaceful coexistence of capitalism and socialism. Consequently, the Chinese line influenced a section of communists in India and they too started fighting the pro-Soviet group, though they were not very prone to follow the Chinese model of revolution either. The Chinese were also happy to see that a section of the communists supported Chinese position during Sino-Indian border skirmishes. However, the party was not split on supporting Chinese position on these border skirmishes. Though that created a furore, only very hardcore leaders of the future CPI(M) like BTR, Basavapunnaiah, Sundarayya and Pramode Dasgupta put forward arguments in favour of China believing that the communists could not attack another free country and Mao Zedong could do no wrong. Many others like Jyoti Basu or EMS never shared their views. They were in favour of strengthening India's border security. Basu stated:

> "Our stand is clear. I think India's border defences should be strengthened and my party will not hesitate to put in all its efforts for the defence of India's freedom, irrespective of the political character of the attacking country."[1]

Thus it was not true that the full party had allegiance to China, though even today the CPI(M) is often accused of working in China's interest. While it is true that it would like enhanced Sino-Indian relations, it cannot go against Indian position on any sensitive issue like China trying to make Arunachal Pradesh a disputed territory. Even in 1962, only a few radicals had some anti-national tilt, and for them the whole party had carried for decades a bad name.

Whatever, Sino-Indian border skirmishes only broadened the rift that had already existed in the party on the point of ideological division based on the rift of the Soviet and the Chinese parties. The pro-Chinese section leaders were arrested, and it was alleged that some pro-Soviet leaders collaborated with the police to identify them. Whatever, the main point of debate was on the line the party would pursue in internal matters. Under Joshi's influence, Ajoy Ghosh's leadership and SA Dange's advice, the undivided party had accepted the line of national democratic revolution and was going soft on the progressive section of the Congress. But the architects of the CPI(M) wanted a line of militant agitation and total anti-Congressism. We have seen the difference of attitude towards the Congress stemmed from identification of the character of the ruling class: while the CPI thought that the Congress represents (small and medium) national 'bourgeoisie', the architects of the CPI(M) believed the Congress represents big 'bourgeoisie'.

For this viewpoint the faction that later formed the CPI(M) was known as the 'Leftists' and those who would stay in the CPI were known as the 'Rightists'. The 'Leftists' believed that by abandoning the possibility of waging a war against the ruling elites (the capitalists, the landlords and the political leaders), the other section was deviating from the path of Marxism–Leninism and was collaborating with the capitalists. The CPI(M) was for revolution as opposed to peaceful or democratic transition to power. They had partial faith in democracy in those days and sought to make it more perfect: but they also believed that the ruling class would not allow it and they would have to take up arms at a later date. A glimpse of a portion of an article by EMS Namboodiripad will make the point clear:

> "There is no question of the ruling classes permitting the 'peaceful replacement' of their regime by a new popular democratic regime. The only question is the method through which the ruling classes would try to subvert the popular democratic governments. Marxist-Leninists should therefore carry on a simultaneous struggle both against the negative attitude to the struggle on the parliamentary arena as well as against the illusions of a 'smooth and peaceful' advance through the parliamentary path disseminated by right opportunism."[2]

It simply meant that the party would try to carry forward people's struggle against the elite through democratic means as long as possible, but would be prepared for a Chile-type situation, where the democratically elected government was turned over by the army backed by the US. Such preparation of course meant preparation for launching, if under attack, guerrilla warfare. This strategy is just the opposite of the path the Nepalese Maoists followed in recent times.[3]

It was not only Chile that convinced them of this: they had their own experience of their government in a state (Kerala) being dismissed in 1959, two years after winning the mandate of the people. They believed, and it was evident later on, that CIA had a role in it. The CM who faced the dismissal was EMS himself, and he escaped the fate of Allende for he was ruling only a state within a country, and was functioning in an overall democratic set-up. EMS was anti-Congress, and naturally so. While a section of central leadership was dreaming of proximity to the Congress, leaders of Andhra Pradesh, Kerala, West Bengal and some pockets of different states where the party had a base had to fight the Congress. So, despite taking a Centrist position in the tussle between the Leftists and the Rightists inside the party, EMS was vehemently against the Congress, and had no hesitation to say openly that the enemy of the people were 'the ruling classes symbolized by the Congress government at the Centre' (from the preceding line of the article by EMS quoted earlier).

Naturally, the CPI(M) was for waging a relentless battle against the Congress, as opposed to a softer attitude towards the Congress or a section of it proposed by the 'Rightist' section of the party. Some of the CPI leaders found greater danger in the communal forces and strived for a better-shaped Congress in the 1960s and 1970s. They took a position in those days that the CPI(M) took in the present century. The CPI(M) followed them after a gap of nearly three decades, and has embraced the same political fate that the CPI had suffered from 1977. It is strange that though the CPI was wiser than the CPI(M) in many other things, they made the near-fatal mistake twice. Their pragmatism was evident in reaching certain decisions much before the CPI(M). They understood in the 1950s that the general mass associated with them and particularly the leaders of Indian communist movement will not be able to carry guns and fight. They combined their theoretical knowledge with nationalistic feelings, and realized that Indian communist movement had to shun the jargon of the West and find indigenous root. Still they failed. There can be only one explanation for this: communists caught poor and common man's imagination for their fighting spirits, they were rejected by the mass in the avatar of a docile compromising force.

Whatever, the CPI(M) said publicly that the CPI did all this under the influence of the Soviet party. The allegation was of course true: in lieu of all sorts of help (I repeat, all sorts of help imaginable) to the CPI, the Bolsheviks constantly nudged the Indian communists to be soft towards the Congress, because Moscow could foresee a close political and trade relation with India. But the ideological difference, probably better to say the difference of the mindset, was not the only question. They were many other things. Death of Ajoy Ghosh, the then general secretary and the installation of a staunch 'Rightist' SA Dange to that post, the acrimony between the two sections of the party during the days of repression on pro-Chinese section in 1962, and personality clashes were some other important factors. Letters allegedly written by Dange to the British in the 1920s expressing willingness to serve them became a major issue. When the split became imminent, the leaders tried to find out which faction was dominant in his state. Thus Jyoti Basu, who presumably had no faith in the firebrand line of the breakaway fraction, joined them after a period of hesitation, for he could foresee that the CPI had no future in Bengal. AB Bardhan, who became the general secretary of the CPI nearly 40 years after the split, was mentally with the breakaway fraction, but stayed in the CPI as the other section had no presence in Nagpur region of Maharashtra. In Bengal, stories abound with differences between Pramode Dasgupta, the organizational architect of the CPI(M) in Bengal, and Jyoti Basu, the popular face of the party.

***

Finally, from a national council meeting held on 11 April 1964 walked out 32 members of the body.[4] They accused Dange of 'anti-unity and anti-communist policies'. Their accusations were not false, for Dange was not interested to keep the main architects of the CPI(M) in the party. Those who walked out were P Sundarayya, M Basavapunniah, P Ramamurthi, EMS Namboodiripad, AK Gopalan, Pramode Dasgupta, Muzaffar Ahmad, Harkishan Singh Surjeet, Jyoti Basu, T Nagi Reddy, M Hanumantha Rao, DV Rao, N Prasad Rao, G Bapanayya, AV Kunhambu, CH Kanaran, EK Nayanar, VS Achuthanandan, EK Imbichibava, Abdul Halim, Hare Krishna Konar, Saroj Mukherjee, MR Venkataraman, N Sankariah, K Ramani, Jagjit Singh Lyallpuri, DS Tapiala, Dr Bhag Singh, Sheo Kumar Mishra, RN Upadhyaya, Mohan Punamiya and RP Saraf.

They then organized a convention in Tenali, Andhra Pradesh in the month of July (7–11) with 146 delegates, claiming to represent 100,000 CPI members, deliberated upon the recent past and future of the party. They claimed they were the real party and so they retained the name the CPI. The convention decided to convene the 7th Party congress of the CPI in Calcutta. The convention displayed portrays of Mao Zedong, but a section of the party protested and banned slogans like 'long live Mao'.

About this convention, Jyoti Basu wrote in his political autobiography (*Memories: The Ones That Have Lasted*):

> "Thirty-two members walked out of the meeting of the National Council in protest. Incidentally, Bhupesh Gupta also took part in this protest but did not attend the Tenali Convention. The 32 members who walked out of the council meeting issued a statement later describing what had prompted them to take this unprecedented step. They said that the political resolution placed at the National Council meeting had made it clear that the revisionists would not take up class struggle as a main policy and instead go in for compromise.... Of the 146 delegates, all but 10 of them had joined the party 15 years back while the rest had joined before 1935. All of them were well-known leaders in their respective states and had done a lot to establish the communist movement. The appeal that was made at the convention elucidated how the Dange loyalists had imposed the policy of 'Congress–Communist unity' on the entire party and how anybody who dared to oppose this had been expelled."

The appeal of the 32 members concluded:

> "Those who are worried about the results of this step may please understand that we have been forced to take this position and that this does not please us. We are still anxious to avoid taking this step. This is why we harped on unity (at a time when that could have been realized). But this endeavour of ours has only met with opposition.
>
> We appeal to all of you to cooperate with us. Please help us in reorganising the Communist Party to make it a unified platform of the labour class and uphold the revolutionary tradition and history of the Indian people".

Interestingly, the convention also discussed the Sino-Indian border dispute and adopted a resolution that said, *"There is no alternative to a peaceful dialogue to solve the border dispute"*. And strangely, they decided to observe (on 5 August 1964) the 75th birthday of Muzaffar Ahmad.

The Calcutta congress was held between October 31 and November 7, at Tyagraja Hall in southern Calcutta. It was called the 7th congress of the party. The Dange group too convened a Party congress of the CPI in Bombay. So, from 7th congress onwards two parties separately carried on the legacy of first six conclaves of the undivided party. Later on, the Leftist group added the word 'Marxist' in parenthesis only for contesting election, for which they were allotted a different symbol. In Calcutta congress, the CPI(M) adopted its own programme and elected P Sundarayya as the general secretary of the party.

The declaration of the seventh congress of the CPI(M) said:

> "The seventh congress of the Communist Party of India declares that all those who assembled for the convention are the real representatives of the communist movement. The Dange group does not have any right to call itself the Communist Party of India.
>
> A total of 422 delegates represented 1,04,421 members throughout the country; this constitutes 60 per cent of the total members who attended the sixth congress.
>
> Conferences had been organized at the regional district and provincial levels before this congress. A scrutiny has revealed that 14 out of 19 units in the states have joined this congress. Nine of those who had joined hands with the Dange group have also attended this congress.
>
> We are also aware that a majority of those who have not participated in this congress have not listed themselves as members of the Dange group either. We are sure that those members who are attached to the Dange group will reconsider their position. The first phase of the struggle against the revisionist policies of the Dange loyalists have begun with this congress...."

Thus the party was split after internal strife for many years. Now there were two communist parties. One was to toe the line of Joshi, probably going too far than what Joshi imagined in his younger days. The other party quintessentially followed the line of Ranadive, though somewhat moderating it.

The CPI(M) started from a jubilant position, 1964 onwards, with this image of a 'rebel' who could not be pacified till the society underwent a thorough change. And this helped them win applause, empathy and salutes from the poor people who were in vast majority. Their strongholds became even stronger. A large intellectual section sympathetic to the pro-poor agenda of the communists embraced them, and through time they became the sole claimant of communist tradition. Most of the CPI(M) top leaders lived in the communes in the party offices, and was accepted by the bottom half of the population as friends and guides. A testimony to this fact is their presence in constituencies like Ambedkar Nagar of Uttar Pradesh, where the lowest rung of the Dalits voted for the CPI(M) till late 1990s, though they never had won the seat.[5]

The reaction from the people added to their enthusiasm. The time too was different. In those days, the US was seen as a real villain in almost all Third World countries, except in a few like Pakistan that accepted its tutelage from the beginning. The US was playing havoc with the weaker countries, totally disregarding internal democracy and sovereign rights of people of those countries. The US Army and the CIA looked like a notorious group of marauders, trying to establish their supremacy over the whole of the globe. They invented an apparition called the communist to justify their action against any country, as though they were the exorcist. They acted even on suspicion. This was best proven in the case of Jacobo Arbenz Gunzman, who was elected President of Guatemala in 1951 with 60 per cent votes for his reform agenda. He was not a communist. He was for capitalism with a human face, without shades of the US colonialism looming large on its economy. Suspecting him to be soft towards the communists (a charge which later could not be proved even after browsing through all possible documents of his government), the CIA organized a coup against him and ousted him from power.

But then there was Fidel Castro and Che Guevara to pen a success story in Cuba. Revolutionary zeal was abounding in different countries. And the CPI(M) cadres and leaders dreamed of a revolution in India.

If we look back at those days, the story of the CPI(M) seems to be almost a tragic story of a beaten self, of a rebel who lost both his cause and his zeal in the face of harsh, trouncing reality. They got increasingly restricted to three states, and most disturbingly for the communist movement as a whole, they lost the fourth one that was as solid a bastion of the communists as the other three—Andhra Pradesh. But the split of 1964 and then the departure of the Naxalites dealt a severe blow to them. In 1962, out of 43 Lok Sabha seats the state then had, the undivided Communist Party won 7 (the Congress 34, the Swatantra Party 1 and Independent 1), and came second in 10. They were the clear second force there. In the assembly election held in the same year, they contested in 136 seats and won 51, while the Congress contested all 300 seats and won 177. The Swatantra Party contested 141 and won 19. The CPI got about 19.53 per cent votes, while the Congress secured 42.25 per cent and the Swatantra Party got 10.4 per cent votes. Ten years later, in the assembly election of 1972, the CPI contested 59 and won 7 (5.98% votes), the CPI(M) contested 32 and won 1 (3.18% votes). Interestingly, the CPI was still respectively second force in the state among the political parties. But actually the second position went to Independents, who won 57 while the Congress won 219 seats. The number of seats won by the Independents was a pointer to the vacuum in political space that was later filled by the Janata Party and then by the Telugu Desam Party floated by the legendary actor-cum-leader NT Rama Rao. It also showed that the space of the undivided CPI remained vacant for a while, but as vacuum could not exist, it ultimately went to the regional outfit.

The loss they suffered in Andhra Pradesh hemmed in the possibility of becoming a major player at the national level. On the other hand, this same Andhra Pradesh, through time, became the major base of the Naxalites (now known as the Maoists) and helped it spread to other regions.

The split reduced the influence of the communist to a great degree. The communists, who got second highest percentage of vote in national election in 1962, started getting less number of seats in other states apart from West Bengal, Tripura and Kerala. In 1962, the CPI contested 137 seats and on an average got about one-third of the votes polled in these constituencies. A detailed analysis would show that there were about 100 seats that they could have targeted and cultivated, and remember it was their individual strength, without any understanding with anyone. Today, the communists cannot even think of winning more than 50 seats on their own, despite their phenomenal growth in West Bengal and Kerala.

It sounds astonishing that even in a place like Delhi, communist candidate got 9.1 per cent vote from Outer Delhi constituency in 1962. In Mainpuri of Uttar Pradesh, their candidate lost to the Congress only by a few thousand votes after pocketing 21.6 per cent votes. In Jhunjhunu of Rajasthan, their candidate got 26.67 per cent (came third) while the winning candidate got 30.21 per cent. The following table has the details:

States	**Seats Contested**	**Won**	**Percentage of Votes**
Andhra Pradesh	20	7	21.04
Assam	4	0	7.06
Bihar	16	1	6.38
Kerla	14	6	35.46
Madhya Pradesh	3	0	0.9
Madras	14	2	10.24
Maharashtra	6	0	4.05
Mysore	3	0	1.54
Orrisa	2	0	5.11
Punjab	4	0	4.72
Rajasthan	5	0	2.99
Uttar Pradesh	18	2	3.63
West Bengal	24	9	29.38
Delhi	1	0	2.14
Manipur	1	0	8.13
Tripura	2	2	51.2
Total (All India)	**137**	**29**	**9.94**

That was 1962. In those days, when they fought independently, without any understanding with any 'bourgeoisi party, without any seat-sharing arrangement, they won 7 seats from Andhra Pradesh (the Congress got 34), while scoring 9 from Bengal and 6 from Kerala. Bhartiya Jan Sangh (BJS), the earlier avatar of the present day BJP got 16 seats and 6.44 per cent vote, whereas the communists got 29 seats and about 10 per cent vote and were in second position on both counts.

But in the next election, after the split, the scenario started changing. In 1967, when the Congress fared worst since Independence and somehow scraped through the halfway mark, the CPI got 23 seats (5.11% votes), and the CPI(M) won 19 seats (4.28% votes). But the communists were overtaken by the Swatantra Party that got 44 seats (8.67% votes), by the BJS that got 35 seats (9.31% votes), and even by a regional Tamil party DMK that got 25 seats (3.79% votes). The Samyukta Socialist Party got 23 seats (4.92 % votes). Had the communists been together, they could still retain the claim to the major opposition space, for the party that would emerge two decades later as the main opposition to the Congress would have been far behind them.

Since then, the communists never got 10 per cent votes again, and in 2004, when seat-wise they were most successful, the CPI(M) got 43 seats but only 5.66 per cent vote. The CPI, which has eclipsed since its siding with Indira Gandhi in the 1970s, got only 10 seats and 1.41 per cent votes. In contrast, the BJP (the earlier BJS) got 138 seats and 22.16 per cent votes. This shows the opportunity that the communists lost.

And this loss had eaten upon their nerves, their convictions and their mindset.

***

Oblivious of what lies in the womb of future, the CPI(M) started its journey from 1964. With the firebrand image they succeeded in attracting poor people's imagination and capturing a place among a large section of the intellectual class, particularly after the failure of the Naxalites to achieve anything before being crushed by early 1970s. But this second split that marked the exit of the true radicals from the CPI(M) in the late 1960s damaged it heavily. If you look at the growth of the Maoists in today's India, if you take note of their geographical spread, you would understand how much the second split had harmed the communist movement.

This second split too was on ideological ground and again inspired by China.

Only three years after the first split, China abandoned the CPI(M) and supported the ultra-Leftist group that had joined the CPI(M) after the split. This group was pro-China and had strong unwavering faith in armed struggle. This group was shocked when the CPI(M) too participated in election in 1967 and then joined hands with the CPI, just three years after the split. Before that a section of the leadership was portraying a picture of revolutionary practices to be undertaken, and many in the party believed that armed rebellion was really an option. There were even questions about participating in elections. But more shocking developments for the far Left came after the elections. The electoral battle was fought between the two communist parties hurling choicest political abuses at each other. But, after the election both the parties came together to form governments in states like West Bengal. In some other states, the CPI participated in combined opposition governments while the CPI(M) provided outside support. We will revisit the significance of 1967 in next sub-section again. Here, we pass on to the 'revolutionary' developments that took place after it.

It all started in northern Bengal, where a virulent Marxist called Charu Mazumdar was for a fairly long time carrying on a campaign—including writing 'historic eight documents' and such other documents—for an armed rebellion. Finally, in Naxalbari the tribal people and tea garden workers revolted, killed a police sub-inspector and made preparation for a long fight. This happened at a time when in Bengal the communists were in the government led by Ajoy Mukherjee, a rebel congressman who had formed the Bangla Congress. Police then open fired on the people and killed five persons including women and children. It is said that initially Pramode Dasgupta welcomed the development, and the central leaders of CPI(M) then operating from Calcutta thought of supporting this movement. But very soon they realized that things were going beyond their control. Chinese Communist Party came out openly hailing this 'spring-thunder over India' and denounced the revisionist CPI(M) leadership. The attitude of the party leaders came to a point diametrically opposite to what it was initially. Dasgupta raised questions about the inefficiency of police in finishing the Naxalites off and asked whether police guns were capped with '*nirodh*' (condom).

It seems that the dependence on police-administration and using it to the hilt started from Pramode Dasgupta. Though they could not stay in power for long in those days, their pro-establishment tilt became clear. This was in stark contrast to Dasgupta's theory of partisan war that he was propagating after the split in the party. The CPI(M) was rattled by the Chinese position. The Communist Party of China (CPC) supported Naxalites continuously for a couple of years. Then it realized the movement was just spreading armed anarchy and came out to condemn the 'annihilation' theory of Charu Mazumdar. But, the CPI(M) never recovered from the shock, and in a way it helped them to shed their dependence on foreign communist parties. It helped the CPI(M) to theorize the situation within the country independently and to keep equal distance from both Soviet and Chinese parties. They refuted theoretical positions of China in their papers and accepted the Russian position of peaceful transition though they did not spell it out.

The Naxalites initially made a strong base amongst the radical sections of the students of Calcutta. Large number of students left their education to join revolutionary activities. While many of those students left Calcutta and went to rural areas to learn from the lives of the poor and to enthuse them in taking up arms, Majumdar's 'annihilation line', a dictum that Naxalites should assassinate individual 'class enemies' as a part of the insurrection, created confusion and gave birth to anarchy. The Naxalites started hunt for individual class enemies and killed landlords and moneylenders in the rural area and university teachers, police officers, politicians and others in the cities. Jadavpur University and Presidency College of Kolkata became the nerve-centre of rebellion that then spread to Delhi's prestigious St Stephen's College, alma mater of many contemporary Indian leaders and thinkers. Simultaneously with Bengal, Andhra saw similar uprising, and while in Bengal the fire was doused quickly, it was Andhra from where it spread like a wildfire. In that age, sporadic events were reported also from pockets in undivided Bihar, Uttar Pradesh, Kerala, Orissa and some other states also. Then state repression in its most barbaric form came down upon them. With no human rights movement in those days, it is hard to estimate how many young boys or girls were killed, maimed, tortured in Bengal and in other states. But the rebellion was crushed and the state was happy that the fire was finally extinguished. Equally happy were the CPI(M) party leaders and cadres. Nobody thought the Naxalites would reappear like the proverbial phoenix, first in Bhojpur (Liberation and PU) in the 1970s and then in Andhra Pradesh (PWG) and in south Bihar with Dakshindesh [Communist Party of India (Marxist-Leninist)] turning into the Maoist Communist Centre (MCC). Gradually, the movement spread to one-third of India's land mass within three decades (People's War Group was formed in 1980), and formed the CPI(Maoist) by merging all major groups.

For a long time, when the Naxalites were growing in other areas, the CPI(M) was almost insulated from direct contact with this rebels whom they consider as anarchists. In Andhra Pradesh too the difference between the two groups of Marxists became very, very wide. But, the CPI(M) forged close contact with the Nepalese Maoists when they decided to follow parliamentary politics. It was another matter that Nepalese Maoists resented the most active CPI(M) leader's guardian-type attitude and that ultimately created a little distance between the two parties. Whatever, the Indian Marxists were eager to forge proximity to the Maoists of Nepal expecting this would have some effect on Indian Maoists. They know that if the Indian Maoists take part in democratic politics that would get the Leftists to a far better position than today. The CPI general secretary AB Bardhan feels the Naxalites are their estranged comrades and can be brought back. However, the Naxalites have identified the CPI(M) as their number one enemy in Bengal and so the distance is not likely to be bridged.

But, apart from the organizational loss, particularly in Bengal and in Andhra, towards the end of 1960s a bigger loss for the CPI(M) was betrayal by China. This virtually orphaned the party and left them shell-shocked, though in the long run it helped them as only after two decades the communist world with its theory of prosperity and invincibility vanished.

***

Now, once again back to 1967.

We have earlier seen that in pre-Independence days the Congress Socialist Party and the communists came very close, but could not stay together. Then in 1952 elections, communists came very close to forming government in the Madras state, Travancore and Cochin. The United Front led by the CPI was in a position to stake claim in both the states. In Madras, out of 309 seats the Congress got 152 and the CPI got 62. If the communists could act swiftly, they could head the first non-Congress government in India by taking help from all non-Congress parties and Independents. But that did not happen, basically because the communists were not sure about rounding up all non-Congress forces in their van. In Kerala and West Bengal they were the main opposition party. The Socialist Party (by then, they had shed the initial 'Congress' from their name) did much better and got more than 10.5 per cent vote (the CPI got 3.29% votes), though seat-wise the CPI got 16 and the Socialist Party won 12.

Since then one person led the Socialist Party or a section thereof steadfastly towards more glorious days. This person was Ram Manohar Lohia. It is interesting to note (particularly keeping Nandigram in mind) that when Praja Socialist Party's government of Travancore and Cochin resorted to firing on the agitating estate workers, Lohia stated clearly that a people's party had no right to misuse its powers to unleash repression against its own people. He demanded that the Praja Socialist Party (formed after a merger) government should resign immediately. Other bosses of the party did not agree and finally in 1955 the Praja Socialist Party took disciplinary action against Lohia.

No wonder that under this man the socialist movement in this country, despite its various set-backs because of the socialists inability to live together with each other, would go very far.

Lohia believed that the gap between the rich and the poor could be resolved by banning big machines that hindered scope of employment. He felt both capitalism and communism were unsuitable for India as both relied on large-scale usage of heavy machines. He strongly believed that mere change of ownership would not bring about equality, simply because mechanized big industries would not be able to provide for employment of all the people. The solution he put forward was utopian in nature, but he identified the basic problem rightly and was searching for a solution. Even decades later, we still do not have a solution to that problem. Maybe a middle way, between Lohia's thoughts and the process of development we witnessed, could bring some relief to a much greater number of people. Recently, before the 2009 election, the Samajwadi Party led by Mulayam Singh Yadav all of a sudden brought up the issue of computerization in its manifesto and claimed that it was shrinking employment opportunity. It was unexpected from the Samajwadi Party since it was known for its proximity to some big industry and business houses. In reality, it was the last remnants of Lohia's thoughts still working somewhere in their minds.

Again, Lohia was keen to establish women's rights. He was for Hindi as the official language at national level and mother tongue at state levels. He was for people's participation in the building of the nation. But Lohia's genius, irrespective of all his sincere and honest thoughts, was in identifying caste division as the deadliest evil of our society and raising the slogan of '*pichhde pabe sau me saat*'.

Just like today, even then talking about caste was not fashionable, not elitist. The elitist attitude was to ignore the reality of the land and deny the existence of caste division that disenabled the majority of people from taking up opportunities of better life. Thus, caste control served two purposes. First, the forward castes' absolute control over decision making, or their dominance over resource and wealth, education and employment and cultural activities, remained intact even after Independence. Second, it blocked the path of aspirations growing among the underprivileged. So, the elites, both Rightist and Leftist, ignored caste, and made talking about caste a taboo by branding all such talks as 'casteist'. They denied the truth that a similar model of development would not be able to uplift both poor among the forward castes and poor among the backward castes. In this environment, Lohia was an exception who spiritedly based socialist politics on caste. The man who was proud of speaking in Lok Sabha the language that Nehru thought 'market Hindi', hardly cared for the dominant view. He was a non-conformist, a world citizen (who fought against injustice even during his tour to the US), a colourful leader of the mass without any source of income. He put forward solid arguments for his thoughts on caste: *"Caste restricts opportunity. Restricted opportunity constricts ability. Constricted ability further restricts opportunity. Where caste prevails, opportunity and ability are restricted to ever-narrowing circles of the people."* In his theorization, caste was congealed class, and class was mobile caste. He felt the country was deprived of fresh ideas because the realm of ideas had monopoly of the forward castes. Even in the narrow world of the forward castes (assumed to be less than 15% of the population), a tight compartmentalization among Brahmins and Baniyas allowed the former to dominate in the intellectual arena and the latter in the business, and further narrowed the capability of the society. So, Lohia proposed affirmative action to include those 60 per cent of population (the backward people) who could not compete with the forward castes otherwise.

Lohia actually saw through what would come of India in the future. As Niranjan Ramakrishnan had put it:

> "Full of unforgettable phrases which would characterize a point of view, he captured who was a member of India's ruling class in with near-mathematical precision that have not been bettered in three decades—'high-caste, wealth, and knowledge of English are

the three requisites, with anyone possessing two of these belonging to the ruling class.' The definition still holds." [The Che Guevara of Nonviolence]

His politics of assertion by the backward castes started changing the polity by mid-60s. Many in the present generation do not know that it was not VP Singh or even Bindheswari Mandal (of Mandal Commission fame) who brought in this politics of assertion by the disadvantaged. It was Lohia. His politics and anti-Congressism got a great boost in 1967 when in almost all major states the Congress lost and the non-Congress governments came to power. However, he could not follow it up as in the same year he died at the age of 57.

Another 10 years later, the socialists merged themselves in the Janata Party, and after the BJP went out, they dominated the party for another decade before splintering off into smaller parties. But what the media described as 'Mandalization of politics', which was actually politics of assertion, has come to stay. This politics of assertion is definitely a Leftist plank, only if it can go down to the bottom. Lohia's legacy was followed by leaders such as Laloo Prasad and Mulayam Singh Yadav who fell victims to the corrupting power of politics and, to survive, they encouraged criminalization of politics. Till now, an exception is Nitish Kumar. But the politics of assertion should not stop at Yadavs or even Kurmis, it should go down to all castes like washermen, fishermen, barbers and those castes who are at the bottom half of the Indian social ladder. Till the time all these castes, the Dalits (erstwhile untouchables or Scheduled Castes), aborigine (*Adivasis*) , the poor Muslims and Christians are not empowered fully and brought at par with the forward castes in respect of education, employment and other cultural fields, a fight against the system has to be continued. That can be done by the Leftists only. By denying to avail themselves of this excellent scope during Lohia's days was a great mistake of the communists. About this we may again refer to Namboodiripad:

"It is now full 32 years after the respective lines of the CPI and the Socialist Party were put to the first test of electoral support. The rich experience gained in this period has taught the CPI(M), the CPI and the various socialist groups into which the original CSP got divided the lesson that they should unite their forces and, together with other democratic forces fight the ruling party's drive towards authoritarianism and for the preservation of democracy, they should base themselves on the mobilization of the working class people independently of the bourgeoisie.

In this struggle for the unity of Left opposition, the ideological difference between the communist and socialist movements should nevertheless be borne in mind.

The communist movement in India arose over six decades ago, as part of the international proletarian movement and with all its ups and downs, stuck to that position; the mistakes and deviations, which no doubt crept in, were overcome, due largely to its basic character, proletarian outlook on international and national questions.

Although to a large extent influenced by the international proletarian movement, the various socialist parties, whose origin should be traced to the formation of the CSP 50 years ago, were, and continue to be, by and large non-proletarian democratic parties.

The two together could make a big contribution in the pre-war years, but drifted apart during the war and after. The unity of action, which has of late been developing is no doubt a positive sign, but it should not make anybody blind to the gulf that still separates the two (proletarian and non-proletarian) trends.

Let it be stated in conclusion that the CPI(M) is itself conscious of the need for eternal vigilance and continuous struggle against the non-proletarian trends that may crop up in a mass revolutionary party of the working class. Hence the emphasis laid in the party documents on continuous ideological struggle against Right as well as 'Left' deviations the use of the method of criticism and self-criticism, without which the party cannot develop itself into a mass revolutionary party of the working class.[6]

Now, 25 years after EMS wrote the article, no sane person believes that the CPI(M) still carries proletarian trends. At least, nobody in Bengal and Kerala believes it. The character of the party have in other areas, like in the growing influence pocket of northern Rajasthan, is different, no doubt. But such pockets are few and far in between. Otherwise the party is known as a Centrist party which the Rightist elites felt could be dragged towards Centre–Right position by offering cosy political deals.

However, it could have been different if they could realize and grab the colossal opportunity that 1967 offered to all opposition parties. The Jan Sangh (the present BJP) steadfastly utilized all these opportunities. The socialists too took advantage of it and grew. The CPI squandered away everything by going with the Congress. The CPI(M) brought in their doom by vacillating all the while. Only in the 1980s they realized that socialists could be their natural allies. Thereafter, VP Singh played his historic role and gave a boost to politics of assertion that by then had shown its strength in Left-ruled Bengal. Laloo Prasad and Mulayam Singh gave it further boost in Bihar and Uttar Pradesh. Another man, Kanshi Ram (who was another stalwart comparable to Lohia) was in those days creating the base for another and a new round of politics of assertion of the Dalits and the most backward castes. Once again the Left missed the opportunity of going with Kanshi Ram (who too was against the communists for their forward caste tilt). A plethora of opportunities came up in Indian politics in 1980 and 1990s where the Left could have played an altogether different kind of interventionist role. That could have been anti-elite intervention. But they dithered, got possessed by the ghost of 'communalism' and dived at the feet of the Congress in 2004.

In all these, their confusion, their unclear perception about themselves, and the consequent directionless politics played a defining role. It got aggravated by their continuous victories in West Bengal. Now we move over to that.

***

The confusion stemmed from conflict between their primary and secondary support bases. In other words, it was a contradiction between the compulsion of governing a state (which implies identifying with the establishment) and spreading the party in other areas.

Let us see it in perspective.

They made a dent among the people in Bengal, Tripura and Kerala: but due to their organizational failures (unlike the Naxalites, their cadres were unwilling to move out to the areas of weakness across the state borders). They failed to even retain their positions in states like Bihar, Andhra Pradesh, Tamil Nadu, which are just neighbouring areas of those three states. Thus, the CPI(M) became a party of Malayalis and Bengalis. This was their primary support base. By primary base I mean the people who voted for them and made them victorious in a constituency. Through time, the CPI(M) created a strong but limited support base on the basis of their anti-Congress and pro-poor plank. It was not comparable to the geographical area of influence of the undivided party, but Bengal became a classic case with astounding electoral success without break over three decades (1977–2008), and gave them something to showcase to the whole country and even outside world.

But beyond the boundaries of these three states they had another support base that could not be translated to electoral victory. This base consisted of a motley band: workers organized under various trade unions, intellectuals including professors and students of colleges and universities, and common men who had faith in the Left as a friendly or even a protector force. The trade unions, both of the AITUC [the CPI] and the CITU [the CPI(M)], formed a large base of dedicated supporters who would have loved to vote for the party if only it had any chance of winning elections. The hinterland of a factory from where the workers came was a large area, and generally the workers were voters from villages or towns. They did not vote for the communists because they hardly had any presence there. To transform this support base what was needed was to make a strong presence in the rural areas. But, the CPI(M) never had any strong political organizations in states other than its strongholds. The other communist party ceased to be reckoned as a serious political force since 1970s when they went with the Congress. So the whole Leftist intellectuals shifted to the CPI(M). Many writers and poets, dramatists, filmmakers and other prominent people of cultural world in West Bengal, Delhi, Uttar Pradesh, Kerala, Tamil Nadu or Maharashtra were Leftists and communists. Even today, Left union dominates the elitist university of this country, the JNU (both Prakash Karat and Sitaram Yechury are products of this university). This secondary base gave the Left a prestige much beyond their actual (or primary) support base. Again some segments of population, particularly the Muslims, lent them a rare respectability as the story of Bengal being a communal-riot-free state travelled the length and breadth of the country. Could the communists earn such credibility among the Dalits and the *Adivasi* population, they would have been in a very advantageous situation.

I said that there was a contradiction between the primary and the secondary base. What was that? The primary base, since 1977, was compelling the party to deliver. The party had to undertake such works of governance so that people are directly benefitted, so that people can see tangible change.

But that called for compromises.

The system in which the state government was working was a capitalist system. Thanks to Jawaharlal Nehru, there was a strong public sector in the country. But the age of public investment, unfortunately for CPI(M), was coming to an end by early-80s. The only alternative for a state government was inviting private sector. But that was not possible, given the ideology they had followed. According to their ideology, the private capitalists were enemy of the people. We have to keep it in mind that they were earlier even not sure why they should take up the reigns of a state even after securing majority. After the formation of the CPI(M), when the first opportunity to form a government (in Bengal) came, there was a debate in the party on it. Finally, it was decided that such opportunities would be utilized only to give people some relief while constantly harping in their ears that unless the system changed, no fundamental difference could be made.

In fact, it was this rebellious nature that had won them their support base. The core of this practical and ideological strength was the CPI(M)'s pro-poor line of thinking which they placed before the country in various garb of terminology strewn with jargon. The crux was simple: they talked of the exploitation of mill and farm labourers by the capitalists and the landlords, they identified the Congress as the biggest salvaging force of the rich. And they had exclusive right over such position as no other party put so much stress on these points. The socialists, whose history is replete with occasional union followed by many splits, raised some of these issues, but their main plank was different. Thanks to Ram Manohar Lohia, their stress was on uplift of the backward population, but their struggle was not so much against the rich. The other major opposition political force, the Hinduites were perceived as a party of the upper castes (*tilak-tarazu-talwar*), and poverty was not an issue for them. The Congress was, in the eyes of the people, the establishment.

Thus, the communist had somewhat exclusive position as far as poverty and exploitation in the society was concerned.

The basic understanding of the communists had these components: (i) the world is dominated by the imperialist forces on prowl for new markets and victims, (ii) capitalism is on its deathbed and has no means to be liberated from the crisis, and (iii) a socialist world order and a revolutionary change in India was not far. The second point was very important for them. They believed that the end of the world of capitalism was not far off. What was needed was to resist the international imperialist forces—the USA and the MNCs—and to attack the national 'bourgeoisie' as hard as possible. The rest would follow, they were sure.

That injected dreams in their eyes and culminated in a conviction that victory of socialism was not far off. It hardened their faith in the axiom that unless the whole system was changed nothing great could be achieved.

Due to this understanding they suffered from a dilemma: what to do in those states where they had attained majority. The advantage for them in earlier days was presented by the Congress by not allowing them to rule for long. Their governments were dismissed. So, it gave them an opportunity to behave like the opposition even when they were in power. Meanwhile, they decided that during the time of enjoying power in a state they would work for providing 'relief' to the people by measures like land reforms (giving sharecroppers a permanent right over the land tilled by him, distributing surplus land to the landless poor, and ensuring payment of stipulated minimum wages to the agricultural labour), and strengthening the bargaining power of the workers in mills and all sorts of offices.

In an overall perspective, the party lacked clarity in understanding itself. They broke out from the CPI(M) in 1964 to fight the Congress more vehemently and to prepare themselves for a revolution. But very quickly they set the same peaceful means to attain power as their road, which in those days many communists felt un-communistic. That was why the Naxalites broke away. But the others, those who were in the CPI(M), wanted to satisfy themselves that they would be able to change the system someday by coming to power through democratic means. They decided to live day to day, waiting for another day when they will be successful to seize power at the union level. 1967 ushered in a period when in many states the non-Congress governments were formed along with West Bengal and Kerala. Their central commitee prepared a report called 'New Situations and New Tasks' in that year and a glimpse of it will give an idea about it:

> "Our ministries, without either entertaining undue illusions about giving relief in a big way, or courting despair that nothing can be done under the present set-up, should always bear in mind that they as the Party's representatives, should strive to tender our bona fides to the people. Any failure on this score compromises the Party's political line in the eyes of the people; adversely affects the independent mobilization of the people, and their activities; and all this in turn, will not help us to resist and overcome the vacillations, wobbling and sometimes even possible backsliding of some democratic parties in the UFs and their respective governments. In a word, the UF governments that we have now are to be treated and understood as instruments of struggle in the hands of our people, more than as governments that actually possess adequate power that can materially and substantially give relief to the people. In clear class terms, our Party's participation in such government is one specific form of struggle to win more

and more people, and more and more allies for the proletariat and its allies in the struggle for the cause of 'people's democracy' and at a later stage for Socialism."

In other words, their governments should create such an image of themselves that they would be conceived as the friends of the toiling masses. It was conjoined with a stern warning that any vacillation in this regard would be treated as compromising the basic tenets of the party.

Now a part of the primary mass base and the secondary mass base took it for granted that this parliamentary path was just a ploy, and nothing more. It was like the concept of Shankarachariya that this world is an illusion and only truth is God (*bramhasatya jaganmithya*). For the communists, the parliamentary path was an illusion and the truth was revolution. On the other hand, for getting support of the people doing something concrete was necessary. Before going into further details of this contradiction, we take a pause to study in detail about the party's outlook as late as in 1980.

***

An article 'Working Class and Bourgeois Parliamentary Democracy' by Ramdass appeared in their magazine *The Marxist* in 1980 that shows what was their attitude till then:

> "The Communist Party of India (Marxist) does not hold that the working class can win state power through elections or by the Party's representatives participating in parliaments, legislatures and even in state governments. It has always held that electoral victories are only formal victories.
>
> It is exactly what the Maoists believe. But why were they in parliamentary politics then? Only to achieve certain political purposes, such as:
>
> ...the Party is trying to achieve-isolating the main party of the ruling classes, advancing the ideology of the Party, liberating the working class and the people, especially the peasantry, from the grip

> of bourgeois ideology, increasing the confidence of the people in themselves and against the bourgeois—landlord government led by the big bourgeoisie and so on. For this, purpose, while the struggle outside goes on, while the revolutionary ideological political work among the masses continues, parliament and legislatures are used as auxiliary forms for exposing the exploiting regime and the exploiting classes. In this the Party follows the Marxist-Leninist teachings about making revolutionary use of bourgeois parliamentary institutions.
>
> .... To say that parliamentary activities should be combined with extra-parliamentary work; that parliamentary activities should be subordinated to the revolutionary work among the masses is one thing. But to scoff at making use of bourgeois democratic rights to advance the cause of the revolution is to adopt a totally erroneous position."

This article shows their attitude towards governance of the states. What it enlisted as credits of the state governments or the aim of ruling the states may sound ridiculous today, but in those days it used to be quite seriously discussed by the party members and propagated to both primary and secondary bases:

> "We are attacked for participation in these governments on the ground that whatever relief given by these governments to the people strengthens constitutional illusions among them and give them the feeling that basic changes can be brought about through parliamentary means. The experience of these governments shows just the contrary. These governments have record totally in contrast to that of the Congress governments. It is only in these states that the repressive machinery of the state, the police, etc. is not used against struggling workers, to help landlords against agricultural workers and sharecroppers. These are the states in which full democratic rights, including the right to strike, are guaranteed to government employees. In these states, serious efforts have been made to implement land reforms in favour of the rural poor and curb the vested interests in the rural areas, the sharecroppers are given legal protection against eviction and ensured their share of the produce, the agricultural

workers are helped to get the fixed minimum wages. At times of natural calamities, these governments try to give maximum relief to the people within their limited resources.

These are all benefits for which people in the Congress-ruled state are fighting and the CPI(M) and other opposition forces are leading struggles. The people are asking for some relief from the growing burdens that are being imposed on them. Is it necessary that the Left Front Governments of West Bengal and Tripura try to relieve the economic distress of the people to some extent? Does this limited relief solve any of the basic questions? Or does it make the people realize more quickly that unless the entire set-up is changed, no radical improvement can take place in their condition, and, with the confidence of protection from the Left Front Governments, carry on the struggle for the basic aims with even more determination?

Any reformist understanding in regard to the utilization of bourgeois parliamentary institutions by the party of the working class will lead to serious opportunity mistakes, as it happened in the case of the Communist Party of India. It was after a long-drawn struggle in the united Communist Party of India on the strategy and tactics of the Indian revolution that the party split two decades ago. The CPI took the programmatic position that the national democratic revolution it envisages and the new state that comes into existence will not be under the leadership of the working class but under the joint leadership of the working class and the bourgeoisie. The CPI leaders also declared that the parliamentary path was the only path for the Indian revolution. This had its own consequences."

So, the government was only for furthering the image of the party which remained imbedded in the idea of revolution.

That idea was utopian and could not be carried forward in reality. The reality came to haunt it in a bizarre way. When the Bills that the West Bengal government passed, like on land reforms, was not cleared by the Central Government, it gave them new agenda to raise finger at the class rule at Centre. But then a time came when Centre stopped seeing them as a threat and started cooperating with them. It created a completely new situation and called for new ways to carry on the fight in the name of communism. However, none was available. The indications were clear that they should try to live as a Left party, a pro-poor and anti-elite non-conformist party, and should not try to carry forward the impossible 'mission communism'.

The CPI(M) was, however, in favour of having the best of both the worlds.

***

The enemy stopped considering them as an enemy. They were to challenge the system: now system challenged them to prove that they were against the system.

It created a new crisis. As though to abet the crisis, people of West Bengal voted for them in consecutive elections.

So the party had to put before the people new examples of enmity of the capitalist system. But, none was available from the reservoir of socialist wisdom. So, certain issues were raised and blown out of proportion. One relevant issue was freight equalization policy. Bengal and Bihar had iron mines, and this iron was taken to the factories in different states. Capitalist economy says, the closer the factories, the less will be the cost of carrying it. So iron will be cheaper near the mines. It will attract the investor to put up their factories near to the mines. But Nehru being a socialist of sort, thought this will hamper the prosperity of distant states through industrialization. So he equalized the freight so that every factory got it at same price. This tampering in free run of capitalist economy was disadvantageous to West Bengal. Strangely, the CPI(M) picked up this socialistic policy of freight equalization as an instance of 'step-motherly' behaviour of the capitalist government at the Centre. This became a big issue in Bengal and strengthened the support base of the CPI(M).

This was the first fraud with the ideology for the sake of better governance of Bengal. The issue was chauvinistic. But it was given a Leftist ideological colour. The issue was simple: putting Bengal in disadvantageous position by disallowing the principles of free market economy, and could be raised by any government, be it Leftist, Centrist or Rightist. However, this was projected as a Leftist issue. And the opposition Congress party failed to counter it either by supporting it (by taking more chauvinist line), or by opposing it (by taking socialist line).

Jyoti Basu, then prodded the party to adopt two-pronged strategy.

First, he asked the party to accept joint sector as the need of the day. It was a departure from the old line of allowing state sector only. Joint sector was private-public partnership, where along with the state an investor will come from the private segment. That would open the road of private investment and prosperity of the capitalist. But if that was not allowed, there would be no big new industry in Bengal. This was the first major dilution of ideology that the party discussed in mid-80s. Strangely, it was BTR who sided with Basu and explained why this was the only way out. The almost decade of continuous rule had put the party face to face with the reality of people's growing aspiration. People now demanded employment and other opportunities. So, the party gave a nod to joint sector. This helped Basu to plan Haldia Petrochemical and other units to provide for some employment. However, these things were blown out of proportion to present before the people a picture of such a bright future that was clearly unreal. What happened with Nano project in Bengal was just a repetition of this Haldia thing.

Second, the party planned another slogan: more power to the states. This slogan moved the Leftist intellectuals also. It was seen as though a move to devolution of power that would go down to the people ultimately. Panchayat was already in place in Bengal and in those days the system was working excellently as a means of power sharing by the lowest rung of the people.

The 1980s was the time when the juggernaut of Indian political system started moving, taking unexpected directions. The regional parties started growing in strength, number and stature. Akalis were there in Punjab and Dravidian parties in Tamil Nadu for quite some time, then NT Rama Rao emerged as a strong leader and swept Andhra Pradesh, through agitation the AGP came to dominate Assam, and so on. All these forces rallied behind Basu's demand for more power to the states.

Some years thus passed with these themes. But nothing concrete emerged out of them. Some extravagant policies like free universal education (ignoring the point that it was just instance of superfluity for the rich) drained the exchequer. The economy was stagnant. Industrial sector was decaying. And there was no Leftist slogan available any more. No inspiration could be drawn from the outside world where Soviet Union had vanished. It was only pessimism, only stagnancy.

Thus the party was left in a precarious position. They were liable for the state's development. And the only way out then was inviting private investors. But the party's central leadership and the majority fraction was not prepared to go that far. So Basu took an unprecedented step. Without informing the party, he placed the 'new industrial policy' for Bengal in 1994. The party leaders sulked. But they had little option before them. The man, who by then had led the party to win four assembly elections consecutively, was too big for the party to take any adverse action.

That was the turning point. From the utopian dream of revolution, the party came down to stark reality. They started with the premise that without total change state governments could not achieve much. While they still take recourse to that, their whole ideological position was diluted gradually, and their outlook on economic development changed. But, still the old mindset remained alive. All the compromises were done under heavy compulsion, for it was not possible for the party to denounce parliamentary politics and take up arms. The only alternative left was what Basu did. Theoretically, it was simply a strategy of survival, postponing the revolution for another day. At practical level, there were many other questions, but we will not go into those.

***

However, such compromises were not fully acceptable to the secondary base. That started shrinking. The contradiction between primary and secondary bases became acute by mid-90s. The intellectuals, and the supporters outside Bengal demanded ideological purity. For Bengal, what was needed was development. The two could no more go hand in hand. Still, the only criterion that could have bridged the two was a strong pro-poor mindset. Let us examine it in detail.

Development encompassed everything: development of health, education, roads, communications, safe drinking water (particularly as arsenic pollution was assuming a dangerous dimension), electricity, and employment. The state government needed money to invest in all these. That was why industry was necessary. Employment in industries was of secondary consequences, for that alone would never solve the problem of unemployment and underemployment. People had to be shifted from agriculture to non-agricultural sector, but not necessarily to big industries, which is not possible either.

But from 2005, Bengal government went for development of big industries which alone could in no way solve the problem of unemployment. And they made it a sort of jihad. But if they were sincere, if they were really concerned about people's problems, they could have gone sensibly on industrialization as all the states of India go, and could have focussed on rural and small industries that have much more potential to generate employment and attack underemployment.

The CM of Bengal and other leaders often took shelter behind Jyoti Basu while implementing the neoliberal policies. As Tata Motors project in Singur showed, finally they had reached a point when their primary aim was not augmenting revenue generation, but to create the most favourable environment for the interest of the investor. That a few other states also do. But to achieve this they went to any extent. As though it was not enough, at the height of doing this they took recourse to a theoretical presentation of 'building capitalism'. Then 90-plus Basu was fielded to support their opinion. It created so much confusion that Prakash Karat, the general secretary had to clarify. The statement that Karat issued will not be out of place here:

> Prakash Karat, General Secretary, Communist Party of India (Marxist) has issued the following statement:[7]

> "The remarks made by Com. Jyoti Basu on the nature of capitalist development in West Bengal and the role of the Left Front government in this regard has been reported in a confused and contradictory manner in the media. On the basis of these reports, some political leaders have also come out with equally confused and misplaced reactions.
>
> Com. Jyoti Basu has explained the economic development in West Bengal and the role of the Left Front government on the basis of the perspective of the CPI(M). Only those ignorant of the programme of the CPI(M) can talk of the Party saying 'goodbye to socialism and welcome to capitalism'.

It is necessary to instruct such critics as to what the CPI(M) programme sets out:

(i) Based on its programmatic direction, the CPI(M) joins state governments knowing fully well that it has limited powers within the Constitution. Utilizing these limited powers, Left-led governments work to protect the interests of the working people, initiate welfare measures and within the limited spheres where it has some powers, put in place policies which are different from that of state governments run by bourgeois parties. The CPI(M) knows fully well that in the states where the Left is in government they cannot build socialism, but undertake some alternative policies within the capitalist system. Land reforms within the constitutional limits was one such step undertaken in West Bengal, Kerala and Tripura.

(ii) Even though the Left Front has been in office for thirty years in West Bengal, capitalist development has been taking place there as in the rest of India. What the state governments can do is to help strengthen the struggle for alternative policies advocated by the Left and democratic platform at the all India level.

(iii) The CPI(M)'s goal is for the setting up of a people's democracy, which is a step towards the eventual goal towards socialism. This, as Jyoti Basu said, cannot be done by the three state governments ruled by the Left. The advance to socialism will be realizable only after the Left and democratic forces are strong enough to build an alternative at the national level.

(iv) Till then, in the states like West Bengal, Kerala and Tripura, the Left-led governments will strive to put in place policies, which benefit the working class, peasantry and other sections of the working people. Working within the capitalist system, facing a situation where the Central Government imposes neoliberal policies, the Left-led governments have to undertake industrialization and economic development in such a manner where the interests of the workers and the poorer sections are protected.

It is amusing to see some leaders of the BJP and the Congress portray this approach of the CPI(M) in simplistic terms of socialism versus capitalism. For them socialism only denotes a slogan to be used as a smokescreen for promoting the interests of big capitalists and foreign finance capital. Joining them in the criticism is the Revolutionary Socialist Party. Unlike the CPI(M), the RSP has declared socialism to be its immediate goal. But one may ask why the RSP has been, in all these years of being in Left-led state governments, working to implement some reforms and welfare measures within the capitalist system?

The record of the Left-led governments in West Bengal, Kerala and Tripura stand testimony to the fact that the Left and democratic alternative advocated by the CPI(M) and the struggle to ensure a degree of social justice within the framework of an all India capitalist model of development has found increasing support among the people. That is why the three states are today considered to be the bastions of the Left."

You can be sure that Karat did not issue the statement only for the media: his real target was his party and other left parties as well.

***

A year ago, it seemed that everything they stood for in 1964, all the reasons for which they split the party, had changed, except their theoretical position and their jargon. It was obvious that the vast majority of the party had no faith in those theoretical postulations of 'people's democracy'. These people, however, successfully grabbed the plum positions in the government or other institutions. Some of them became important party officials also. Only a miniscule section of the party leaders still believed in working for 'people's democracy'. That section included old-timers and maybe, people like Prakash Karat. The economic policy the party supported during 2004–08 had however raised strong question marks about Karat.

All through this book we have studied this change. We have seen what happened just after the election results, we have examined what happened during the days of their support to the Congress government and in immediate aftermath of withdrawal of support, and we have examined how these recent stands (supporting the Congress or adopting neoliberalism) marked a complete break from the past.

Now let us move over to some important points related to its survival. We need not discuss whether they can survive if they continue to follow neoliberal policy. Today nobody is bothered about the CPI, because that party long back gave up its identity by supporting Indira Gandhi. Similarly, if the CPI(M) sacrifices its identity, no one will be interested in whether it survives or not. And it will gradually lose its secondary base. So what is most important for its survival is (i) whether it can fight corruption, caste discrimination and take positive attitude towards novel developments like environment protection and human rights; and (ii) whether fight against communalism leaves them with any other option other than building up a third alternative. Both these questions throw up challenges to be anti-elitist, and no one knows whether the party has the ability to do so.

References

1. *The Statesman*, 31 October 1962, as referred to in the article of Sankar Ray, *Mainstream*, 16 July 2008.
2. From *'Chile and the Parliamentary Road to Socialism'*, 1973.

3. Though during a certain phase a section of the Nepalese Maoists contested elections, in general they carried on guerrilla war and after securing a strong base declared 'People's War' against the monarchy. They the elites were compelled to negotiate with them, and they are now in charge of the affairs after contesting elections.
4. The CPI changed its decision-making body's names from politburo and central committee to national executive and national council. It was a part of their trying to be nationalistic.
5. I visited the constituency when Mayawati was in the fray, and it was her election agent who told me that they would get three-fourth of the Dalit vote, leaving the bottom one-fourth. I was surprised to hear this and wanted to know which was the party that would take away the lowest rung of the Dalits from the Dalit queen. The man answered: the communists. I found those communists in the villages. There was no leader from outside. They were all locals, the most wretched people. The candidate was from them and they were his campaigners. I could not communicate with them well for they spoke in local dialect that I could not follow properly.
6. *The Marxist*, 1984.
7. Press Statement, 7 January 2008.

PART IV

Future: Dangers and Opportunities

Nine

Burden of Organization

AN ICEBERG cannot sink the Titanic'. It appeared in a blog of one British newspaper, or maybe, a newsmagazine. About the New Labour of Tony Blair and Gordon Brown, someone wrote that their attitude was like propaganda solved all problems. Suppose they are in charge of the Titanic and the news comes that it has been hit by a huge iceberg and is sinking: they will get up and say, 'There is a perception that the ship is sinking and we have to go to the people on board and change all that.'

I am sorry that I have forgotten who wrote this: must be some great analyst. His remarkable description of the mindset of the Labour, which at one point of time was a Leftist party, perfectly fit with the mindset of the CPI(M) leaders of today.

After they lost badly the Lok Sabha polls, the Bengal CPI(M) declined to accept that it had anything to do with the new reality of Bengal. They pointed finger at the central leadership and claimed the debacle was due to the faulty policies of the central leadership. They claimed that the call of forging a Third Front had not gone down well with their supporters, and the Congress regime of 2004–09 had engendered a surge in the largest party's popularity. Neither was true. The voting pattern of the people of

West Bengal or Kerala or Tripura was never affected by the feasibility of formation of a Third Front during 1977–2004. So, even if it is assumed that it affected them in 2009, there must have been some other reason behind that. Again, there was no major surge in the Congress votes. The Congress had got, in 2009, 206 seats while securing 28.55 per cent votes. In 2004, it got 145 seats with 26.7 per cent votes. So it was about 2 per cent increase in vote share that brought 61 additional seats. I have earlier explained how it could happen. But that is logic. When someone decides to change the perception that the Titanic has hit an iceberg and is sinking, logic does not work. It is true that the Kerala party has not taken shelter under such bizarre and ignorant generalization. But, they also imagined factors to lay the entire blame at the CM's door.

Surprisingly, in Bengal, there was a clear indicator already in existence. In July 2008, Panchayat election, the opposition came very close to the Left as far as the lowest tyre of Gram Panchayat was concerned. The opposition had won 1,479 Gram Panchayats against the Left's 1,597 (some 116 were undecided). Compare the figure with the year 2003, when the Left had won 2,311. And this was in the rural area where the opposition had lost out for last 30 years. With the battle being equalized in the villages, it was only predictable that more than half of the seats at the assembly or the Parliament level was gone. True, at the higher levels of Panchayat the opposition could not do se well. But with the battle either tilted towards the opposition or hanging in balance in East Midnapur, Hoogly, South and North 24 Parganas, Maldah, Murshidabad and North Dinajpur, it was truly 50:50 for the whole of Bengal, particularly if the cities were added. Even the pro-CPI(M) media cautioned the party about the verdict[1]. Thus there was no scope of misreading the verdict of 2009. And yet the state CPI(M) misread it. We know they did it deliberately at the behest of Yechury, and their aim was to remove Karat from the helm of the party.

A few weeks after the Lok Sabha polls, 16 municipalities went to polls on June 28. The Trinamool Congress–Congress alliance won 13 of the 16 municipalities. Five years ago, out of these 16, they had only five.

This time the opposition wrested nine from the Left. Four seats were retained, and one was lost to the Left.

What did it show? And I have discussed earlier the debacle they faced in the 10 assembly seats where by-election took place on 7th November. The CPI(M) lost all its seats.

But, as late as on 21 November, when Yechury was asked[2] why his party was sinking in India, his answer was: *"We have said that the Third Front we proposed was not credible. That was why we lost."*

So naïve! Their Titanic (I am sorry, the appropriate word should be 'dingy') was sinking and they were trying to change that perception.

This effort to change the perception stems from dependence on a well-built and well-knit organization. They had decided to convince the people that the CPI(M) was losing Panchayat and municipal elections, assembly by-elections and Lok Sabha elections all because they had decided to forge a Third Front! No other party can risk playing such trickery with the people, because they do not have an organization on which they may depend to make the black white.

Traditionally, the communists have imagined their party as the 'vanguard of the proletariat', and to make it so they put maximum stress on building a strong organization. In India, the organization was first built up through trade unionism and that created a flutter both among the British rulers and Indian political elite. But that waned through time. However, a mass base, particularly a rural mass base, started growing after Independence. We have seen how the party's policy was dictated by some foreign bosses from the beginning till the 1960s. That made the party directionless and implanted seeds of confusion in the party. The party was split in 1964 and then the CPI(M) became the mainstream. While the movement lost out in almost all the states through the 1960s and 1970s, it amassed more velocity in West Bengal, and also in Kerala and then in Tripura. As it grew in stature, it went on building the organization in these states.

What this organization does? The loose organizations of all other parties try to mobilize people during the voting seasons and occasionally try to educate people on various issues. On the BJP's behalf a joint machinery of the RSS and the party tries to rouse communal passion in the minds of the people and also spreads various rumours. But the RSS net is not so strong even in Gujarat as the CPI(M)'s in Bengal. In last decades, the CPI(M)'s organization has perfected in three things: making the police and civil administration an extension of the cadre (the local administrators work as instructed by the local committee); controlling every sphere of social life (including schools, colleges, clubs and other various organizations); finishing off an iota of rebellion with brute force. Thus it became not only a combination of the executive and the judiciary; it became something more. You cannot keep your house under lock and key for years together: that will be occupied by the local cadres. You cannot get employment in schools and colleges or in government and autonomous bodies without a clearance from the local party office. You cannot form any association without the party's nod. You cannot visit your state freely, for 'outsiders' are not welcome in the CPI(M) dens. The party was the last word. It is still the last word in some districts, where the Maoists (with similar faith in organization and with same organizational capacity) are taking on them.

Through time additional responsibilities were taken up by the organization. As the party started amassing huge immovable property[3], the individual members also started converting their clout into money and assets.

Now, the population under the Left rule was in a dilemma. They developed dislike for the party swarmed by dishonest people (and almost always, with a few brilliant exceptions), but had no way to organize themselves or rally public opinion against the Left. The degree of control varied from district to district, from region to region, and between the rural or semi-urban areas and the big cities. But, it was there everywhere. And it took a really significant dimension in Bengal in last 15 years.

This was most true about Bengal, but not less applicable in case of Kerala. Had Kerala been ruled by the Left for continuous three decades, the situation would have been the same there. With its history of fighting militancy, and a mixed population of Bengalis and tribesmen, Tripura is somewhat different and that is why we shall not bring that state in this discussion: but the characteristic of it is no different there.

Being a party without any organization worth its name, the Congress could not stand by the people of Bengal. The leaders of the party started submitting before the Left[4]. Much later, Mamata Banerjee came up to challenge the Left. She came out from the Congress to accomplish her mission. But, she had no ideology, no programme and no alternative to offer. So, she was appealing only to the mass who were already anti-Left, who had voted against the Left and who in some places could not do so out of fear of retribution. The CPI(M) organization rightly identified her as enemy number one, and constantly attacked her personally (including a physical assault on her) and politically. Their propaganda succeeded in making people believe that she, and her politics as well, was whimsical, irresponsible and disastrous.

If things had gone that way, it is doubtful how long the Left would have ruled Bengal. Without any political foresight, Mamata Banerjee was vacillating, sometimes joining the BJP-front and sometimes aligning with the Congress. Her support was on the wane, and Buddhadeb Bhattacharya assumed he had got a providential chance to rule over a state where a divided opposition would ensure his perpetual victory. So he went berserk. This gave Mamata Banerjee her first real chance. It was not because she had changed or had done something positive. She just started opposing the Rightist policies of Bhattacharya, mainly forcible eviction of the farmers. Then she added some Leftist points in her agenda like opposition to privatization or surrender before the industrialists. This brought her votes to the extent she could not imagine even a couple of years ago.

So, the Left brought its nemesis by its own deeds: Banerjee only fished in the muddy water.

The communists believe that their cadre reach their message to the people, organize the mass against the capitalists, and brings feedback from the lower level to the higher levels. But when the communists become friends of the capitalists, and when the cadre does not know anything about the basics of the ideology they are supposed to follow, they just become a delinquent force. Suppressing people and making money become the aim of their life.

It is inevitable, that such cadre force cannot alert the party about its growing unpopularity. Again, for the cadre, only the flag is important, not the ideology. It does not question ideological bankruptcy. It works for retaining the supremacy of the party. Thus it makes the party more unpopular among the mass. It does not happen till the party follows a positive ideology, which may be invalid as a theoretical framework, but still is pro-poor, pro-underprivileged in nature.

Exactly this has happened in Bengal. Kerala is a little different. But in Bengal, it is likely that the opposition, if united, will come with two-third majority in 2011 assembly election.

And you see the leaders. They believe the iceberg that has hit their Titanic cannot sink it. A liability in the true sense.

So, the organization that the communists build up so meticulously and depend so heavily on, cannot serve any great purpose. It cannot forewarn the party about its growing unpopularity and thus cannot act as a check on the leadership. It cannot question ideological bankruptcy. Rather the monolithic organization carries along it a negative value. When the party becomes unpopular, it tries to suppress the people, and thus make it more unpopular. So, it is not an asset for the party, it is a liability.

Even earlier, on thousand and one occasions the reality the party imagined was wrong, and they realized it many, many years later. That is why their history is replete with confessions of committing mistakes. Their assessment of Gandhi, Tagore and Subhas Chandra Bose was wrong. Their assessment of Quit India Movement was wrong. Their assessment of Independence was wrong. Their opposition to computerization was wrong. Their abolishing English till Class IV in Bengal in the 1980s and 1990s (true that it was done by many others states also, still) was wrong. The list can be enlarged endlessly. In no case, the organization could play a meaningful role in rectifying the mistakes. Just like any other party, a communist party is led by a few. In 99 per cent cases, the central committee blindly endorses the view of the politburo, and the Party congress endorses the view of the central committee. So, ultimately only politburo matters. And the general secretary matters the most. The organization that goes down to the local levels plays no role in determining the policies. It only executes the diktats of the upper echelon of leadership.

The popularity of the party depends on the policies decided at the top. Land reforms, siding with the rural and urban poor, increasing the wages of labour and the pay hike of the teachers and state government staffs and the likes were decided by the top leaders and implemented by the party's governments in all the three states. In others states, the party fought with whatever strength they had for such changes. This gave them a definitive character, and the cadre went ahead with zeal and dedication to spread the message and organize people in support of it. Till the 1980s, at least a few of the local level leaders also had some understanding of Marxism. The party was not confused. It was facing challenges of governance and the whole party came together to find a way out of it. Demands of more power to the states, strengthening public distribution system, thrust on universal education and free treatment of illness were the issues that the whole party adopted to pursue. Occasionally, someone found fault with this line and left the party. But there was overall unity and unanimity. That was why when Basu came up, in the mid-80s, with the proposition of accepting joint sector as the instrument for industrialization, even Randive accepted it. The party was lagging behind the time, but the effort to find a way forward was honest, and the party machinery, i.e., the organization, was acting on behalf of the poor and underprivileged. The rural gentry was against the party, a large part of the bureaucracy was against the party, the urban areas were against the party: so the party had to fight the opponents. The party organization had a positive value.

By the mid-90s this unity in the party started falling apart. Basu came up with his industrial policy (1994) without consulting the Delhi party and set a dangerous precedence. The lesser and younger leaders of the party were encouraged by this, without understanding that what Basu could do would not behove them. Then Basu lampooned the decision of the party to reject the proposal of leading the Central Government. It further encouraged the young Turks of Bengal. Finally, they started working as an independent unit since 2004. Bhattacharya kept Karat in good humour, and started preparing for a revolt. His assessment was simple: the party would never go beyond the three states, and so it was prudent to adopt such policies that would keep it in power. The organization in Bengal started to follow this logic. In earlier times, the principles were more important than power, as it should be with any Left party. Now power became the single-most important criteria and the whole organization (in Bengal) followed this line. It condoned Bhattacharya's over-thrust on industrialization, came up with those arguments for industrialization that the capitalist world had brought a century ago, and for their every failure blamed the Trinamool Congress leader. Thus, a cadre working at the local level almost turned himself into a joker.

So, in modern times, the CPI(M) organization is only an instrument of carrying the orders and silencing the people, and also a rumour mill. It has great similarity with the RSS, but is more efficient. This is true about both Bengal and Kerala.

In the 1990s, the politburo decided to decline a uniform pattern of political alliance all over the country, and decided to make it a state-specific issue. So, somewhere it could ally with a party opposed to the Congress (like the TDP), and in another state it could align with a pro-Congress party (like the RJD). Strangely, later they extended this same principle in case of their governments. Kerala was free to pursue an anti-liberal policy, while Bengal was given freedom to go ahead with pro-liberal policies. This was a symptom of growing confusion in the party and waning authority of the central leadership. Only 15 people were at fault. But that resulted in a pro-Congress organization in Bengal, and an anti-Congress organization in Kerala.

Now, because of this nature of the organization of Bengal, it will not be easy for the party to rectify the mistakes, better to say the sins, of recent past. If a purging has to start, that should start with the heads; but then if it has to continue, it will have to throw out at least 80 per cent of the people of the party organization in Bengal. Neither is possible. It would have been possible had there been no extremely well-organized party machinery in place. The organization thus blocks the path of rectification.

Again, the cadre and party offices in local areas do not serve any positive function in a parliamentary democracy and mostly stand as symbols of unconstitutional authority, of interference and terror. If the organization was of any value, it would have understood long before that they were fast losing ground. Actually, the organization does not help much in providing correct feedback as the organizational people meet only their comrades, and the common man do not open up before them. Their attitude towards the common man is that they will educate them. About his industrialization plan and his mode of functioning, many times in last few years the Bengal CM had said that if the opponents came to him for discussion he would have convinced them about the rightness of his decisions. From the top man to the lowest rung this is the attitude of the CPI(M): with their limited knowledge, and that too from biased sources, they feel they knew everything and those who oppose them are ignorant people. Under the circumstances, if a CPI(M) man approaches a common man, the latter will not open up before him.

Well, probably people have now convinced the CM and the party that they were wrong. And the organization had failed to gauge the mood of the people. Both Bengal and Kerala party went haywire in their assessment of the situation.

In Bengal this organization consolidated the mass at one point of time. That was a time, particularly 1970s and early 1980s. The party-men had worked for decades and had developed a strong bond with the poor people. Rural poor was with the Left. Then in the towns and small cities a section too was with them for reasons explained earlier. But the party did not want to stop there. It vied for the support of other sections ignoring the inherent contradictions between those other sections and their own base. Thus *Khet Majdoor* (agricultural labour) wing of the party was developed everywhere except in Bengal. In particular, the party was eager to have the whole of the middle class with them. By then administration had gone down to the Gram Panchayat level. Even for a birth certificate or a death certificate one needed the cooperation of the Panchayat. It gave the Left further leverage. With time, irrigational facilities and agricultural output also increased. It gave birth to rising aspirations in the minds of the better-off people. On the other hand, the facilities through the government projects could not satisfy everybody. Those who did not get the facilities, or got less of it, started turning against the party. So two segments of population—those who were better off and those who did not get much facilities—started drifting away from the Left. However, the process was slow. But, the signs were clear. The Left's vote peaked in 1980 Lok Sabha elections (54%) and thereafter started declining. But till 1989 they got more than half of the votes polled, except in 1984 Lok Sabha elections held after the assassination of Indira Gandhi. The Left got 52 per cent in 1982 assembly election, 48.5 per cent in 1984, 52.9 per cent in 1987 assembly election and 52.3 per cent in 1989 Lok Sabha election. But in 1991, it came down to 48.9 per cent in assembly election and 47.1 per cent in Lok Sabha election. After one-and-a-half decade of Left rule, the support was steadily declining. Again, in 1996, it showed a slight improvement: it was 49.4 per cent in the assembly election and 48.3 in Lok Sabha election. But again, in 1998 Lok Sabha election it was 46.6 per cent, in 1999 it was 46.8 per cent votes. There was definite decline at least by 7 per cent votes since 1980. Some sections of people who were not getting enough benefits from the Left, turned against them. So the party machinery wanted to punish them by pursuing a policy of deprivation. It further alienated people. Chinks developed in the rural base.

People have tried to break open this suffocating environment time and again. In the mid 1990s, in the Keshpur–Garbeta region the people revolted with the help of the Trinamool Congress and the Maoists. That was the first case where people used arms to counter the arms of the CPI(M) goons. But they failed. The whole region is so terrorized even now that no one dares to oppose the Left openly. Second time it happened in Nandigram. The party spoke of presence of Maoists there. They spoke of armed goons. But finally they reclaimed Nandigram in 2008 by the help of their goons. The CM hailed the action openly. The Maoists had to make retreat in face of the fire-power of the attackers.

The party started a lie-campaign. Bizarre theories were propagated at the local levels. The hand of CIA staged a comeback in Left parlance after a long time: it was restricted, however, in Medinipur district. The CIA, the Maoists, the Trinamool Congress, the BJP, the Naxalites, everything was put in the same basket to make out a demon of the Nandigram resistance. This lie-campaign, in which one could clearly see the shadow of Joseph Goebbels' principles of propaganda[5], was aimed at vilifying the people of Nandigram. The worst part of it was bringing the question of 'outsiders' participating in the struggle. Yechury presented this point before the reporters during the parliamentary party briefing day in and day out. Forget about Che Guevara, forget that Yechury himself is a Rajya Sabha member from Bengal despite being an 'outsider' in his own yardstick. The simple question is what can prevent any Indian to show solidarity with any movement in any part of India? A leader who has a democratic mind could never bring forward this point. You and I have as much right to organize people of any part of the country as Yechury has. But democratic decency cannot be expected from the communists for they do not follow democratic principles. It stems from their faith in organizational control of an area. Principle-wise, this is very close to the concept of liberated areas of the Maoists. The only difference is, the Maoists do it without participating in election and thereby fail to earn a sort of approval like the CPI(M). Whatever, the CPI(M) organization has earned notoriety in the regions it dominates, particularly in Bengal, for its lie-campaign. It only added to the acceleration of the downfall.

Thus, the organization, with its firm faith in Stalinist principles of finishing off the opponents at any cost, did irreparable damage to the party's image.

What happened in Nandigram? As the news spread that large-scale land would be acquired in Nandigram, many CPM people rebelled against the party. These people were the backbone of the movement. They knew how the CPI(M) party machinery worked. They knew how the CPI(M) silenced the opposition. In fact, they were the CPI(M) soldiers. But, many of them did not have proper papers of the land they held and would not have been compensated if their land was acquired. They started building up resistance in the same way as the CPI(M) operated. Haldia Development Authority headed by Lakshman Seth put a notice for land acquisition. Later, it was claimed by the state government that the Authority had no authority to put up the notice. But—and here was an example of the nasty tricks of the communists—the villagers were not supposed to know that. The party wanted to gauge the mood and the real situation by doing this. But, the notice gave the rebel communists their required ammunition to mobilize the locals.

Democracy failed the people of Nandigram when they were tortured for months for their rebellion. But the people became victorious. Though elitist media has never discussed it, the truth is that Nandigram had raised serious doubts about the maturity of Indian democracy. It had raised a very important question: if people do not get justice from the democratic system, what alternative they have other than taking up arms and creating liberated zones? Even the people having full faith in democracy had to adopt violence in Nandigram to secure their future. Nandigram was not only about land acquisition: it was about survival in an environment where the state and all of its institutions had failed to give people any protection from semi-fascist attacks. Gujarat pogrom was another such incident, though of a much larger magnitude. Lalgarh, or other liberated zones of the Maoists, are another form of manifestation of people's accumulated distrust. If we turn blind eyes to these incidents, we will be failing democracy and our children's future.

Now, compare this situation with Kalinganagar of Orissa where people were resisting the proposed steel factory of the Tatas. There also it went on for years and police resorted to firing on 2 January 2006 and killed 12 tribal people. The movement is still alive there. But, it had not affected Navin Patnaik's party elsewhere in Orissa to any great extent. In Orissa, the Biju Janata Dal had no cadre army that would attack the villagers for months and years. It was a fight between the villagers and the administration. In Bengal, it was basically people of Nandigram versus the CPI(M) party machinery assisted by the police. Had there been no significant role of the party organization, the damage would have been much less, simply because people's sympathy for the resistance movement would not have grown like wildfire. In fact, the movement would have died down much earlier.

So, from every conceivable aspect, the Stalinist organization of the CPI(M) and its Goebbelsian lie-campaign does not help the party. On 15 June 2009, something happened in Lalgarh and most papers carried a report the next day. A double-storey white house was razed to ground by the people's committee that was protesting the atrocities of the police force and the CPI(M) people. Newspapers had it that the house stood earlier as a symbol of opulence in an area poverty. That house belonged to Anuj Pandey, the zonal committee secretary of the CPI(M). That means he is a block level top leader of the party. Though the papers wrote that the house belonged to him, I doubt it. It must belong to his brother, or cousin, or if he is an aged man, to his son. That is the tactic of the CPI(M) cadre force. A few days later a joint operation of the state police and paramilitary force began in the area to finish off the resistance, which was gradually slipping down to the hands of the Maoists. The Centre asked the state to start developmental efforts in that area. Though the joint operation has not achieved much in last five months, it may ultimately crush the Maoists and re-install Anuj Pandey and his cadre force ousted by people's committee. But will that really help the CPI(M)?

We may reach the conclusion that if the CPI(M) can rid itself of the likes of Anuj Pandeys and the cadre force, if it can dismantle its Stalinist organization and turns into a true mass party, it may survive as a democratic party. But the Stalinist mindset is too deep-rooted in them. Let us now see how it diminished the image of Prakash Karat.

The Organization diminished Karat too.

The CPI(M) has lost much of its ground today because of its organization: its excesses, its involvement in corruption, and most of all, its interference in the socio-economic life of the people. It has not created any better culture, but has created a lot of clutter around it. This type of organization is dangerous for a democratic society, and for any party operating in democracy without any ulterior motive of upturning it.

The Stalinist organization has not only done in the party in Bengal (while doing so in Kerala), it also diminished the image of Karat in public eyes. The organization in Kerala is in the hands of the anti-Congress neoliberals, many of who are not known by the people for their probity in public life.

But, as Vijayan had taken command of the whole party in Kerala, the national party was being compelled to protect a leader who was accused in a corruption case. This had stripped the party of all its claims to probity in public life, and had brought it down to the level of all other parties. According to newspaper reports, after the election, Prakash Karat placed a proposal before the politburo seeking removal of Achuthanandan from all positions while retaining Viajayan.[6] It was also reported that the proposal met stiff resistance from Manik Sarkir (the CM of Tripura), MK Pandhe and Sitaram Yechury. One newspaper said Brinda Karat, who is the most prominent woman leader (and happens to be Prakash Karat's wife), also opposed this. Prakash Karat took this position to have Vijayan with him, and thus proved moral values are less important to him than his organization. It shows how a Stalinist organization gobbles down the upright comrades and best values.

In simpler terms, Karat had thrown away his image of a man who has faith in probity in public life to win over the Kerala party organization. Why has he done so? He knows the majority of Bengal unit is against him for pursuing an anti-US policy and withdrawing support from the government. So he needs Kerala with him to overrule West Bengal in the future. Thus the organizational structure and its compulsions converted an ideologue with high moral positions to someone as cheap as any other politician.

Years ago, Sundarayya, the first general secretary of the CPI(M), relinquished his post as he felt the party was putting too much stress on electoral politics, was turning into a mass party, and was neglecting the essential organizational preparation for a future revolution. He thought the party should guide the mass towards revolution while retaining the character of a 'proletarian' party. In those days, communists spent their time in meaningless debates over whether the factory workers are the only revolutionary class or even the agricultural worker can play a revolutionary role. Just 20 years ago they failed to realize that the units where they were building their revolutionary brigades would put its workers at such a comfort level that they would rather turn to the BJP. Sundarayya raised his issues in the 1970s, and by the 1990s organized sector workers turned towards the Right. Whatever, Sundarayya was trying to turn the tide against time. Once more, Karat is trying to do that by making the party organization supreme.

In a democracy, the party organization is subservient to people's will. The Stalinist party organization has no *locus standi*. It is a dangerous body that turns into be-all and end-all. It reflects the totalitarian mindset of Stalinist communists. The party organization cannot claim any legitimate place in public life, except for campaigning for the party candidates and propagating the party view or building public opinion. It is a devilish idea that the party will perform parallel governance and will control the socio-economic-political system. That is anathema to civil liberty. The way it has been built in Bengal and Kerala, the way Karat loves to see it, is anti-democratic. Its activity is not much different from that of the Maoists' organization.

Definitely, Karat is the most controversial character in Indian politics. Earlier, I have projected him as the man who could revive the CPI(M) and could bring it back to the path of socialism. Not Marxian socialism, but to Leftism. Though many people believe that Karat was hand in glove with neoliberals of the party, I argued why I would give him benefit of doubt. But here I must say that he has inherent tendencies of becoming a party bureaucrat. He has never won, and cannot win any election even if he wishes to fight one, unless Kerala party makes arrangement for him to win (even that is a distant dream now). Great leaders of his party—EMS Namboodiripad and Jyoti Basu—were legitimate popular leaders. Karat has no legitimacy in that sense. Neither Surjeet had. People who cannot win a popular election are not leaders.

There is no other party where the top leaders of the party cannot win election and prefers to be the boss by taking shelter under the party organization. Manmohan Singh is not a leader of a party. He is a chosen executive head. His second term gave him indirect legitimacy as people had voted (though roughly only one person in every three) for the UPA knowing well that Singh would lead it. In fact, it was Sonia Gandhi who lent him this legitimacy by announcing before the poll that he was the party's Prime Ministerial candidate. In a democracy, popular leaders are supreme and legitimate representatives of the people. Only they have the right to decide the fate of the people.

Karat had the chance to hit the organization and weaken it, so that a section of people cannot take control of the party from the states. If the dependence on the apparatchik—who has no concern for the ideology or the ideal—cannot be diminished, the party will not have a bright future in a democratic set-up. This is the sphere where one has to change with time and maturity of Indian democracy. Karat could risk going against Vijayan on the point of probity: that could have made him a tall leader in Kerala. But, being in charge of the organization for more than a decade, he suffers from a psychological disorder concerning the supremacy of the organization. He feels the organization is important to carry on propaganda and get the required feedback from the lowest level. Neither of the two purposes will be served by the organization. Karat has failed to understand that and has diminished his image by standing with Vijayan on Lavalin case. He did so, because he is not a popular leader. He got scared as Sitaram and Bengal conspired against him. He cannot appeal to the people directly. So, the only way out for him is to survive through the organization. That prodded him to sacrifice his image of probity. It is not known whether Vijayan is guilty on that particular Lavalin case: probity demands he should step down from the public life till he is cleared of the charges.

Karat had earned his post as the best deserving candidate. But the organizational principles that he and his predecessors used to earn the top posts have become obsolete in a modern democratic country. If Karat wishes to be a leader, if he has any ambition of deciding the fate of the country, he must contest elections and lead the party from the front. A back seat driver like the Sarsangchalak (of the RSS) for the BJP, and party bureaucrats of the CPI(M) are the same.

But the indications are, Karat has no courage to lead the party from the front. That is why he will always put stress on the organization, a Stalinist and anti-democratic totalitarian organization.

However, if things do not change, this organization may spell doom for the party.

References

1 See on net the article titled 'Wake Up call' that appeared in the *Frontline*, 7–20 June 2008.

2 He was addressing a Press conference on International Meeting of the Communists and Worker's Parties in Delhi.

3 The buildings of the party and the CITU and various bodies affiliated to it, spread all over Bengal, are worth thousands of crore rupees. Some people believe it is worth tens of thousands of crore rupees. But it cannot be accounted, as mostly these are in name of various trusts controlled by the CPI(M), or are just under illegal occupation.

4 A section of the Congress was nicknamed *tarmuj* (watermelon), a fruit which has a green skin, but is red inside.

5 The *Wikipedia* article on Goebbels says, he used modern propaganda techniques to psychologically prepare the German people for aggressive war and the annihilation of civilian populations. Among other propaganda devices, he accused many of Germany's ethnic and national minorities (such as the Poles, the Jews, the French) of trying to destroy Germany, claiming that Germany's belligerent actions were taken in self-defence.

6 The *Indian Express*, 6 July 2009.

Ten

Total Lack of Political Direction

THOUGH WE have discussed the burden of organization in details, it is unlikely that the CPI(M) will get out of this in near future.

Leaving that, a debate is also necessary to fix a definite programme and political direction of the party. Before the naked eyes, the Left stands as the most opportunist political force. The Congress does not go with the BJP. The BJP does not go with the Congress. But the Left has gone with both these parties. In 1967, it supported those state governments where Jan Sangh was in the ministry. In 1969, it tacitly stood behind Indira Gandhi. A few years later, the CPI went away with the Congress. But the CPI(M) remained anti-Congress and in 1977 supported Janata Party government despite the fact that Jan Sangh was one of the constituent of the party. Again in 1989, both the CPI and the CPI(M) supported VP Singh whose government was entirely dependent on the BJP. In 1996, the whole Left supported the United Front government supported by and dependent on the Congress. In 2004, they directly supported a Congress government.

This lack of political direction is rooted in lack of a strong political base. It is true that despite having no political rivalry with the BJP on the ground (they have exclusive geographical regions under their sway), in last 15 years the Left has steadfastly opposed the BJP on ideological ground. But, there is no guarantee that it will not go close to any outfit that may come out of the BJP with certain moderate agenda. A conflict of interest on the ground is a guarantee against this. Prakash Karat could not have succeeded to take the party out of the Congress orbit only because the party has conflict of interest with the Congress in Kerala and in Tripura. When Yechury planned a rebellion against Karat just after the election results were out, he could not garner support from Tripura (Kerala he did not even try) for the same reason.

But there is only an outside chance that the CPI(M) or the Left will grow, in next two decades, in states apart from the three where it has a foothold till now. The question is, how can the CPI(M) have a definite political direction.

Despite their claim of faith in communism or change of the system, no one believes that the mainstream Leftists are really committed to such things. Everybody knows those words are simple eyewash to mislead people. People do not expect it from them. But, people who knew about them believed for long years that the Left would fight for socio-economic changes. Simply put, they believed the communists would try to eliminate poverty in real terms; they believed the communists would fight to end exploitation by raising and ensuring minimum wages; they believed the communists would ensure dignity of the people who were backward in every sense of the term. But, the experience of Bengal shows that the communist of today can throw all these in the air and follow a pure neoliberal policy. Karat's argument that a state has to follow a central policy is childish, for no other state killed and tortured its farmers for months, often using the police and often using the party machinery, as the CPI(M) did in Bengal. As a consequence, the CPI(M) now stands the risk of being marginalized in Indian politics.

Unless the party can find a real agenda for socio-economic changes and implement that when in power, it will never become a meaningful force in Indian polity. It may rule a state, a Central Government dependent on it may spring up occasionally, but many other parties have such credits in their accounts. That is not meaningful existence. But then, even the Congress Party is trying to follow a path that may, over a period, if pursued sincerely by Sonia Gandhi or her son, bring in certain socio-economic changes. So this cannot be the sole agenda for a Leftist force.

What the Congress will not do, the Leftists should do. The Congress will not fight the humongous extent of corruption in the country. Now, it is no more black money that denotes this corruption. Individuals are now earning hundreds and thousands crore of rupees of white money through corrupt practices. A policeman taking bribe from a lorry driver is just a drop in the sea. Corruption, huge corruption, in high places involving hundreds and thousand crore of rupees, is the biggest threat before Indian democracy. A Leftist party should come out to fight this. Till now, the record of the Left in India is abysmal in this regard. When Jayalalitha, then involved in corruption charges, came out of the BJP alliance in 1999, HS Surjeet was gaga about it. In fact, he was instrumental in Jayalalitha's switching sides. When I asked him how he could go along with a person allegedly involved in corruption, he said the main task before him was to defeat the communal forces. 'Corruption can be fought later', he told me categorically. This attitude besmirched the Left's credibility. And now, Karat's strong defence of Vijayan has put the last nail in the Left's coffin. Whether the Left would go for burial, or will emerge out of the coffin again, depends entirely on their credibility in the eyes of the people. Unless they launch real fight against corruption, people will never believe that they are different. If they are not different, they are just an 'also ran' force.

Again, the Left forces all over the world are against American hegemony, both economic and political. Now, even from within American mainstream, voices have been raised against their hegemony-centric attitude. American President Barack Obama himself has described the Iraq War as an unjust one. All over the world sane people have opposed such hegemony of the US and have tried to keep their countries free from the corrupting influence of the US administration as far as possible.

The Leftists have tried, in different countries, to curb the US economic designs from unfolding in their countries. It is true that no country in the world can do without interacting with the US, for it is the heaven for technology, science and knowledge, and also of internal democracy. Despite many shortcomings of its democratic institutions, it has the maximum ability to resolve internal contradictions and conflicts through interactions, sensitiveness and dialogue. But that does not mean a country should capitulate before continuous efforts for aggrandizement of the US ruling elite.

It is rather strange that the CPI(M), along with the other Left parties, supported a government led by a pro-America Prime Minister. It is stranger that a section from within the party dissented when the CPI(M) decided to withdraw support on the question of succumbing to the US pressure (I strongly believe that this gamut of relationship was the main cause of their irritation, though Karat and company's immature politics failed to bring the whole before the people and highlighted the single issue of Nuke Deal).

Till now, the Bengal party believes that withdrawal of support was suicidal. They would have preferred to live with a pro-US government. One of the state secretariat member, late Subhas Chakrabarty (who was a very popular man and reflected the mood of the common party workers to a large extent) even said that 'if one wishes to fight imperialism in Indian context, one should join hands with the Congress party'. If anyone gets opportunity to talk to different CPI(M) leaders privately, one is sure to find many such absurd and even bizarre theorization doing the rounds among them. Abdullah Kutty of Kerala discovered merit in Narendra Modi's governance, but Kerala unit quickly expelled him. According to insiders, Bhattacharya too is an admirer of Modi though he has never stated that publicly.

Such ideological bankruptcy is the end of the road for any organized force, and is the root cause of rejection of the communists all over the world. So, if the CPI(M) and the Left cannot decide unanimously. their attitude towards the designs of the US elite, both governments and capitalists, it is sure to lose all claims to Leftism.

Again, trying to implement in India what one has learnt from the history of distant countries, equating the BJP with the Nazis, copying concepts of Russian or Chinese 'front' politics, or following other parties of Europe or Latin America will do them no good.

Earlier, we have seen how the debate on relationship with the Congress had besmirched the communist movement for all the decades of its existence. The CPI(M), however was rather free from it. Despite a short stint of hobnob with Indira Gandhi after she suddenly went for bank nationalization in 1969, the Marxists remained anti-Congress at core. This helped them, to a large extent, to be seen as a small but a potential alternative player in national politics. It gave them status. Whenever a regional party rose in any state breaking the monopoly of the Congress party, it looked towards the Left. The only exception was the Shiv Sena with a strong Hindu ideology.[1] In the 1980s, when Jyoti Basu created quite a flutter in national politics by demanding more power to the states, almost all the regional parties joined him. Even Akali Dal, a religion-based party, was with them. These regional parties later sided with VP Singh who dubbed the Left as his 'natural ally'. Everything went right till 1998. The CPI(M) was at the centre of a so-called Third Front. In reality, there was no Third Front till the 1980s. It was the 'Second Front' which used to dethrone the Congress either from the states or from the union level once in every 10 years—1967, 1977, 1989, 1996. On first three occasions the Left joined hands, either directly or indirectly, with the Jan Sangh and its later avatar the BJP to put the second front at the South Bloc. Things changed in the 1990s when the BJP rose to a new high and started a vigorous communal Hindutwa movement that ultimately demolished the Babri mosque. It was a savage act and the popularity of its leader was a threat to liberal democracy. But, the CPI(M) lost faith in the people of the country too early. Whatever, the erstwhile 'Second Front' turned into a sort of Third Front in 1996, a crippled Third Front that took support from the Congress. It did not work, thanks to the Congress. Then the BJP came into power and the communists shrunk in fear.

No other anti-BJP party lost nerve. Sonia Gandhi, the number one target of the BJP remained calm. She even lent support to the BJP government when it brought legislation on certain subjects initiated in the previous regimes. But this cooperation stopped after the Congress gave its nod to the Insurance Regulatory Bill. In March 2000, after almost two years of the BJP-led NDA rule, everything changed. First Narasimha Rao, the real architect of liberalization in India, himself raised questions about the way India was liberalizing, and then Sonia Gandhi initiated the shift in the Congress line, making it pro-poor and giving the hue of a Centrist party.[2]

Sonia initiated the process from a speech she delivered in a rally organized in Ramlila ground of Delhi, and then the Congress attitude in the Parliament on disinvestment and certain measures on the WTO underwent sudden change. Sonia explained to her party that she had extended support only for those legislations that the Congress was committed to from a prior date, and that period was over. So, now it was time for repeat of *'garibi hatao'* (eradicate poverty) plank of her mother-in-law. The Leftists within the Congress were happy. And the CPI(M) was impressed. HS Surjeet and Jyoti Basu saw a new Congress that could be befriended. By then, the party had changed its old and consistent position of equal distance from both the Congress (which it felt the main representative of the ultra-rich of the country) and the BJP (which it felt was both pro-rich and communal): they had identified the BJP as the main enemy. This theoretical shift gave them further impetus to embrace the Congress.

Here, they became victims of self-delusion for the second time.

Why? First, they did not have actual strength on the ground to take advantage of the situation. Like PC Joshi, they were dreaming of riding a wild elephant and controlling it. The Congress is not a tamed elephant for them. It is a wild one which will not waste a moment to trample them under its feet. Or, more dangerous for them, the Congress may beat them with a hard stick whenever necessary, and provide them a carrot when it becomes necessary. The situation would have been different if they had real strength on the ground to bring a hundred MPs from five-six-seven states, either as an individual party or as a cohesive unbreakable front.

Secondly, they were actually playing in the hands of the Congress while imagining that they were influencing the Congress. Whatever real success they had (like stalling disinvestment) only added to the bitterness. The other things that the government did and the Left tried to take credit of, like hundred days' Employment Guarantee Bill[3] were actually Sonia Gandhi's plans. These would have been implemented anyway, with or without the Left. This is simple. The Left is not with Sheila Dixit's Delhi state government, and yet she provided houses to many poor of the national capital and earned their votes to become chief minister for the third time in a row. Similarly, the Union Government will go on doing things that will earn them poor men's sympathy. That will not stop them either from taking measures to help the rich to become richer, by hook or by crook. One day it will be SEZ, robbing millions of their land, hearth and home; the other day it will be NREGA, providing millions their sustenance.

Third Front is the only alternative.

Thus, it was a repeat history in 2004, and so it ended in a farce for the CPI(M). Repeat, because the CPI had earlier gone through this experiment and lost everything it had. Thus, it was pure self-delusion on the part of the Left. But at what cost?

The CPI(M) lost its high seat in the polity. It was a party that had the potential to change the nature of the polity by rallying various parties against the major player of the day. For first 27 years, its main target was the Congress, the then biggest player. Then it started shifting its position. Still it was at the centre of all anti-Congress anti-BJP parties. Its own record in opposing both these parties was impeccable. It played the unofficial role of the convenor of the Third Front. But when the BJP came to power, the CPI(M) increasingly played a role of a junior partner of the Congress. It was working for strengthening the Congress. After years of efforts to weaken the Congress, there was a sudden break. In 2004, it could have aligned with Samajwadi Party and together they could have extended issue-based support to the Congress. But it ditched the Samajwadi Party, abdicated its age-old role of leading the Third Bloc and accepted an insignificant position by joining hands with the Congress. Ironically, when it tried to wrest its lost prestige, Samajwadi Party ditched it and went with the Congress to save the day for the government.

Now, the CPI(M) and the Left is alone and irrelevant. No party trusts it anymore. The credibility they earned through decades of efforts of the earlier generations stands badly mauled.

Seen from the total perspective of Indian polity, the Left can keep itself afloat only when it leads a Front that fights both the major parties of the day. If it goes with the Congress, it becomes just one of the many junior partners of the major party. When PC Joshi stressed on the need of helping the progressive section of the Congress, then there was at least real theoretical possibility of steering the polity towards a desired direction. When both the Communist parties supported Indira Gandhi, they could at least get the satisfaction of steering the country close towards the Soviet bloc. Indira Gandhi did it in her own interest, yet that suited the communists. But, when they repeated the experiment in 1991, the Congress was taking a definite Rightward turn. Maybe that Rightward turn was the only option of the day, maybe the selfish interest of a few also played its game; maybe, it was both. But there was everybody to praise it, and a Left force was not needed to join that chorus. People look at the Leftists only to hear their dissenting voice so that they could judge whether they themselves can weigh the actions of the government. Otherwise, who is interested to hear what Laloo Prasad says, or what Mulayam Singh says? The latter met APJ Abdul Kalam to have his opinion on the Nuke Deal and then announced (only to extend support to the Congress) that it was good for the country. What could be more ridiculous? If Left loses its dissenting voice, it will have no difference with Laloo Prasad's or Mulayam Singh's parties.

The government the Left supported directly in 2004 had at least three men (Prime Minister Manmohan Singh, Home Minister P Chidambaram and Deputy Chairman of Planning Commission MS Ahluwalia) at the top who believed India should always stay close by the US. So, the government was essentially pro-US and thereby opposed to the Leftist worldview (that essentially stipulates end of hegemony or domination, both political and economic). Thus, supporting this government was riddled with essential contradictions and the CPI(M) lost its way, gradually shifting to the Rightist orbit. It had to be so, as it was the only possibility.[4] The other possibility that some of the Left leaders dreamed of, that they would be able to drag the Congress to somewhat Leftist path, was a figment of their imagination. The Congress took that much pro-poor measures that it needed to strengthen its base in a democracy where vast majority is poor. The Congress will take such measures in this term also when no Leftist is around.

The CPI(M) sought the best of both the worlds. Some of its leaders felt that the party would be able to retain its character of being the rallying point of the 'third alternative' while having influence on the Congress-led government. But, ultimately it lost both the worlds. Its adventurism put paid to all its political ambition. And the party is still divided on whether the third alternative is its only recourse. A section of the party loves the Congress, loves to busk in the reflected glory, loves to even join a Congress government and assimilate all the advantages of being in power. For them, like all other parties, joining a government is be-all and end-all. For them, even Leftism is a burden.

The CPI(M) has not only lost its old status, its internal squabbling has come in the open badly. All the journalists who cover the Left know about the bitter relation between Karat and Yechury. After the electoral debacle, Buddhadeb Bhattacharya skipped one after another politburo meeting, sending signal that he did not care for the central party. The CPI(M) is now a badly divided house bereft of its halo. Precisely for these reasons, no party any longer will admit the natural leadership of the CPI(M) in forging a Third Front. Mulayam Singh Yadav and Laloo Prasad had in the past also defied the writs of the communists. Then a section of the 'Third' parties joined the BJP government. While the CPI(M) tried to wean them away and succeeded in case of two important parties (the Telugu Desam Party of Andhra Pradesh and the Biju Janata Dal of Orissa) in recent times, its *locus standi* has taken a severe beating. With its house divided, it will not be easy for them to regain the old position even in the long run. Their words do not carry any weight any more. The mad effort of Prakash Karat to bring down the government after withdrawal of support has further exposed their weakness.

It is unfortunate that this has happened when the political reality of the country is offering another great chance to the Left to rise high. The BJP is on the wane. That party is likely to be further weakened. Hindutwa as an ideology may turn a burden for them. The party may split and the larger section may turn up with a new face: a Rightist party (as its president Rajnath Singh has described it recently) without Hindu chauvinism at its core. If it happens, that new avatar will be best suited to be an important junior partner of the Congress. It may suit the Congress as well, because together they may garner majority in the Parliament. That means, for the Congress, the end of dependence on smaller parties. That means no role for the Left. That means no hindrance in the path of following neoliberal policies that are close to the heart of the Congress leaders. And that also means a large vacuum in the opposition space.

Even otherwise, this space is being created with the weakening of the BJP. If the progressive forces fail to occupy it, naturally it will go either to the ultra-Right (as it is happening in Maharashtra), or to ultra-Left (the Maoists).

For decades, the CPI(M) leaders tried to forge a Third Front to occupy this space. The space was not open then. Interestingly, this time a vacuum is being created not for the third alternative, but for the only alternative. Weakening of the BJP has presented the CPI(M) and other regional outfits with a golden opportunity. But the Left will not be able to take advantage of it unless it takes an oath of equal distance from both the Congress and the BJP.

We may give them the benefit of the doubt for all their fears and capitulations during the BJP's heydays. But, apart from the changed political scenario, Karat's own analysis, if extended logically, calls for shift in party's stand now. When Surjeet (then general secretary) advocated a line of equal distance in the Chandigarh Party congress (1995), the majority led by Karat rejected it. Even before that he had found the traits of the BJP correctly[5].

Communalism is of course a danger before the country: but equating the BJP with communalism is overestimation of the Rightist party.

And, for a real Left party, there can be no alternative to charting out a third course, of being distant from both the main parties, the Congress and the BJP. Both those parties are neoliberal and both of them play the communal card. The Congress tries to play it softly. It wants to appease both the communities. The BJP is more communal and mostly try to get the support of the Hindu majority.

But, even if we suppose that the CPI(M) once again decides to have equal distance with both the major parties of the day, the question remains whether people will endorse it. Here people do not mean the people of West Bengal and Kerala or Tripura. The question is whether the people of the country will see the 'third' force as an alternative?

The Left cannot enthuse the people with an alternative programme for its own house is so badly divided, for its own record is so slippery. No one knows when it will be in which camp. It cannot even decide what should be its alternative programme. It has no fixed position. We know what the Congress stands for. We do not know what the present Left stands for. We do not even know whether it stands for forcible eviction of farmers from their land, or it stands for the rights of the farmers and all other poor and vulnerable sections.

In short, what they had earned in 50 years, they have squandered in five years. Their credibility is almost nil in the eyes of the people. For next many years, they will have to rebuild them if they want to occupy the opposition space along with other regional outfits. There is only an outside chance of their being able to do so.

The world has changed. Forcible eviction of the tillers, herdsmen or villagers from their land has given birth to the Maoists in remote regions of the country. This armed movement feeds on every economic and social injustice, and the establishment will not succeed to exterminate it till justice—social economic and legal—reaches every home. The need of the time has provided an excellent opportunity to the real and democratic Left forces.

But it is hard to imagine, post-Nandigram, that the CPI(M) will ever be able to fit in that category again. Its love for the Congress since the beginning of communist movement is finally gobbling it down. And, it still looks like unaware of the self-help movements, unaware of various NGOs working honestly on the ground (like Aruna Roy's organization), and importance of people like Medha Patkar who has contributed a lot in harnessing weaker people's consciousness. They not only arrested Medha when she went to Bengal to protest Nandigram and Singur, like the BJP they started slander campaign again her.

Curiously, the CPI(M) has started talking of a 'third alternative' in recent years. The third alternative, they argue, will emerge out of pro-people struggles on the ground. This sounds great. A real Left can emerge only in this way. But, who are the parties whom the Left hopes to get along with it in this movement? I do not know of any such party. In fact, despite the CPI(M)'s heavy influence, the two United Front governments (1996–1998) went ahead to continue the neoliberal policies. It was one of the reasons that frustrated a section of the party and gave them opportunity to speak in favour of aligning with the Congress. So, as an afterthought, it seems this the concept of 'third alternative' is just a means to put off the politics of Third Front, or maybe an effort to give it a decent burial. Interestingly, this concept was proposed by Surjeet and was always eagerly supported by leaders like Yechury or Bhattacharya. According to insiders, when it was deliberated upon in Delhi congress in 2005, Karat tried his best to scuttle this move. In fact, the highlight of that Party congress in Delhi that was held just a year after extending direct support to a Congress-led government was the party's stand on the Third Front and an economic document that spoke of making compromises with globalization. Karat fought and retained the political ground, but lost on economic front. The party did not discard the 'Third Front', though it decided to strive for building up an absurd 'third alternative'.

A third alternative, in the real sense, is only the Left parties, but without Yechury–Bhattacharya group. You decide whether it is absurd or not.

That is why taking recourse to Third Front politics is the only road ahead for any Left force in India. There will be neoliberal parties of smaller strength in it, and that will give the CPI(M) more scope to put forward its own policies.

To grab the opportunities the future still offer it, the CPI(M) will have to go for an overhaul. Its survival probably depends on several factors, like whether it will stop doublespeak, whether it will discard its Stalinist organization and build up a democratic organization, whether it will be able to find an identity for itself so that people will know it stands for what, and whether it will stop switching sides that branded it among the people as opportunists.

References

1 In fact, the Shiv Sena made its base among the workers by weaning them away from the communists. So they had a conflict of political interest on the ground.

2 Almost all the papers and magazines reported the shift. One such report available on net is in the *Outlook* issue dated 27 March: '*Garibi Hatao* Back'.

3 Now known as National Rural Employment Guarantee Act (NREGA).

4 From my personal experience of interactions with Prakash Karat, I feel he had no illusion that his party would not be able to influence the government. That was why he settled for the minimum on economic questions.

5 See his writing on this in the *Annexure* part.

Eleven

Will the Left Survive?

THE PRESENT decides the future. What lies ahead for the CPI(M) can be answered from its present condition. And for the genesis of the crisis it is facing now, one has to look back to the past.

Keeping the question 'what lies in future' in mind, here we shall recapitulate, very briefly, the relevant portion of the CPI(M) or the Left's past.

Long years ago, in pre-Independence days, the communists started their journey. In those days, they had to work under instructions coming from their foreign bosses who had little knowledge about India, and this compromised the communist's credibility severely. In this period, some non-communist Left forces also came up [like Subhash Bose's Forward Bloc, or a Trotskyite force, the Revolutionary Socialist Party (RSP)], but they failed to get a foothold in national politics. The communists, however, despite their juvenile vacillations and strange mistakes, became a force to reckon with. This was primarily due to their dedication to the cause of the poor and unprivileged people, and the sacrifice they made in everyday life or in laying down their lives.

Yet, the differences in international communism led to a split in the Communist Party in 1964. There were also some other factors in it: relation with the Congress, personality clashes, and overall approach towards Indian democracy. The pro-Russian group retained the name CPI, but its proximity to the Congress had it face its Waterloo: within 10–15 years of the split, the CPI lost its relevance in Indian polity. It never regained it, and if still it gets any importance in national politics that is mainly due to the presence of its veteran leader AB Bardhan. The only other nationally-known leader of the party is Gurudas Dasgupta.

But, after the split, the CPI(M) emerged with a different image: it was seen as a revolutionary, pro-poor and anti-rich force that could change the system. This image kept it alive and kicking.

The split, however, shrunk the communist base severely. The CPI(M) survived in West Bengal, Kerala and Tripura. From the time of the CPI, occasionally the communists came to power in Kerala and in Bengal, but its governments were regularly dismissed. The tradition continued in the 1960s also. Then in 1977, it came to power in Bengal all on a sudden. Its leaders were not prepared for this, and were ready to concede even 55 per cent assembly seats to the Janata Party. Due to obstinacy of Prafulla Sen to have more, the understanding broke down and the Left (without the CPI) swept the poll. The leaders still thought that the government would be dismissed as soon as the friendly government of the Janata Party would be out of power. That was why the Bengal leaders were too eager to make compromises to keep Morarji Desai government at saddle. But the national party overruled the Bengal leaders (just like in 2008) even in 1979. In 1980, the Congress came back in Delhi, and the CPI(M) took it as a foregone conclusion that its government was going to be dismissed.

But that did not happen. Year 1982 saw the Left's return to power in Bengal with a thumping majority (of both seats and votes). More than half of the people supported them. The Left Front government had by then started implementing land reforms, which was an administrative and legal step, and worked for empowerment of the people which was a political step. To consolidate this, Panchayat elections were held and that created a new enthusiasm among the people. They sought to give people relief, for they did not believe they will be allowed to rule for long years, and took remarkable steps for the poorer and unprivileged or underprivileged segments of population. They were unpopular in big cities and massively popular in rural area.

But, no one came forward to dismiss their government.

That was the time when socialism was still an alternative to capitalism, and continuous lie-campaign of the USSR and China had it believable that socialism would triumph over capitalism. The CPI(M) too believed in it. They were pro-China, but China ditched them and supported the Naxalites who sprang up from within them in the late 1960s. The Chinese party condemned the CPI(M) as a revisionary force. This made them more neutral as far as the international communist divisions were concerned, and also made them independent of foreign influence. But, they were to find out ways to rule a state satisfactorily while waiting for the final triumph of socialism in India and all over the world. Meanwhile, they came to power in Kerala also in the 1980s, and the same problem arose there too.

By then, Sundarayya (the first general secretary) had left the party headquarters after being fed up with his party's obsession with elections and electoral politics. He felt the party was ignoring its organizational built up for revolution. With him the overzealous revolutionaries were out of party's leadership. Now, general secretary was EMS Namboodiripad, who was more in the mould of a confirmed Leftist and a firm believer in democratic socialism.

By then, obsessed with its organizational capacity and invincibility of its ideology, the Left had lost opportunities to align with other socialist forces to make a dent in the national sphere by their own right. They dreamed of a day when they will be a major player in India, and were satisfied with their ability to intervene in the system politically. But the time was changing, and the new reality started sinking in with an awful finality in them. Politically, they started aligning with other forces like the Telugu Desam Party or the Janata Dal. On the economic front, they stated realizing the role of private capitalists in pre-socialist stage.

At this juncture, it was Jyoti Basu who came up with his pragmatic line. He advocated promotion of joint sector in Bengal and the party accepted it after a debate. It was a major shift as it marked acceptance of private capital by the CPI(M). Basu's proposition was supported by Randive, the man who just after Independence made a futile attempt for armed revolution. Soon thereafter, the communist world crumbled before their amazed eyes, and capitalism hit back with vengeance. It was now the age of neoliberalism: a time for liberalization. Even China had given up socialism, and while trying to camouflage its acts was actually following the capitalist path.

Then, after 15 years of great political success, the first chinks started appearing in Bengal. Stagnation was setting in: neither any new political initiative could be thought of to renew people's faith in the Left, nor any new economic agenda could be conceived of. It was frustrating for the whole party. The main question was how to get out of the stagnation. The communists failed to think of newer ways to augment the success it had already achieved. In this scenario, Basu prepared his document for industrial development in Bengal. In this document, placed in the state assembly as the industrial policy, he advocated and welcomed private investment in Bengal. Many of the central leaders, and the majority section led by Karat, could hardly consume this pragmatic step of the Bengal government. Kerala party supported Karat as it had not faced the problem so acutely, for there the Congress had ruled for more time than them, and private investment had enjoyed enough patronage.

The hardliners—majority comrades of Kerala and most of the other state units and the frontal organizations—retaliated in 1996, and denied Basu of premiership of the country. The clash between the two sections, liberals headed by Basu–Surjeet duo and hardliners led by Karat, was now in the open. Basu openly stated that the refusal was a historic blunder. A debate started within the party and demands for more modern outlook, both in organizational matters and in politics, came to the fore. It affected party's base in Bengal further. It became a divided house. It was Basu and Surjeet, minority group in the party, who still abided by the majority decision and saved the party from a split. Basu continued as chief minister and Surjeet as general secretary of the party.

But then Basu sought retirement due to age and his failing health and the party had to concede it. Bhattacharya became the Bengal CM. In Kerala, arose Pinarayi Vijayan. Gradually, neoliberal thoughts started to influence the party more vigorously. Old stalwarts were no more around to lead the party. Surjeet and Basu, the last of the old guards, raised the bogey of fighting communalism, and the exaggerated danger got acceptance in the minds of the middle class. Karat was compelled to toe the line. Finally in 2004, the party extended support to a Congress government. Then Surjeet became critically ill. Karat took over the reigns of the party. The neoliberal section of the party now started their offensive.

Only two leaders of the older generation, Achuthanandan and Pandhe, still sought to resist the onslaught of neoliberal thinking in the party. But Karat was on the defence, the day was carried by Bhattacharya and Yechury.

But then Bhattacharya–Yechury went too far. They rushed in where the hardcore Rightists feared to tread. This landed them in Nandigram. While the central party supported SEZ, national big players' entry in retail, and many such other steps of the neoliberal government at the Centre, Bhattacharya trampled the rights of the farmers in Bengal to provide all facilities to the industrial barons. Media hailed him as an avatar of Deng Xiao Ping, the establishment was too pleased, and nobody realized that what Bhattacharya and Yechury were doing were expressions of frustration. They had lost faith in the words written in the document of the party they belong to. That is no offence. But they wanted to follow their new faith while pledging their loyalty to the ideology of the party. That was a fraud on the people.

If politicians have the guts to play it straight, a clear picture arise before the people, and they can choose from the alternatives. Bhattacharya or Yechury did not have that courage to play it straight.

However, it is not only Yechury and Bhattacharya. It is the whole party that is party to this fraud. In the name of serving the people they made attempts to forcibly acquire their land. Ironically, what the CPI(M) did in Nandigram was far more Rightist than any of the Rightist forces of the present India. Forcible acquisition of land or firing upon the protesters was trademark of Indian Rightists. It was, but is no more. Thus, post-Nandigram, the whole party stands exposed. It is a particular mindset that allowed the whole thing there to drag for months and years. It is a Rightist mindset[1], it is a Stalinist mindset.

Meanwhile, in Kerala too, the neoliberal section has taken control of the party. But these neoliberals are different from Bhattacharya–Yechury in two respects. First, they are against the Congress; and second, they are not averse to people's movement against imperialism or MNCs. Kerala party has initiated militant movements in last two decades during which the Bengal party turned itself into 'establishment'. Kerala party has even organized protest against the MNCs or imperialism in this century. It means the spirit has not died in Kerala among the people. But the way the junior leaders of both the state and the central party heckled Achuthanandan has posed a serious question on the future of Leftism in Kerala.

A section of the party now advocates close relationship with the Congress. The present rulers at the Centre are opening the key sectors to the foreign investors and allowing a take-over of our economy by them. People may not understand its significance now. This insidious take-over may take a decade or even a few to have its effects felt in common people's lives. And the bogey of turning India almost overnight into a great economic power will bring in further disaster. This is a dream comparable to Hinduttwa of the BJP. Both work as addictions for sometime, and then start to kill.

It is a farce that instead of fighting this design tooth and nail, a section of the communists want to be a subsidiary ally of the Congress. Like those 'socialists' like Laloo Prasad or Mulayam Singh, these people are making a mockery of the word 'Left'.

This is the 'present' of the CPI(M). Ironically, it is the combination of partisan attitude and Stalinist mindset that is finally spelling the doom for the CPI(M).

The Stalinist organization tried to crush the seeds of rebellion everywhere. The process is still going on in Bengal, particularly in parts of West Midnapore, Burdwan and a few other districts. But this is only adding to the momentum of fall. Strangely, Bhattacharya probably knows that he is becoming more unpopular because of the organization,[2] but he is not capable of changing it.

It is virtually a split party. However, the CPI(M) stands vertically split at the moment.

On one side we have a broad group led by general secretary Prakash Karat, a motley conglomeration of anti-Congress and anti-US forces within the party. A section within this group (like Karat himself and the CITU or Kisan Sabha) is somewhat opposed to neoliberal ideas, but another section (mainly Kerala comrades) is open to it. Karat is compromising with the later, and to retain his majority in the party has become blind to corruption charges against Vijayan and his friends. While his attitude may cost the party dearly in popular elections, it will help him to keep his position intact inside the party. He is likely to have support of the majority of both Kerala unit and mass fronts, and the majority of smaller states including Tripura. That will ensure his smooth sailing in the next party congress to be held in 2011.

The other side compromises of Sitaram Yechury–Buddhadeb Bhattacharya duo. This group is eager to endorse the neoliberal agenda of the establishment with some corrections, and has no qualms about staying close to the Congress or turning the party a critical satellite of the Congress. They have the support of majority of West Bengal, Andhra Pradesh (Yechury's home state), and of Tamil Nadu. A section of delegates from frontal organizations may support them in the next party congress. Still, it is very difficult for them to garner majority support in case they go for unsettling Karat. At one point of time this group tried to stall Chittabrata Mazumdar's induction in the politburo, but failed.

Organizationally, they are on a sticky wicket. On economic issues, they still retain their ability to influence the party's policy as they did in the past few years. They were instrumental in bringing the party on a neoliberal track and had it support SEZ and many such other policies.

The clash between the two groups in future seems unavoidable.

As things stand now, the relation between the two groups is, least to say, bitter. The differences are political, organizational and personal. Karat wants to purge the party of the people whose lifestyle is not communistic! But he himself supports Vijayan. The opposite group is interested in purging Karat from the party headquarters, as was once done with BT Randive.

To delay the clash, both the groups have now signed an uneasy truce. For time being, they are busy showing the world that they are trying to find a cure-all for its recent miseries. They are trying to change the perception that their dingy is sinking. They have taken refuge under the age-old idea of the communists—purging the party of unwanted elements at the lower levels.

Anyhow, the idea of 'purification' that the party has come up with recently is of no consequence at all. The upper layer of the party is full of people for whom the party comes later and self-interest comes first. Twenty years ago, it was impossible to imagine of a leader of the CPI(M) who would not resign from any post, be of the Parliament or of the government, when the party desired so. Jyoti Basu could split the party and yet become the Prime Minister in 1996. This was seriously deliberated upon by the anti-Karat section of the party in those days. But for Basu, self came much later than the party. For the whole of his life, he remained a minority leader in the party, but never fell victim to personal aggrandizement. On almost every single issue, from making adjustments with the present world (like accepting parliamentary democracy as supreme or inviting private players for developing the economy) to changing attitude towards the Congress (supporting the Congress and taking support from it), the party has followed later what he proposed earlier. One may agree to his thesis, one may disagree, but undoubtedly he is the greatest character of

Indian communist movement. He sacrificed the most coveted chair of an Indian politician with calmness of a disciplined soldier.

But for the present 'leaders' of the CPI(M), the self comes first. They are not popular leaders. None of them, except, maybe, VS Achuthanandan.

While no pure 'purification' drive is possible in the party, the fact remains that Karat and company is 'unwanted element' for the other group, and for the official group the most unwanted elements are Yechury and Bhattacharya.

Had there been a situation in 2009 like the UPA coalition had fallen short of majority by the number that the Left could provide, these two groups would have clashed in May 2009 in a way dangerous for the unity of the party. Now, the Yechury–Bhattacharya group is busy mending matters with the Congress. Almost the whole of the party in Bengal believe in the mythical proposition that they would have not lost the election in Bengal had there been no alliance between the Congress and Mamata Banerjee's Trinamool Congress. So they will go whole hog to break this alliance before the assembly poll to be held in 2011. The Left has extended support to the Congress to keep the Trinamool Congress at bay in Siliguri corporation in north Bengal. After losing 2011 election (and it seems, as things stand now, a foregone conclusion), they may try this model for the whole of Bengal. If they manage to get enough seats to help the Congress cross halfway mark by extending support to it, they will eagerly do so. The Congress too may not be too unwilling.

If any such thing happens in the future, it will make the Yechury–Bhattacharya camp triumphant inside the party. It will make the split complete. There will be two CPI(M)s going to two opposite directions in Bengal and Kerala. They still may stay in one party (for the mother party has money and other resources); or they may openly split the party. But the gap between the two segments will become unbridgeable. Even if the situation in Bengal does not evolve in such a way, the clash on the question of proximity to the Congress will haunt the party for many more years.

Any of the alternative scenarios do not reflect a bright future for the Indian Left. It is the saddest part of the recent India's political history. An earlier generation considered as harbingers of change, the great communists whom everybody respected for their dedication, had finally left the party in the hands of those people who destroyed everything they achieved.

Nobody can anymore bet that the younger generation will again turn around and fight for change, fight for the underdogs. How will they, when among them there is no underdog, no leader at all from the weakest sections of the population?

In the past, the national party had always protected the interest of the Bengal party, particularly since 1977. Bengal was its body, while Leftism was its soul. But after 2011, Bengal party will lose that status. It will be free for all. The party may split, or it may decide to follow a certain course. That course may turn up to be Leftist one, may turn up to be a Rightist course, or simply one of compromise.

History may give them a second chance. But, India will definitely change: not only the snazzy India advertised by the elites in their speeches and glorified in the newspapers and magazines and televisions; but even the other India will emerge. History tells us that never ever, in any country, prosperity like New York and poverty like Sub-Saharan Africa could coexist, side by side, for long. In earlier times, it changed through bloody revolutions, and the Maoists are trying that old path. However, given the presence of a mighty army at the disposal of the state, there is little chance of success of such revolution in modern days. It can only lead to colossal bloodbath: it can only create and spread anarchy. The other option is coming up of a new democratic force, dedicated to the cause of the poor, prepared to sacrifice and even lay down their lives while functioning through democratic system.

Long years ago, Mahatma Gandhi shunned violence and adopted '*satyagraha*' to free India from the shackles of the British. He believed the inhuman inequality existing in the country will go after Independence. Six decades after Independence, we find it has only increased. But it will change. With no Mahatma around to launch another '*satyagraha*' to make it curtains to this unimaginable discrimination, it will change through the efforts of thousands of small men and women. The process has already begun in the vast fields, in the remote areas of the country, and it will not stop.

We do not know which force may come up to represent the irresistible urge of the deprived people to change their lives and their future. But the alternative to the Rightist forces would have to raise the issues of the poor. They will have to make a charter of demand which must say unambiguously that the first task of the state is to provide adequate and nutritious food, proper clothing, proper housing and sanitation, safe drinking water, quality medical facilities and social security (for those unable to work) for each and every citizen. This force should fight everyday for this demand, enthusing the people to come out and fight for this. They should take help from everybody who may join them on this issue. They should believe in people's power. This should be their primary agenda. Then they may make their secondary agenda which will include opposition to the US economic designs and all other things that the conventional Left raises. This secondary agenda can be made, or even implemented to some extent, by sitting in the party headquarters. But the primary agenda requires sharing the experiences of the poorer people, living with them and thereby knowing their lives. That will help develop a sense of the 'people's issues' in the minds of the leaders. Only such leaders, thus trained, can create a true Left force capable of launching a second struggle for Independence, this time for the unprivileged, deprived and neglected part of the population, in other words the majority of the population.

Long years ago, the communists were the people who sought to do it. But then they got confused midway. The whole world changed. The Soviet crumbled. The true stories of the heavens on earth were all in the open. The loss of millions of innocent lives was mourned. The communists stood alone, condemned. The Indian communists did not have the guts to charter a different path. Unfortunately for them, at this critical juncture they lost touch with the people. The changed economic reality of the world frustrated them so much that they overlooked the fight that had already begun against the new economic order. The glory of power (in West Bengal, in Kerala, and finally at Centre in an indirect way) blinded them so much that they even shunned their pro-poor stand. They lost their identity. They lost their credibility that was earned by sacrifice and hard work by the earlier generation despite their limitations and their following a flawed ideology.

The Left, now bereft of dedication and commitment, embraced neoliberalist ideas. With the people revolting against it, the Left's Stalinist organization tried best to silence them. People of West Bengal and Kerala knew the meaning of it, and that was why the reaction was so widespread, so deep when the nefarious designs of 'the party' peaked in Nandigram. There is little chance that the people will pardon their sin.

But, that may not be the end of the Left. Over the vast fields of India the new sun is shining. True that the elite are trying to divert attention from the real issues and are picking up only one or two: but they can thus mislead only a section of the urban people. They are all so very concerned about 26/11 that it rebounds everywhere: but they are so callously unconcerned about the unprecedented price rise that is killing people everyday, slowly but definitely. The elite believe only the Taj Hotel and their tiny elite world is India. I strongly believe that a day is not far off when the elite will compel the Congress and the BJP to come together to stifle the challenges from the non-conformists. Of course a bi-polar polity suited them best, for both the leaders (the Congress and the BJP) were their parties. But that did not work perfectly in 2004–08, and with weakening of the BJP a new strategy should evolve from their minds. However, the common man everywhere in this country has become more conscious, and thereby more eager to wage a war against discrimination and deprivation, against the elites who consider themselves the masters.

People in general, like those of Nandigram, are not prepared to be cheated and overrun by the masters yet again. They led their lives but did not yield. After Tebhaga and Telangana, a new chapter was written over the bloody fields of Nandigram. History was created yet another time. In earlier history, the communists stood against the oppressors. In recent history, people resisted the communist oppressors and won. Poor farmers fighting for their rights everywhere in India drew inspiration from Nandigram. The way people of Nandigram (and also of Jagatsinghpura in Orissa) fought and won, had also helped India to change. This is evident from the Union Government's decision to change the law that allowed political rulers to behave like British masters and usurp anyone's land to donate it to the industrialists with the hoax of 'public interest'.

India is changing and will change. The process has begun. It has begun with the midday meal scheme initiated by the Supreme Court, with 'Right to Information' thanks to Aruna Roy's movement, with proposed changes in land acquisition act and many such other small but significant steps. No political party has initiated the process. Better to say, all (I repeat, all) the political parties opposed these efforts, delayed it and still trying to rip off the efforts. Even some bureaucrats (hope you still remember TN Seshan as the election commissioner) have played their role as head of different institutions and have contributed significantly in this process.

In this whole context of changing India, the conventional communists cut the sorriest figure. They initiated this struggle decades ago. When this struggle is gaining significant momentum, they stand on the wrong side of the divide. Maybe, everything is not lost for all of them. A significant vacuum is being created in Indian polity due to the decline of the BJP. Maybe, a section of the CPI(M) and the present Left can still take initiative to transform themselves into a modern, democratic, progressive and truly Leftist force. They may come up to fill the vacuum of the Indian polity.

Or, maybe, they will not be able to utilize this last opportunity. It will be somebody else.

Long years ago they embarked a journey that is still remembered. History gave them a chance. After crossing many a stations and roadblocks, finally they have abandoned their wagon. From the heroes, they have turned into the villains in the eyes of those very people who were with them for such a long time. Maybe, it is the end of the traditional Left.

Maybe, for history seldom gives a second chance.

References

1 Here I must explain one thing. Throughout this book I have used the word Rightist in strictly economic sense. Those who kill people are not Rightists. People have been killed, in thousands and millions, by both the Rightists and the Leftists, by both Hitler and Stalin.

2 While this book was going through the final processing, the West Bengal CM said (on 28 October 2009) that the major problems in the Panchayats are corruption, nepotism and working in party's interest. He urged the Panchayats not to see the colour of the party while identifying the people living below the poverty line. Remember, these Panchayats are ground-level bastions of the CPI(M) organization.

Annexure I

The difference of perception

Bengal and central party's views on electoral debacle

I. The State Committee's view (Statement issued on 12 June)

SEE HOW the Bengal leaders reacted even when the immediate aftershock was already absorbed. Their Bengal committee met on 11–12 June 2009 to discuss the electoral debacle and at the end of the meeting they issued this statement. Relevant portions are quoted below.

> The 13th session of the West Bengal State Committee of the CPI(M) was held on 11–12 June 2009. The main agenda of this meeting was to discuss the results of the 15th Lok Sabha elections in West Bengal and the future tasks in the post election period.
>
> .... In the elections, the Left parties took the initiative to form an electoral understanding with non-Congress, non-BJP parties. However, the Third Front could not gain the confidence of the people. The attempt to unite all democratic and patriotic forces on the basis of an anti-imperialist ideological political stand in order to meet the electoral challenge, was not very successful. In

the absence of a credible alternative force to meet the challenges of communalism and terrorism, the people voted for the Congress for a stable government.

Some initiatives taken by the UPA government under the pressure of the Left also helped the Congress. All these factors affected West Bengal along with the other states in the country. In our state, all kinds of divisive anarchist forces along with the ultra-Left and ultra-Right reactionary forces forged an alliance under the leadership of the Trinamool Congress centering on the issues of Singur and Nandigram. The electoral alliance between the Congress and the Trinamool Congress provided further fillip to this:

...The state committee has opined that the party's organizational weaknesses have been reflected in the election results. Unprincipled activities, lack of mass contact and weaknesses in building up movements on a consistent basis, have all played their part in denting the support of the party among the people. The image of the party has been damaged. The state committee has called for serious initiatives to rectify the shortcomings. In spite of huge attacks against the party, we have secured the support of over 1 crore 85 lakh people in the state. 42 comrades have been martyred since the elections were announced. After the declaration of results these attacks have increased manifold. Through the process of self-introspection, there is an urgent need to strengthen the party and counter such attacks. The state committee also opined that some neglect and sluggishness have crept into the work related directly to the people, particularly to the interests of the poor and working masses. There are shortcomings in the functioning of the Government, Panchayats and municipalities with regard to maintaining proper class outlook.

...The state committee has said that the divisive forces are receiving support of the reactionaries both within the country and outside. There are attempts to create divisions within the poor people by raking up divisive issues. This divisive agenda needs to be resisted with a proper class perspective.

As far as the immediate tasks in the post election situation is concerned, the state committee has said that attempts are being made to mount large-scale attacks on the Party, the Left Front government and the people thereby creating an atmosphere of anarchy and terror in the state. The party has to resist this attack by forging even greater unity both at the political as well as organizational level.

The aim of the opposition is to create divisions within the democratic and working people. The task is to unite the people by breaking these divisions. The party has to reach the people as their true friend. The work for the poor and the working masses should be given more priority in the tasks of the party, mass organization and the administration. Immediate and bold steps should be taken to stop non-communist activities and behaviour at every level of the party.

.... State-wide movements will be organized on the issues of price rise, universal public distribution system, providing BPL card to all poor families, changing the centre defined BPL criteria, expedite the process of granting SC/ST certificates, expediting the programmes for minority welfare and implementation of the rural electrification programme.

Participating in the discussion, General Secretary Prakash Karat said that while the third front has not been acceptable to the people in this election, the necessity of creating a third alternative has not ended. Although the present situation is one of adversity, the Party and the Left will be able to overcome it.

II. The Central Committee statement

The following statement was issued on 21 June:

Election Review

The Central Committee conducted a comprehensive review of the results of the Lok Sabha election. It also made an in-depth study of the Party's performance.

Among the factors responsible for the success of the Congress is that it could utilise the people's concern for a stable secular government at the Centre. The rejection by the people of the BJP's divisive brand of communal politics and Hindutva benefited the Congress.

The support that the Left parties had extended to the UPA for four years also contributed to providing legitimacy and credibility to the Congress-led government. The UPA government had pursued neoliberal policies which have heightened inequalities and failed to tackle the agrarian crisis, price rise and unemployment. Despite this, some of the measures taken such as the NREGA, farmers loan waiver scheme, the Forest Tribal Rights Act and the increased minimum support price for food grains and other crops helped to mitigate some of the effects of these policies and had a positive impact. Some of these steps were adopted due to the Left's pressure.

The spate of terrorist violence culminating in the Mumbai terrorist attack in November 2008 heightened the people's concern for unity and the popular mood was against the BJP's communal platform which sought to divide the people.

The Congress also benefited from the consolidated support it received from the big business of the country who registered enormous gains during the five-year rule of the UPA.

Defeat of BJP

The BJP's defeat is significant because it has failed for the second successive time to win the elections. The main reason for this failure is because the people have rejected its communal platform which was highlighted by the virulent hate speeches of Varun Gandhi and similar propaganda by less prominent figures. The image of a hardcore Hindutva party was heightened by the projection of Narendra Modi as the future leader of the party. The record of the BJP as the opposition party which mainly concentrated on disrupting Parliament and not taking up the main issues affecting the people such as the agrarian crisis, price rise and unemployment led to loss of support for the party.

The Central Committee noted that the emergence of the non-Congress, non-BJP combination which included the Left parties contributed to the defeat of the BJP which was unable to get any worthwhile allies in states like Andhra Pradesh, Tamil Nadu and Orissa.

Withdrawal of Support to UPA Government

The Central Committee was of the firm opinion that the withdrawal of the support to the UPA government on the nuclear deal in July 2008 was correct. This was consistent with the Left's stand against forging of a strategic alliance with the United States.

Non-Congress, Non-BJP Alternative

The Central Committee of the CPI(M) had called for the formation of a non-Congress, non-BJP alternative as against the Congress-led alliance and the BJP-led alliance. This was a correct tactic. These efforts resulted in the electoral understanding forged by some regional and Left parties in Andhra Pradesh, Tamil Nadu, Orissa and Karnataka. However, such an electoral understanding could not be extended beyond these four states and the three Left-led states of West Bengal, Kerala and Tripura. It failed to be a viable and credible alternative at the national level.

Critically reviewing these efforts, the Central Committee felt that it should not have extended the call for building such an alternative to the formation of an alternative government. In the absence of a countrywide alliance and no common policy platform being presented, the call for an alternative government was unrealistic.

The Central Committee reiterated that it will continue to strive to build the third alternative. Till then, whenever required the Party will forge electoral understanding and alliances with like-minded non-Congress secular parties.

CPI(M) Performance

The Party has suffered serious reverses in the Lok Sabha elections. It has won only 16 seats. Nine seats in West Bengal, four in Kerala, two in Tripura and one in Tamil Nadu. The Party has got 5.33% of the vote, which is only marginally less compared to the 5.66 per cent it polled in 2004. While expressing concern about the erosion in the Party's support base in West Bengal and Kerala, the

Central Committee also noted that the Left Front in West Bengal polled around 1.85 crore votes and in Kerala the LDF has polled 67.17 lakh vote. Though there is some erosion, the main base of the Party is intact by and large in these two states.

Review of Party's Performance

The Central Committee conducted an in-depth review of the performance of the Party based on the review reports received from the states.

The Party has registered a good victory in Tripura winning both the seats with the Left Front polling 61.69 per cent of the votes.

Apart from the all India factors, the specific situation in the states of West Bengal and Kerala where serious losses took place were also reviewed.

In West Bengal, the review noted the political, governmental and organizational reasons for the setbacks suffered by the CPI(M) and the Left Front. The review noted that there is some erosion of support among the rural and urban poor and sections of the middle classes. There are shortcomings in the functioning of Government, Panchayats and municipalities based on a proper class outlook. This is due to the failure of the government to implement properly various measures directly concerning the lives of the people. The apprehension about land acquisition has contributed to the alienation amongst some sections of the peasantry.

At the organizational level certain wrong trends and practices have adversely affected relations with the people. The Central Committee endorsed the steps proposed by the state committee to take corrective measures at the organizational and governmental level.

In Kerala, the factors responsible for the poor performance were also analysed. The disunity in the LDF and the Party leadership had an adverse impact on the people; the churches played an active role in mobilizing Christian votes against the LDF; the association with the PDP caused confusion among the people. The UDF and media campaign on the SNC Lavalin case also had its impact. Certain wrong trends within the Party organisation have also had a negative impact.

The Polit Bureau decided to have a meeting of the Polit Bureau on July 4 and 5, 2009 to discuss specifically the organisational matters in Kerala.

The Central Committee reviewed the overall performance of the Party in the rest of the country. It noted the organisational weaknesses in expanding the independent work of the Party, conducting sustained struggles on local issues and the building of the mass organisations. It directed the state units to implement the tasks arising out of the reviews conducted in the states regarding these matters.

The Central Committee expressed confidence that the entire Party would draw lessons from this electoral setback. It will identify the shortcomings in carrying out the political line of the Party and take steps to rectify the weaknesses in the organization. The Central Committee affirmed that immediate steps would be taken in states like West Bengal and Kerala to reforge the links with those sections of the people who have been alienated from the Party for various reasons. The state governments will also take necessary steps to implement measures which are expected of it by the people.

Relations with Parties

The Party will work to strengthen Left unity and maintain relations and cooperation with secular opposition parties on people's issues, for pro-people economic policies and in defence of secularism and an independent foreign policy.

On the UPA Government

The Central Committee reiterated the stand already outlined by the Left parties that they will play the role of a Left opposition in Parliament. The Central Government should take immediate steps to provide relief to the millions who have lost jobs due to the adverse impact of the global economic crisis. Measures should be taken to see that because of the crisis common people are not burdened further. Though the rate of inflation is shown to be negative, the prices of essential commodities continue to be high. The government must take steps to curb price rise. The Government has to take steps to devolve adequate resources and funds to the state governments who have to primarily bear the responsibility for tackling the effects of the economic slow down and pursue developmental and welfare measures.

The CPI(M) will vigorously oppose all such measures in Parliament and outside which seek to push through legislations for increasing foreign capital in the banking and insurance sector and financial sector liberalization. The Party will continue to oppose disinvestment of the profit making public sector units, FDI in retail and higher education and such sectors which are not beneficial for the country. It will press for the adoption of the women's reservation Bill.

Protest Attacks in West Bengal

The Central Committee has issued an appeal to all its Party units and other Left and democratic forces to protest against the widespread attacks on Party workers, offices and supporters in West Bengal by the Trinamool–Congress combine and the Maoists. The Party will conduct a campaign all over the country in solidarity with West Bengal and in defence of democracy.

III. Review of the Election Report adopted by the party in the Central Committee meeting held in June.

This is a sort of political-organisational report which consists of self-criticism. A study of parts of this report will enable us to understand how much self-critical the party is and whether it will help them in the future. Here Kerala is also dealt with in detail.

The review of the elections of West Bengal, Kerala and Andhra Pradesh have thrown up instances of the disturbing erosion of Party standards and communist values. Parliamentarism leading to open violation of Party norms, sabotage of Party candidates, coming under the influence of money or caste considerations; cases of corruption, nepotism and behaviour of cadres alienating the people from the Party have been noticed. Such problems have been reported in other states too.

In West Bengal such alien and harmful trends need to be taken seriously as they will harm the Party organization which has been the pride of the entire Party. In Kerala, the prolonged factionalism has led to various evils flourishing without check. In Andhra, some of the trends in the two strongest districts of the Party need to be firmly curbed. All Party state committees should examine concrete cases of such violation and wrong trends and take specific action to check them. Particular attention will have to be paid to raising the political-ideological level of the members to counter the corrupt influences during election time.

Overall, the need for a thoroughgoing rectification campaign gets further underlined. As decided by the CC in January, 2009, we should take up the rectification campaign document at the earliest for adoption by the CC and initiate the rectification campaign.

... The lack of credibility for the "Third Front" at the national level and the concern for a stable secular government had its impact on different sections of the people, particularly the minorities. Though the all-India trends influenced the elections in Kerala, there were the state-specific factors which decisively affected the elections. A section of the people who had rallied behind the LDF during the 2004 Lok Sabha elections and 2006 Assembly elections moved away from the LDF. Religious and caste leaders actively intervened in the elections in favour of the UDF.

The anti-Communist forces succeeded in weaning away a substantial section of Christian minorities from the LDF. The Catholic Church rallied other churches and openly campaigned against the CPI(M) due to its opposition to the Education Act which sought to put in place some social control over self-financed colleges. Certain other controversies also came up during this period.

Though there is no erosion of our support base among the Muslim minorities, the efforts to expand our influence among them have not yielded the expected results in many areas. The UDF and the media were successful in creating some confusion among a section of the secular minded people that the CPI(M) is also resorting to an opportunistic stand in the matter of getting the support of Madani's PDP to the LDF candidates. It may be necessary during elections to get support from different parties, groups and sections of people in elections, but at the same time, we should be careful to ensure that our secular identity does not get blurred by any such maneouvres. We should have avoided having a joint platform with the PDP during the election campaign. It is to be noted here that the UDF got the support of the NDF or Popular Front which is an extremist outfit involved in communal and criminal activities.

The Party should continue its struggle against using caste and communalism for political or electoral gains. It was this secular stand taken by the Party that helped to expand its influence among the common people belonging to different castes or religions. Any weakness in taking such secular positions should be eschewed.

While the UDF was a united force, the disunity in the LDF was one of the factors for the defeat. The disunity in the Party and LDF had an adverse impact on the people. Some of the statements of Com. VS Achuthanandan during the campaign had an adverse effect and helped the opposition campaign.

The public controversies that erupted in the LDF just on the eve of Lok Sabha elections conveyed an impression in the minds of the people that the LDF was disunited and was fighting each other. It led to the dominant section of the JD(S) going out and opposing the LDF. The dispute over Ponnani seat with the CPI saw public acrimony. All this created frustration and confusion among the supporters and well-wishers of the Party and LDF. As the major component of the LDF, the Party should have taken steps to avoid such differences at least after the announcement of Lok Sabha elections.

Even though the LDF government did many things for the common people, they were not adequately projected and people rallied to support, because of the never ending controversies in the leadership of the Party and government. The opponents of the LDF made use of the SNC Lavalin case to create confusion in the minds of the people. The media used the Lavalin issue as the central issue in the elections.

A section of the media continuously carried out a vicious attack against the LDF and particularly the CPI(M). The anti-LDF media acted as the propaganda team of the UDF and tried to see that the media reports were mainly confined to three issues—Lavalin controversy, PDP's support to the LDF and disunity in the Party and the LDF. They were successful in creating confusion in the minds of the people. The attitude of this section of the media was similar to the so-called 'liberation struggle' days of 1959–1960 in Kerala. Money was extensively used by the UDF in this election.

In some constituencies, the UDF was able to rally students, youth and middle-class employees in considerable numbers. Political-ideological work among the students and youth should be strengthened. The erosion among our traditional support bases in certain areas should be self-critically reviewed and proper lessons drawn for appropriate corrective measures.

The Party failed to assess the magnitude of the setback till the counting day.

We were hopeful of getting more than a majority of seats for the LDF. The Party has to identify why such a wrong estimation was made. It should be examined whether factionalism has adversely affected the organisational work in certain areas.

There are instances of alien trends among some Party members which violate Communist norms. All such and other shortcomings and weaknesses should be critically and self-critically examined and rectified. A rectification campaign should be organized within the Party against all the shortcomings, mistakes and deviations. The disunity and wrong trends should be firmly put down.

Annexure II

A Glimpse of Mindset of the Leaders of Bengal During 2008

FROM THE document on 'Left Front Government, Panchayats, Municipalities and Our Task' adopted in West Bengal state conference, 2008:

> **1.2**... In the context of the policies of economic liberalization pursued by the Centre and the experience of running three Left led State governments in that backdrop, the 18th Party Congress unanimously adopted a document on some policy issues after detailed discussions, providing broad guidelines for the policy direction of the present Left Front governments. This has helped to unify the entire Party. Discussions and political classes on these documents have been organized at all levels of the Party.
>
> **1.3** The massive success of the Left Front in the 14th Assembly elections held in June 2006 vindicated the policy direction of the Left Front government and the positive impact it had in eliciting mass support. The fact that the masses repose deep faith in this programme of the Left Front government, even after being in office for 29 years, was undoubtedly proven by the victory of the

Left Front in 235 seats by securing 50.18% of the votes, with the CPI (M) winning absolute majority.

1.4 Therefore, there is no reason to change the policy direction laid down in the above-mentioned documents. Neither is there any need to reiterate the content of those documents. What is required is an evaluation of the experience of running the Left Front."

1.8... New proposals for establishing large industries have naturally increased the demand for land and infrastructure. Because of the high population density in West Bengal, per capita endowment of land happens to be low. Most of the land is under agricultural use and as a result of the progress in agriculture intensity of cultivation is also relatively high. Since small, marginal and middle peasants in the state own 84% of the land, the process of acquisition of land for industry and infrastructure is a complex as well as sensitive issue. In the recent past, the opposition has consistently tried to isolate the Left Front government, especially the CPI (M), from the peasantry, using this sensitive issue. Land acquisition for building industry, infrastructure etc. has taken place in the past. But we never faced such resistance to development on the question of land. In order to carry forward the programme of development, this issue should be satisfactorily resolved. The fear among the peasantry of losing their land has to be addressed in a serious manner. Although the amount of land required for industries and infrastructure is meager compared to the total amount of land and cultivated area in the state, the matter needs to be considered with seriousness. Besides ensuring adequate compensation, specific planning is required for alternative sources of income for families whose land is being acquired. The local people need to be involved in the process of land acquisition and fixing the compensation amount. Confidence has to be generated among the local people regarding the positive economic and social benefits of the projects for which land is being acquired. These tasks are not only administrative but also political.

1.9 Caution is also required in changing land use for the purpose of industry. Priority should be given to setting up of industries on relatively less fertile land. The Left Front government has already taken steps in this regard. Large industries are mainly being set up on relatively less fertile land not suitable for agriculture, in the regions of West Midnapore, Bankura, Purulia, Asansol, Durgapur and Birbhum. However, all types of industries cannot be set up in these regions. The Haldia industrial region needs to be expanded in order to take advantage of the port facility. Similarly, there are possibilities to build a large industrial region in and around Siliguri and Jalpaiguri in North Bengal. Large areas in and around Kolkata, North and South 24-Parganas, Howrah and Hoogly are traditional industrial belts. These areas are most suitable for technology intensive manufacturing and IT industries. Urbanization is also high in these areas. Large-scale transfer of agricultural land is taking place in these areas in response to market forces. The government has to take planned measures in this regard. Besides, initiatives are underway to develop industries centering around Kalyani in the Nadia district. Overall, besides the development of 6 large industrial regions in the state, initiatives need to be taken in order to develop at least one industrial zone in every district, which will provide all facilities for setting up small and medium enterprises.

Annexure III

Singur Package Offered to Tata Motor

THE PACKAGE (which the government hid from the public initially by saying that it was to be kept a secret) came to light on 11 September 2008. It said that the package offered by some other states to Tata Motors had in it offers of 100 per cent exemption from excise duty for 10 years and 100 per cent exemption from corporate income tax for first five years along with 30 per cent exemption from corporate income tax for next five years. Bengal government said, as it was keen to attract some major auto projects, it 'approached TML to persuade them to locate an automobile project including the project to manufacture Tata small car in West Bengal.' Then, 'TML showed interest in locating the plant in West Bengal, provided the state government gave fiscal incentive equivalent to the value of total incentives it would have received by locating the plant in Uttarakhand/ Himachal Pradesh.' These argument is not verifiable. But when finally Nano project shifted out of Bengal, the Tata Motors officials went for searching suitable land in Karnataka and Uttarakhand, but not found good opportunity in those places. It shifted to Gujarat.

Let us see the highlights of what Bengal said (compiled from media reports).]

- West Bengal 'offered to match the financial incentives (to be given by other states) in equivalent terms and invited TML to set up the small car plant in West Bengal entailing investment of over Rs 1,500 crore (Rs 15 billion) by TML' and further Rs 500 crore (Rs 5 billion) by the associated vendors.
- The state and Tata Motors agreed to 'make best efforts to maximize sale of products from the small car plant'.
- West Bengal also agreed that the computation of the comparison of benefits with Uttarakhand would be changed if there are any changes in the rates of excise duty and corporate income tax during the next 10 years.

The land was acquired in the heart of a vast greenery (where for decades people demanded a canal to solve the problem of water logging, and which was not initiated till it was needed for Tata Motors) beside river Ganga, only because Tata Motors had liked the place. See the details:

- WBIDC acquired 997.11 acres of land to be given for this project. Out of this, an area of 645.67 acres was earmarked for leasing to TML for setting up the automobile project, including the small car plant and another 290 acres for leasing to the vendors to the project.
- WBIDC agreed to provide 645.67 acres of land to Tata Motors Ltd on a 90 year lease, on an annual lease rental of Rs 1 crore (Rs 10 million) per year for the first five years with an increase of 25 per cent after every five years till 30 years.

  On expiry of 30 years, the lease rental will be fixed at Rs 5 crore per year, with an increase of 30 per cent after every 10 years till the 60th year.

  On the expiry of 60 years, the lease rental will be fixed at Rs 20 crore (Rs 200 million) per year, which will remain unchanged till the 90th year. On expiry of 90 years, the lease terms will be fixed on mutually agreed terms at that point of time."

- In addition, 14.33 acres was marked for handing over to West Bengal State Electricity Board for construction of 220/132/33 KV substation and the balance 47.11 acres for rehabilitation activities for the needy families amongst the project affected persons.
- The agreement provided for lease of 290 acres of land to the vendors on payment of premium equal to the actual cost of acquisition plus incidentals. The lease rental payable per year per acre by the vendors was fixed at a rate of Rs 8,000 per acre for the first 45 years and Rs 16,000 per acre for the next 45 years. On expiry of 90 years, the lease terms was set to be fixed again on mutually agreed terms at that point of time.

Now, let us come to the financial incentives:

- WBIDC agreed to provide Industrial Promotion Assistance in the form of a loan to TML at 0.1 per cent interest per annum for amounts equal to gross VAT and CST received by government of West Bengal in each of the previous years ended March 31 on sale of 'Tata small car' from the date of commencement of sales of the small car. WBIDC agreed to continue this benefit till the balance amount of the Uttarakhand benefit was reached on net present value basis. WBIDC will ensure that the loan under this head is paid within 60 days of the close of the previous year (on 31st March) failing which WBIDC will be liable to compensate TML for the financial inconvenience caused at the rate of 1.5 times the bank rate prevailing at the time on the amount due for the period of such delay.
- The West Bengal government agreed to provide TML a loan of Rs 200 crore bearing a one per cent interest per year repayable in five equal annual installments starting from the 21st year from the date of disbursement of loan.

  "This loan will be disbursed within 60 days of signing of this agreement," according to the agreement.
- West Bengal Government agreed to 'provide Electricity for the project at Rs 3 per KWH. In case of more than Rs 0.25 per KWH increase in tariff in every block of five years, the government will

provide relief through additional compensation to neutralise such additional increase."

Experts computed these things in 'present terms of money value' at 2007, and came to the conclusion that the company got the land at about 25–35 crores, while the value of the land was three to four times higher. On an average 10 lakhs were paid as compensation for an acre for acquiring this thousand acres of land (and that was arbitrary and too meagre). Thus the government incurred huge loss on count of land. Then there was huge revenue loss and additional burden of providing huge loan. Simply put, it denoted loss of thousands of crores of revenue. One wonders if 25 such projects came to West Bengal as part of its new industrialization plan, what would have been the burden on the state and whether the state would have survived the burden.

Again, Bengal government did not come out with any document to prove that how the project would have ensured generation of more gainful employment for more people than those who were evicted from that highly fertile land that could have been further developed with a little governmental help. I am not going into the question of the damage to the environment simply because I am not well-trained to discuss that.

Annexure IV

Details about Rizwanur case*

WE ALL know about CPI(M)'s campaign about its great secular credential in Bengal. Emboldened by this secular credential of the system, one middle-class Muslim boy Rizwanur Rahman dared to marry a rich Marwari girl Priyanka Todi. This Marwari family owned Lux Cozy brand. They had connections, and they were furious about the marriage. They wanted their daughter back! The girl's uncle Pradip Todi and Snehasish Ganguly (well-known cricketer Sourav Ganguly's elder brother) went to the Police Commissioner of Calcutta, Prasun Mukherjee, for remedy of their grievance.

Soon Lal Bazar, the headquarters of Calcutta police, swung into action. Rizwanur was threatened by big shots of Calcutta police, including some notorious officers of anti-rowdy department. The department itself is notorious and allegations abound about its extortion racket. According to Bengali newspaper reports coming after Rizwanur's death, many of those men also work as mercenaries. The police officers arranged for Priyanka being sent to her father for a week. But after a week, she did not return.

* compiled by the author from newspapers and the *Wikipedia*

Rizwanur went to human rights activists against this, and also to one honest upright officer, Nazrul Islam, who had been shunted in some unimportant corner by the CM. Rizwanur was planning to move the court.

Before he could actually do so, Rizwanur's body was found lying near the railway track (21 September 2007) and the next day *Anadabazar Patrika* gave a laudable coverage of the incident. But police commissioner promptly announced (on 23rd) that the death was 'definitely a case of suicide or an accident'. It was not clear whether he had any special clairvoyance to know such things, for nobody else knew anything, as even the post-mortem report was awaited. When asked by the reporters about the interference of the police in a personal matter of marriage, the proud CP announced that 'police can interfere in cases where a marriage has taken place between families who are poles apart in social standing'. If you are now seething in anger, you must know that he did not stop there. He himself claimed that police department had done such things in the past, and would do so in the future too. He even dared to poke fun at the Press by asking them if the police would not take up such cases 'who else will do it, 'the Public Works Department?' He claimed that cases of eloping, even by adults, were unacceptable morally and that was why the police swung into action. When pressed on the legality of his comments, the commissioner turned angry and left the conference in a huff. On 24th various newspapers carried this.

Thanks to the Commissioner, the brutal and regressive face of the Calcutta police became public. And Mukherjee was fearless, for he was the favourite of the CM, who was running the police department for about 15 years. The CM had played a crucial role in installing Mukherjee at the helm of Bengal cricket body. He dubbed the earlier president of CAB Jagmohan Dalmia as 'evil power' and fielded his favourite commissioner of police against him. Mukherjee won. By the by, the Todis were also related to cricket. Ashok Todi was under scrutiny for illegal cricket betting, according to cricket correspondents. It was also alleged that Todi was one of the financiers of Mukherjee in CIB election. (*Pioneer*, 7 October 2007).

The media and the people demanded the CP should be transferred immediately. His comments blatantly violated the spirit of Supreme Court's observation also, as the law provides for security against harassment in case of inter-caste or inter-religion marriages. When the protest refused to die down, the CP was removed from his post on 17 October, after a gap of good 24 days that would allow anyone to annihilate all uncomfortable evidences. He was removed when Calcutta burst into protest, and when senior leaders of the party including Jyoti Basu raised questions about his continuance.

Ultimately, responding to a petition, the High Court ordered the CBI enquiry on Rizwanur's mysterious death. The CBI had found that Lal Bazar was the place from where the whole thing against Rizwanur was planned and conducted. The High Court has directed the CBI to chargesheet the Todis and one of their accomplices and four policemen from the police headquarters. The top IPS officers of the CBI however failed to get anything against two top IPS of Calcutta police Gyanwant Singh and Prasun Mukherjee.

But what was the role of police in the whole episode?

After having an understanding with the Todi family, top level police officers of the state summoned the couple several times to State Police Headquarters at Lal Bazar, Kolkata, and threatened Rizwanur of dire consequences if he did not separate from his wife. The couple refused. On September 8, eight days after their marriage was certified, the police summoned Rizwanur again and threatened to have him arrested on charges of abduction if he did not return his legal wife to his in-laws, even though no official case was registered against him. Rizwanur was also accused of stealing a cellphone and other items from the Todi mansion (*Indian Express*, 7 October 2007). It is alleged that after police coercion, Rahman was forced to send Priyanka to the Todi's house for a week that same day. One of Priyanka's uncles, who was present at the police headquarters, signed an agreement on a plain paper in front of a witness that Priyanka would be sent back to Rahman's house after 7 days, on September 15. (*The Telegraph*, Calcutta, 24 September 2007). Rahman died in the afternoon of September 21, about two weeks after his wife was forcefully separated from him.

On 16 October 2007, totally dissatisfied with the state CID investigation, Calcutta High Court ordered a Central Bureau of Investigations (CBI) enquiry. Surprisingly, the very next day, the CM stated that all five suspected police officers would be transferred from their posts with immediate effect.

During the investigations, it was alleged that several people including local goons and also some of Rahman's family members received money from Ashok Todi to sabotage the marriage.

Thus, Rizwanur death case appeared as a bizarre story of money-murder-illegal authority of police racket and industrialist-police-politician nexus. But it did not end there. On 11 February 2009, Arindam Manna, the government railway police officer who initiated the probe into the death of Rizwanur, was found dead beside a railway track. Manna was also on the list of witness that the CBI submitted along with its chargesheet to the Chief Metropolitan Magistrate. The body had injuries on the left eye, right leg and a deep cut on the throat.

Annexure V

Karat on BJP

ANY DISCUSSION on the Bharatiya Janata Party must begin with the question: how is the BJP to be characterized? From 1986 what stands out about this party is its strident advocacy of Hindu majoritarian communalism. But in Marxist terms, while it is necessary to underline its communal features, that alone is not sufficient to define the Party's character. It would not be correct to see the BJP, as many analysts do, as a nationalist party which is right of centre.

The BJP is definitely a Right-wing party, but it is distinguished by its reactionary communal platform. In that sense, it is different from ordinary conservative parties of the Right. Classically, such parties of the Right-wing are characterized by the open advocacy of the interests of the ruling classes and are defenders of the status quo. This stance differentiates them from other ruling class parties who disguise their class interests when putting out their party programmes and strive in varying degrees to build a coalition of support based on welfare state or social democratic prescriptions.

---

* From *The Marxist*, vol X, no. 3, July–September 1992:

In contrast to the conservative Right-wing parties, there is very often the phenomenon of the neo-Right parties which are marked by radicalism i.e., they take to mass politics and launch mass movements with a critique of extant society which break the boundaries of the traditional Right. The mass politics generated by such parties is primarily motivated by a reactionary-sectarian platform which targets an "enemy"—the other ethnic/religious community which is held responsible for all the problems of society. Le Pen's National Front in France registered growth mainly through its virulent campaigns against immigrants and projecting a French ultranationalism tinged with racism; the new parties in Germany are also making a dent in the Christian Democratic base with their chauvinist anti-foreigner appeal; in the middle-east, the parties of Islamic fundamentalism have their mass radical character whether it be the Khomeinism of Iran or the Islamic party in Algeria. Most of these parties flourish when societies are in acute crisis and the traditional ruling class prescriptions to run society have reached a dead end.

The BJP has to be placed at this end of the spectrum in the Indian context. In the political terrain of India, a conservative party of the Right has no immediate foreseeable future. Given the mass poverty, the sharp economic and social inequalities and the compulsions of electoral politics, all bourgeois-landlord parties have to pay obeisance to the slogans of social equality and removal of economic disparities. The BJP in its quest to function as a viable party of the Right in the Indian political milieu has finally arrived at what it considers to be the key to success. Hindu nationalism articulated with an internal enemy—the Muslim minority—gives the BJP its communal character. Alongside this cutting edge to its platform, is the Right-wing character of its economic policy—support to the liberalization and privatization drive. It is the combination of these two features which makes the BJP a unique political force at the national level—a Right-wing communal party which represents the reactionary sections of the big bourgeoisie and landlords.

The BJP came into being in 1980 after the collapse of the Janata experiment. The resurrection of the Bharatiya Jana Sangh in the form of the BJP seemed to be a qualitative transformation wherein the party seemed to mark a break from the old Jana Sangh–RSS ideology. This brief interregnum when the party adopted the plank of Gandhian socialism sat ill upon the RSS dominated cadres of the party. The presidentship of AB Vajpayee (1980–86) saw the underplaying of the Hindu communal rhetoric and the attempt to broadbase the Party's platform by taking up the issues affecting the tribals, Scheduled Castes, the rural and urban poor. The trauma of the experience within the Janata Party and the controversy regarding dual membership (with the RSS) which ended the marriage resulted in the lingering effort to imitate the Centrist bourgeois parties. The 1984 debacle put paid to these efforts. The phase of Indira Gandhi's appeal to Hindu votes and the strong reaction to her assassination, were seen by the BJP as the success of the Congress(I) in stealing its original platform and prospering from it. It must be recalled that the RSS worked to ensure the success of the Congress(I) in many areas in the 1980 elections.

Index

N

O

P

Q

R

S

T

U

V

W